# Bayou

*volume one*

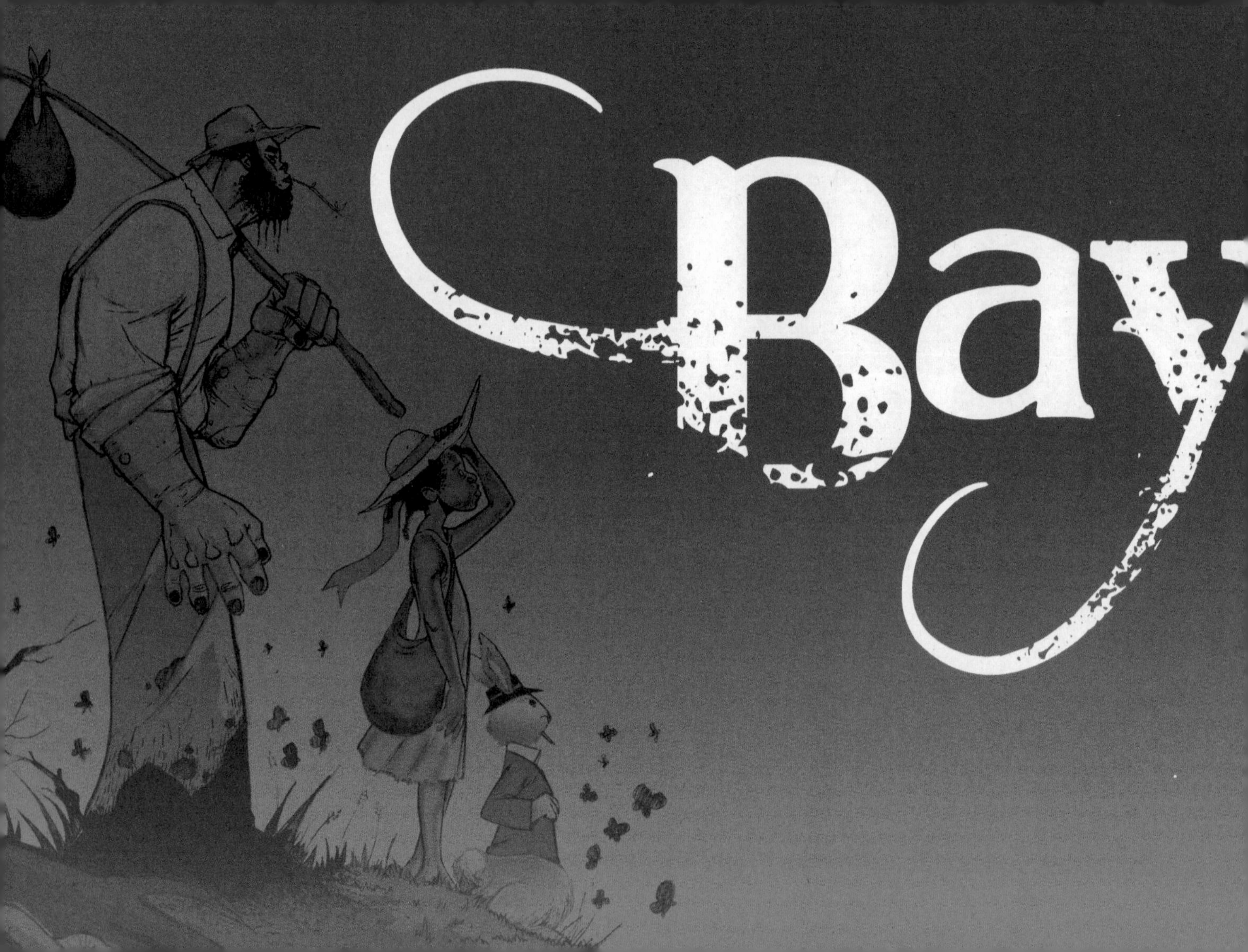
Bay

**OU**

*volume one*

created by *Jeremy Love* colors by *Patrick Morgan*

**Ron Perazza** *Editorial Director-Zuda Comics*  **Kwanza Johnson** *Editor-original series*  **Nika Denoyelle** *Assistant Editor-original series*

**Sean Mackiewicz** *Editor-collected edition*  **Robbin Brosterman** *Senior Art Director*  **Paul Levitz** *President & Publisher*

**Georg Brewer** *VP-Design & DC Direct Creative*  **Richard Bruning** *Senior VP-Creative Director*  **Patrick Caldon** *Executive VP-Finance & Operations*

**Chris Caramalis** *VP-Finance*  **John Cunningham** *VP-Marketing*  **Terri Cunningham** *VP-Managing Editor*

**Amy Genkins** *Senior VP-Business & Legal Affairs*  **Alison Gill** *VP-Manufacturing*  **David Hyde** *VP-Publicity*

**Hank Kanalz** *VP-General Manager, WildStorm*  **Jim Lee** *Editorial Director-WildStorm*  **Gregory Noveck** *Senior VP-Creative Affairs*

**Sue Pohja** *VP-Book Trade Sales*  **Steve Rotterdam** *Senior VP-Sales & Marketing*  **Cheryl Rubin** *Senior VP-Brand Management*

**Alysse Soll** *VP-Advertising & Custom Publishing*  **Jeff Trojan** *VP-Business Development, DC Direct*  **Bob Wayne** *VP-Sales*

DC Comics, 1700 Broadway, New York, NY 10019
A Warner Bros. Entertainment Company
Third Printing.
Printed by RR Donnelley, Willard, OH, USA. 7/01/11
ISBN: 978-1-4012-2382-3

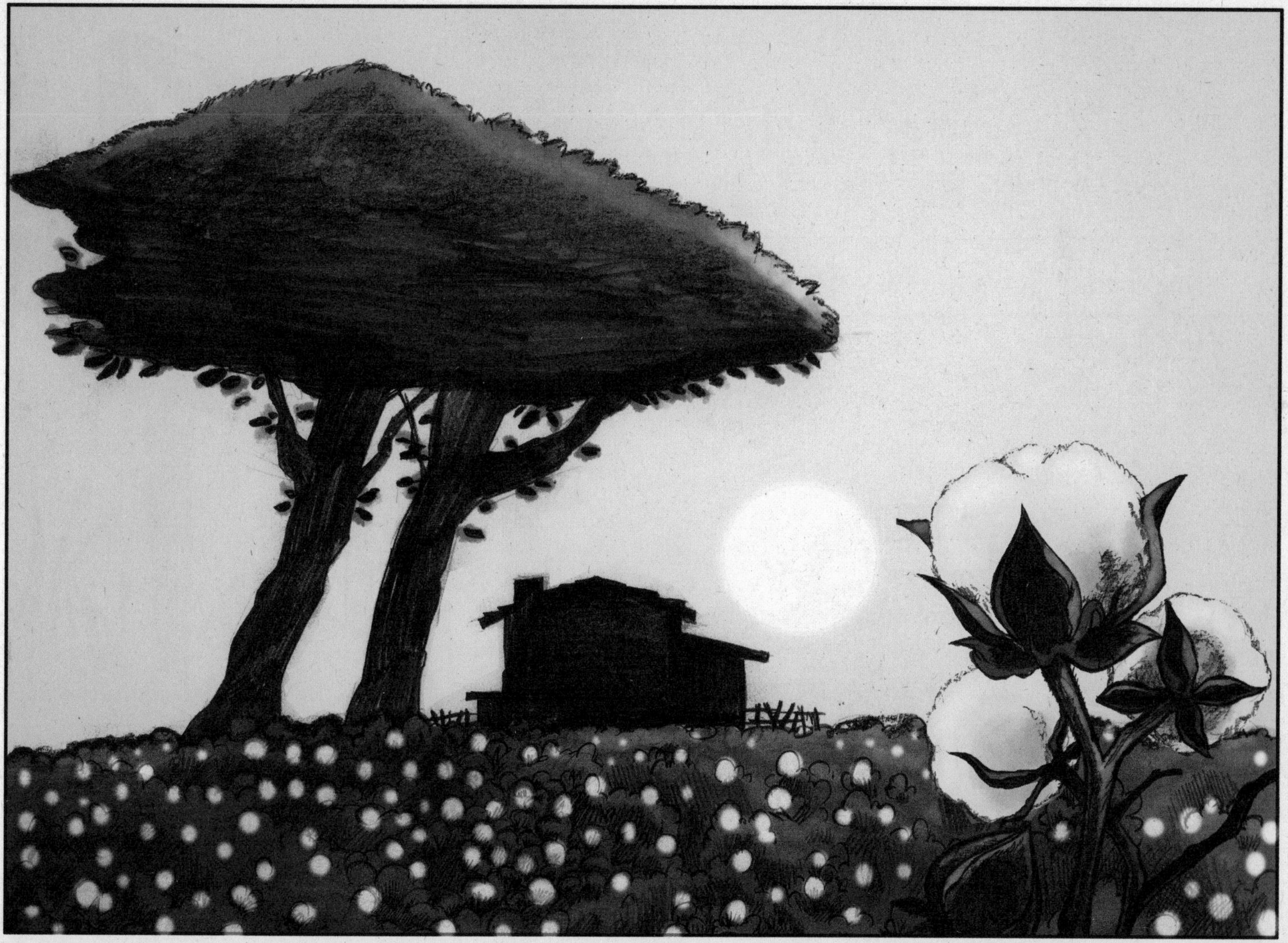

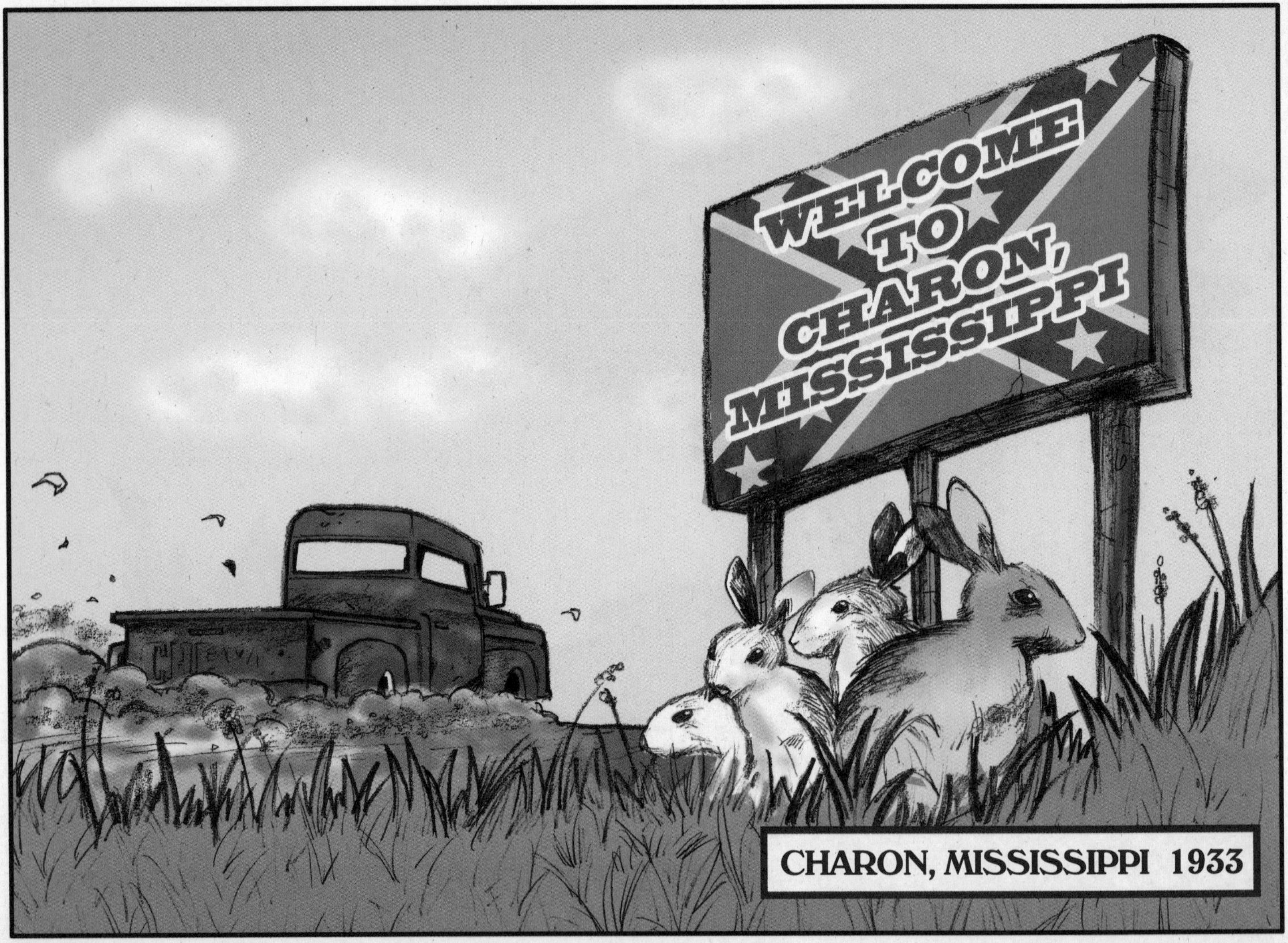
WELCOME TO CHARON, MISSISSIPPI
CHARON, MISSISSIPPI 1933

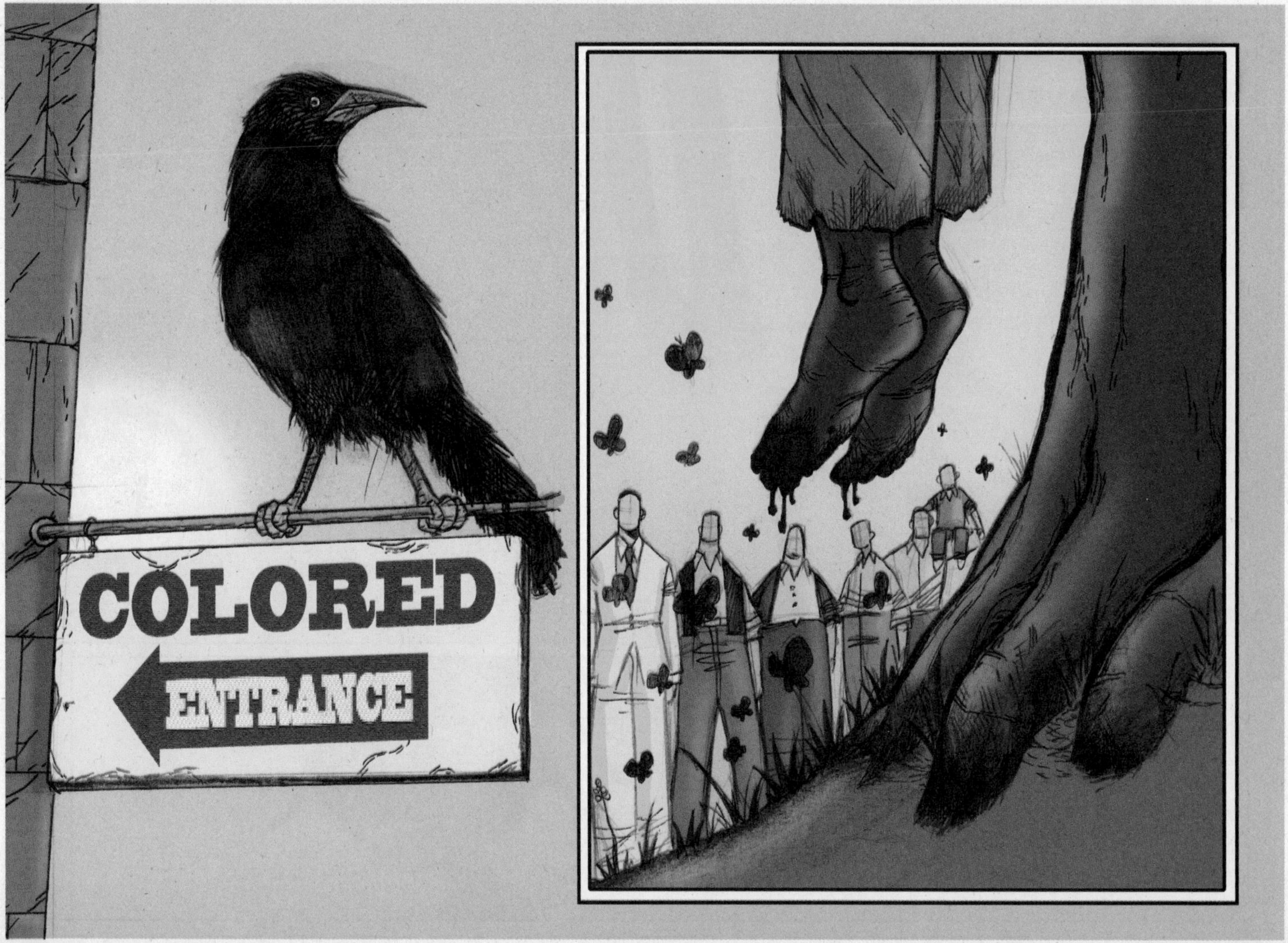
COLORED
ENTRANCE

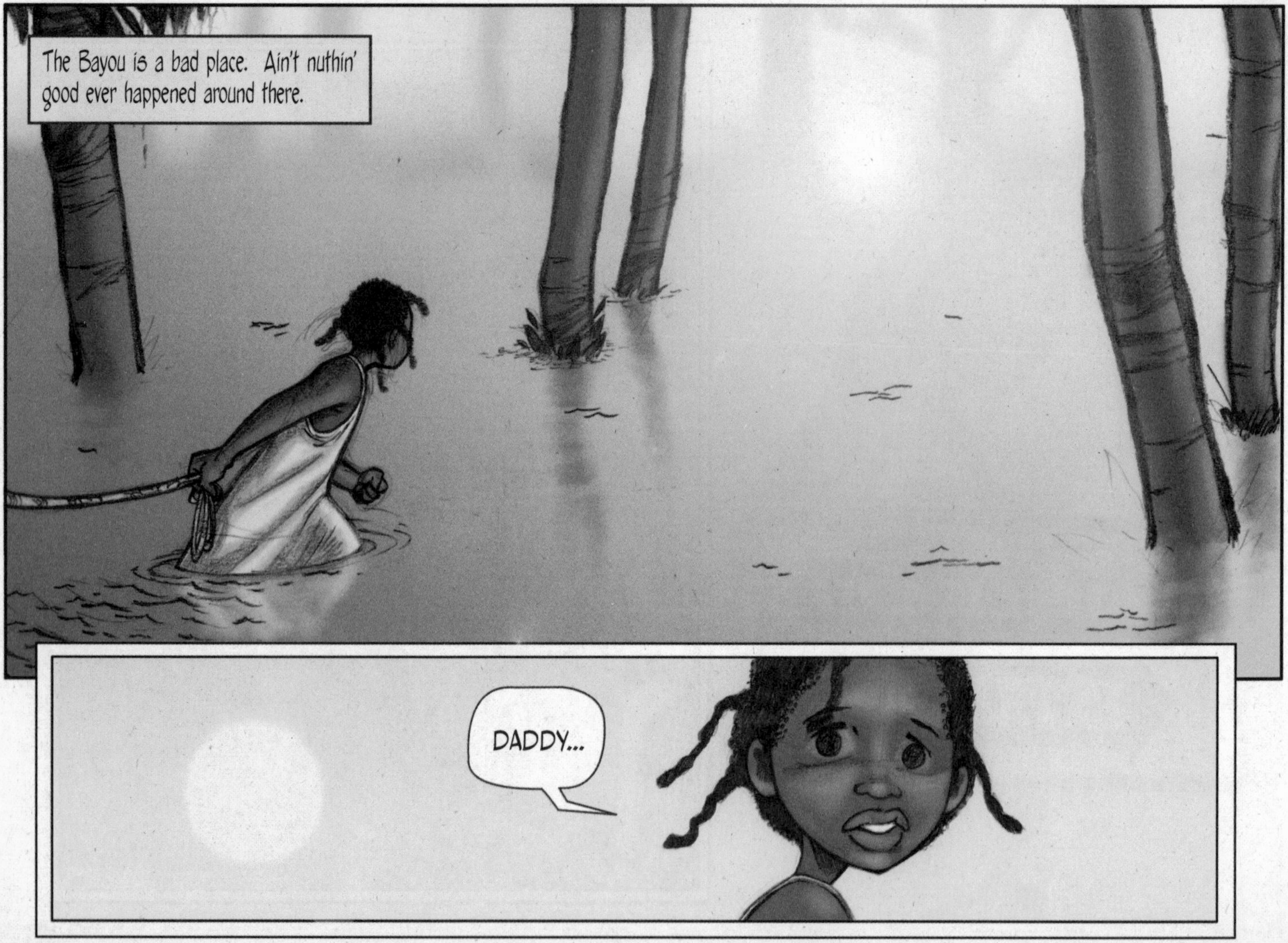
The Bayou is a bad place. Ain't nuthin' good ever happened around there.
DADDY...

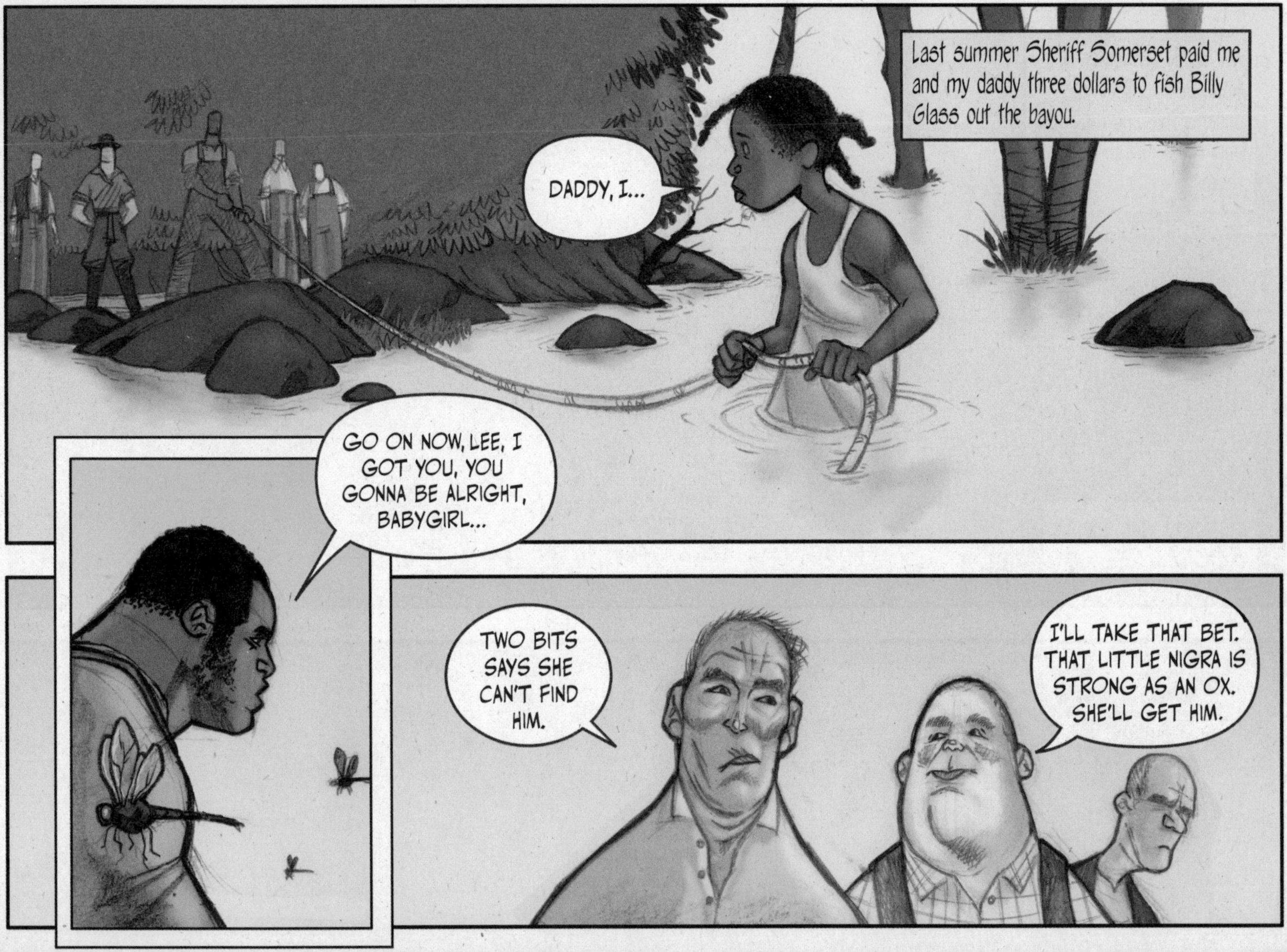
Last summer Sheriff Somerset paid me and my daddy three dollars to fish Billy Glass out the bayou.
DADDY, I...
GO ON NOW, LEE, I GOT YOU, YOU GONNA BE ALRIGHT, BABYGIRL...
TWO BITS SAYS SHE CAN'T FIND HIM.
I'LL TAKE THAT BET. THAT LITTLE NIGRA IS STRONG AS AN OX. SHE'LL GET HIM.

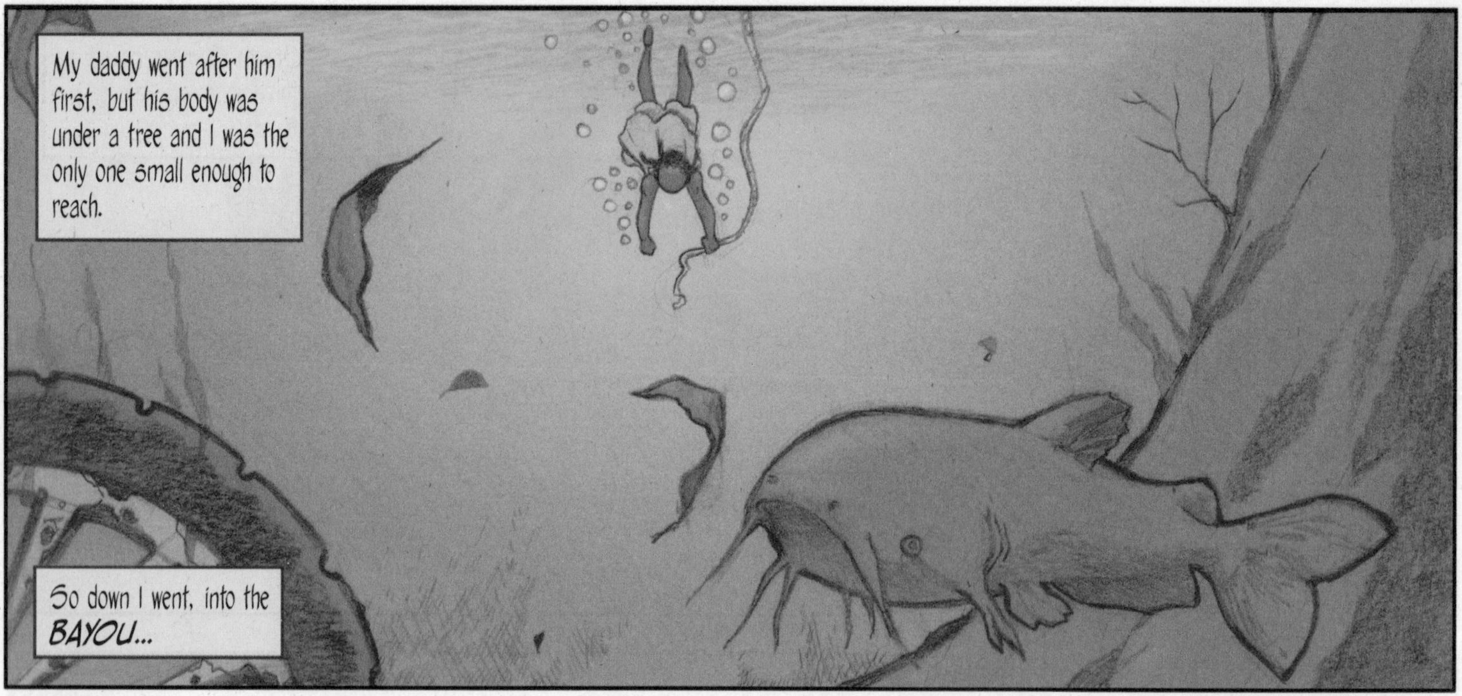
My daddy went after him first, but his body was under a tree and I was the only one small enough to reach.
So down I went, into the *BAYOU...*

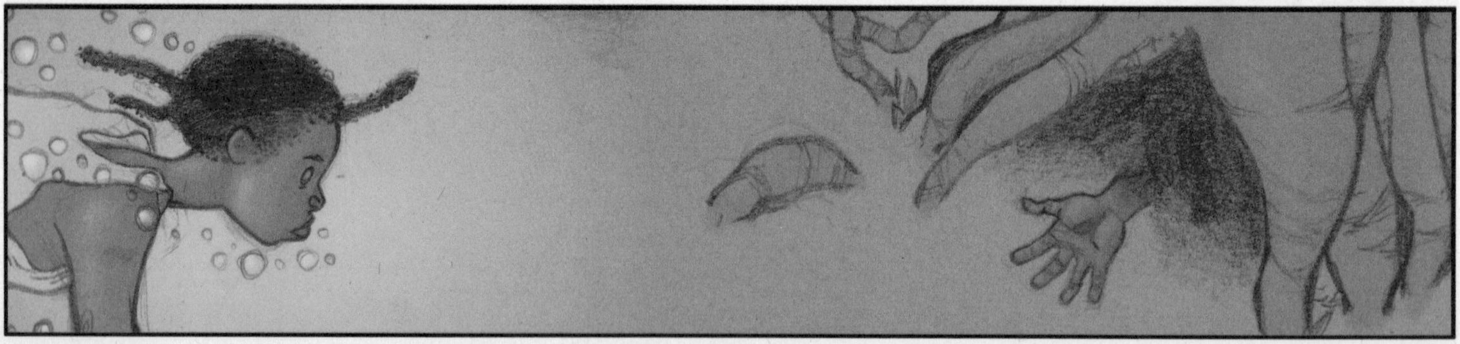

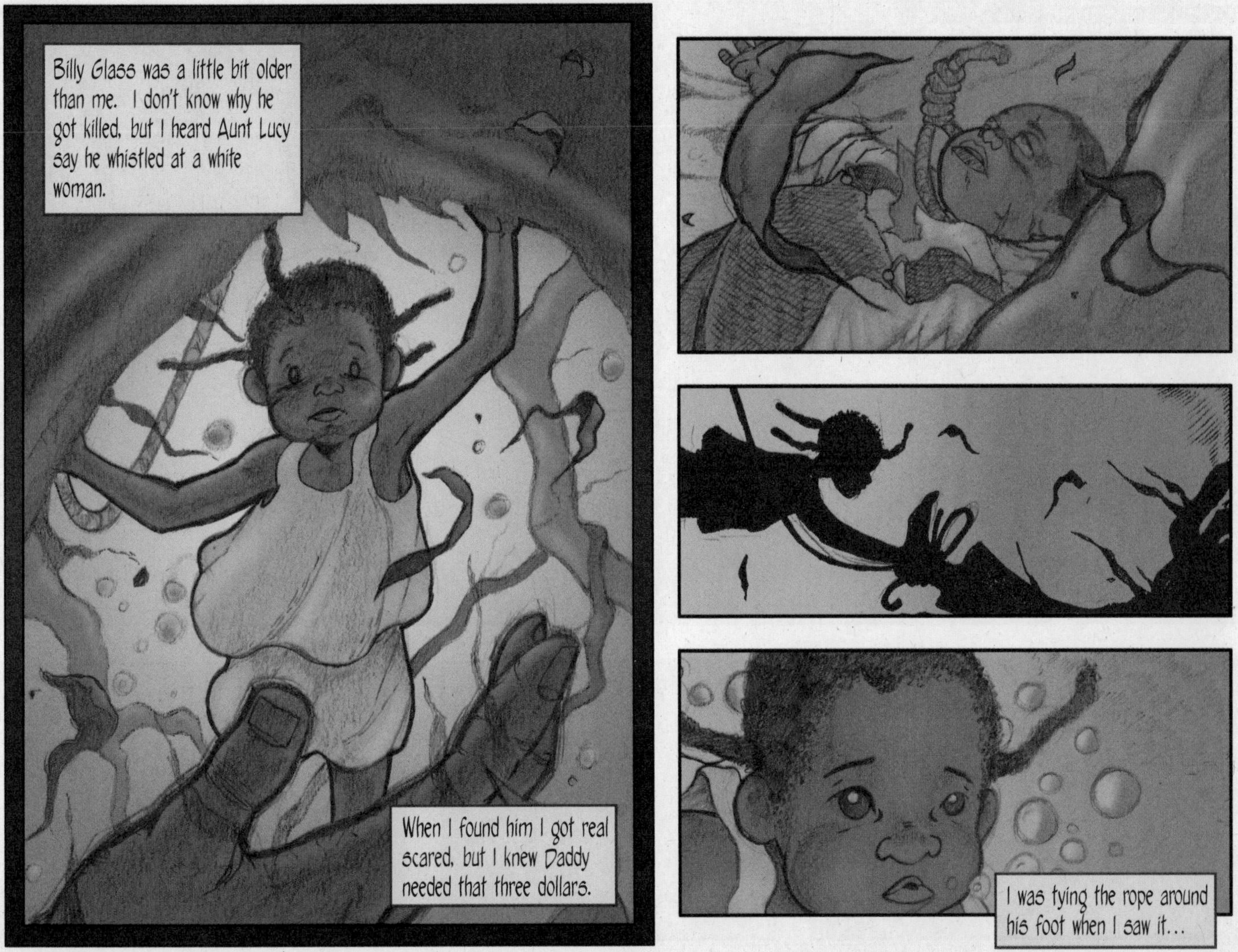
Billy Glass was a little bit older than me. I don't know why he got killed, but I heard Aunt Lucy say he whistled at a white woman.
When I found him I got real scared, but I knew Daddy needed that three dollars.
I was tying the rope around his foot when I saw it...

I figure it was Billy's soul on his way to glory. There was this hole and it was so bright I could hardly see. I wanted so bad to see what was on the other side. But I was scared.

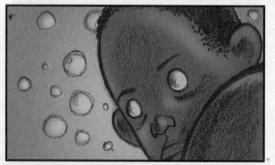

And just like that, it was gone...

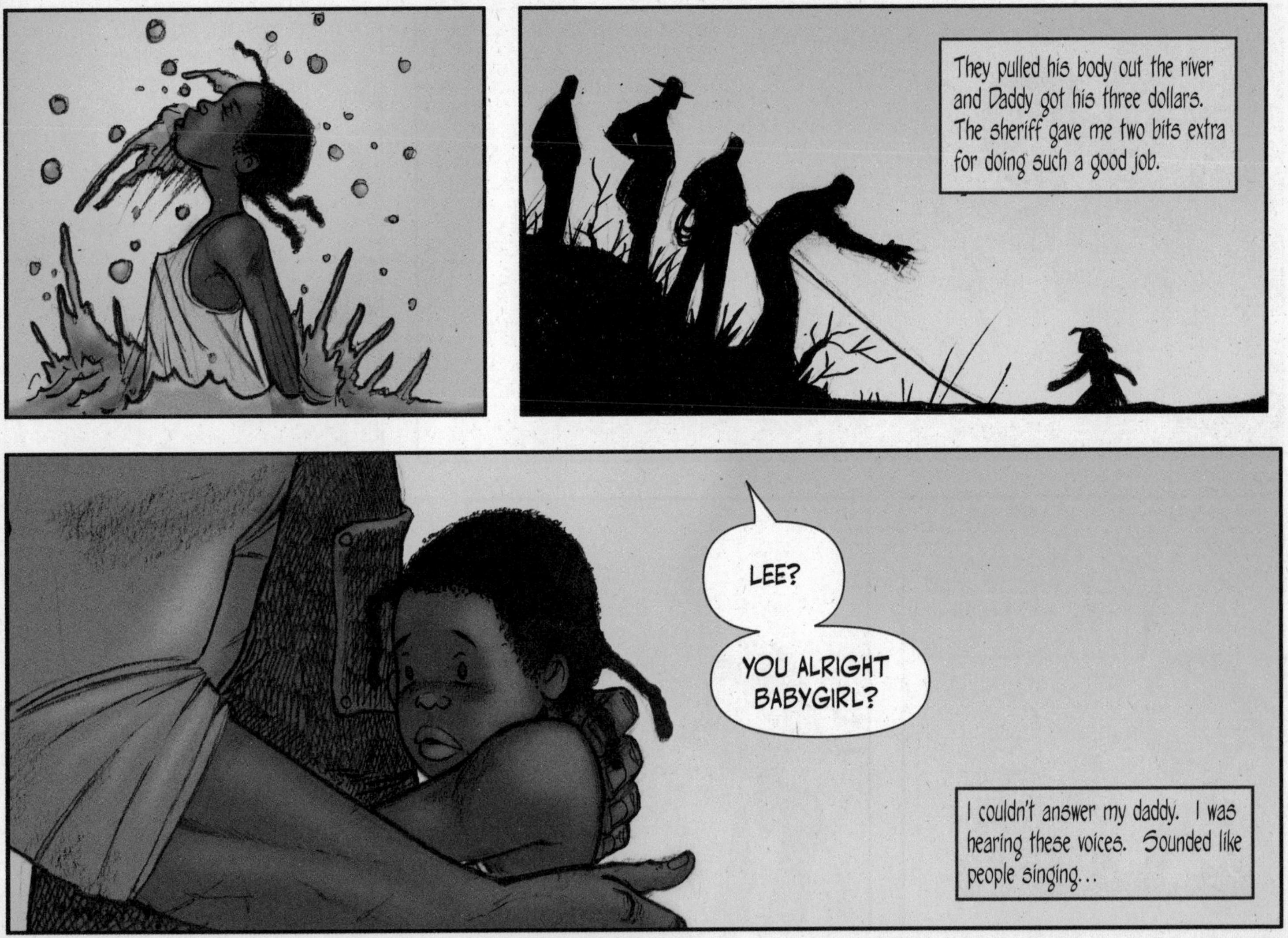
They pulled his body out the river and Daddy got his three dollars. The sheriff gave me two bits extra for doing such a good job.
LEE?
YOU ALRIGHT BABYGIRL?
I couldn't answer my daddy. I was hearing these voices. Sounded like people singing...

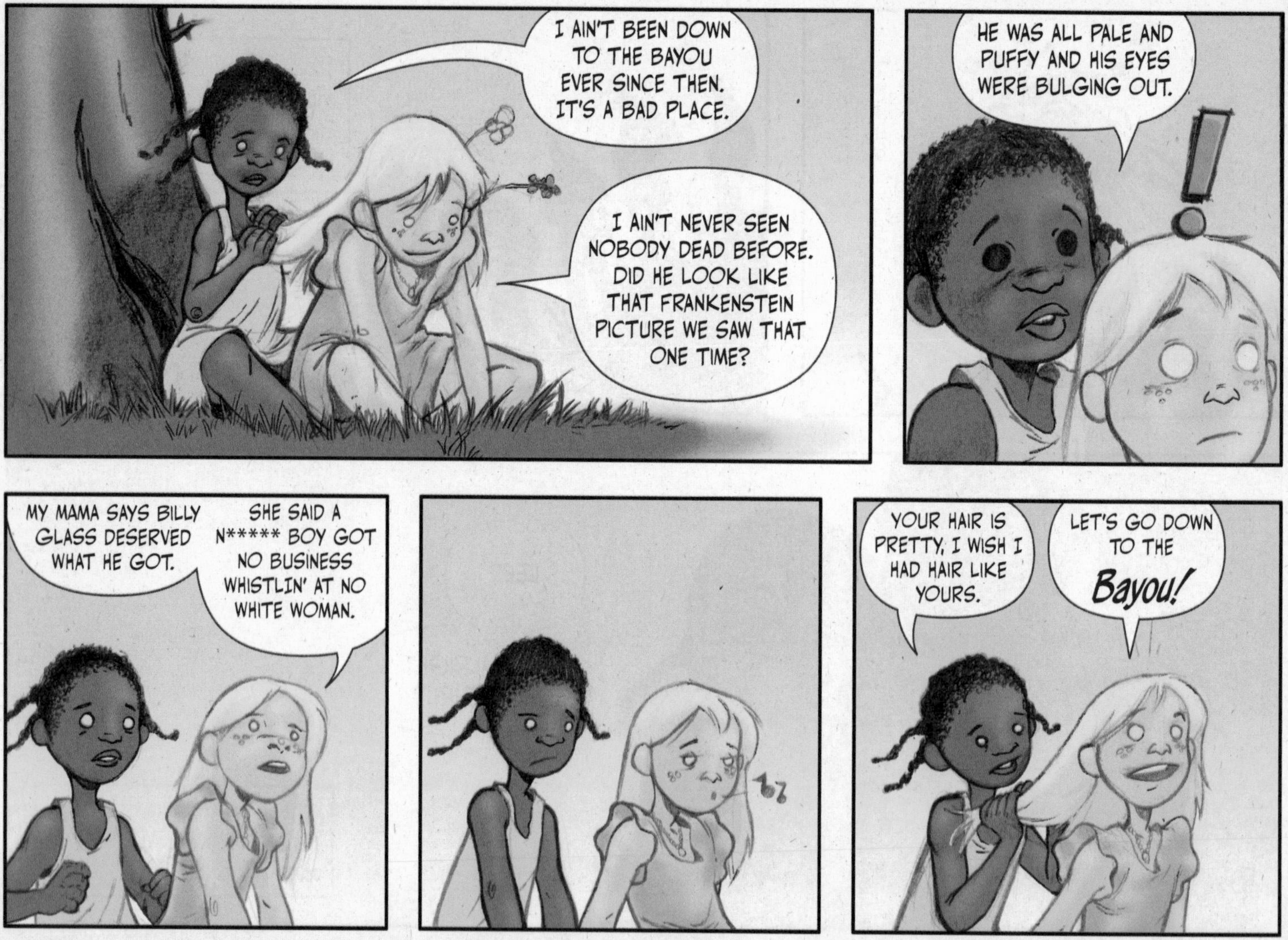
I AIN'T BEEN DOWN TO THE BAYOU EVER SINCE THEN. IT'S A BAD PLACE.
I AIN'T NEVER SEEN NOBODY DEAD BEFORE. DID HE LOOK LIKE THAT FRANKENSTEIN PICTURE WE SAW THAT ONE TIME?
HE WAS ALL PALE AND PUFFY AND HIS EYES WERE BULGING OUT.
MY MAMA SAYS BILLY GLASS DESERVED WHAT HE GOT.
SHE SAID A N***** BOY GOT NO BUSINESS WHISTLIN' AT NO WHITE WOMAN.
YOUR HAIR IS PRETTY, I WISH I HAD HAIR LIKE YOURS.
LET'S GO DOWN TO THE Bayou!

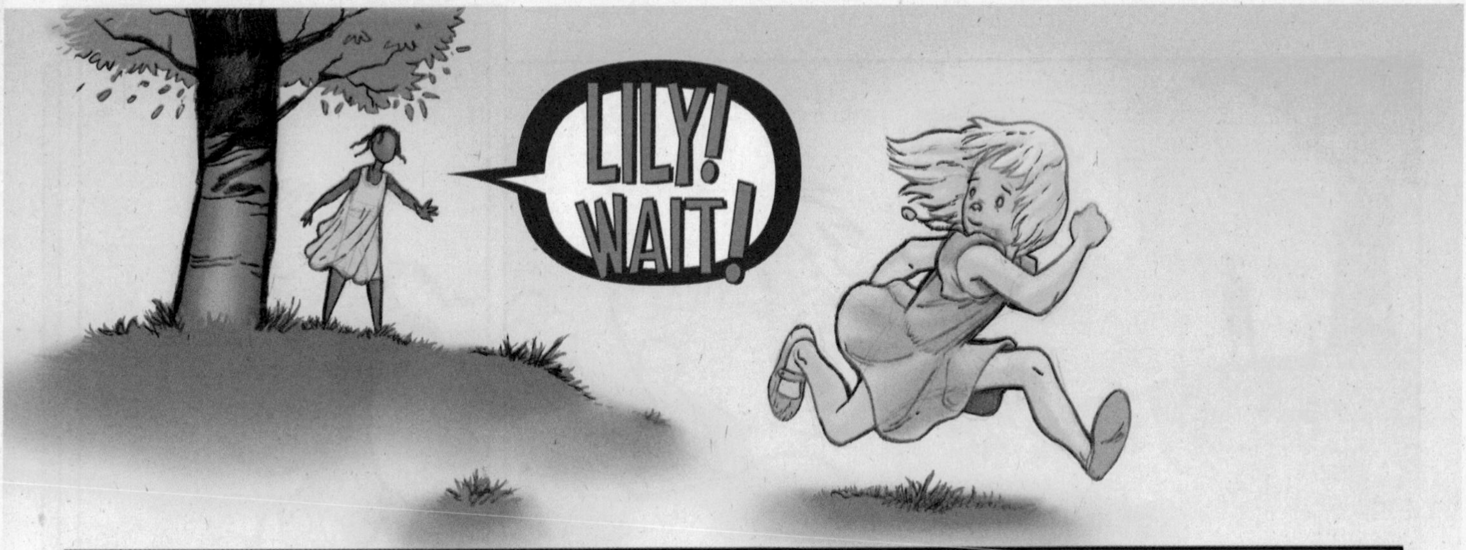
LILY! WAIT!

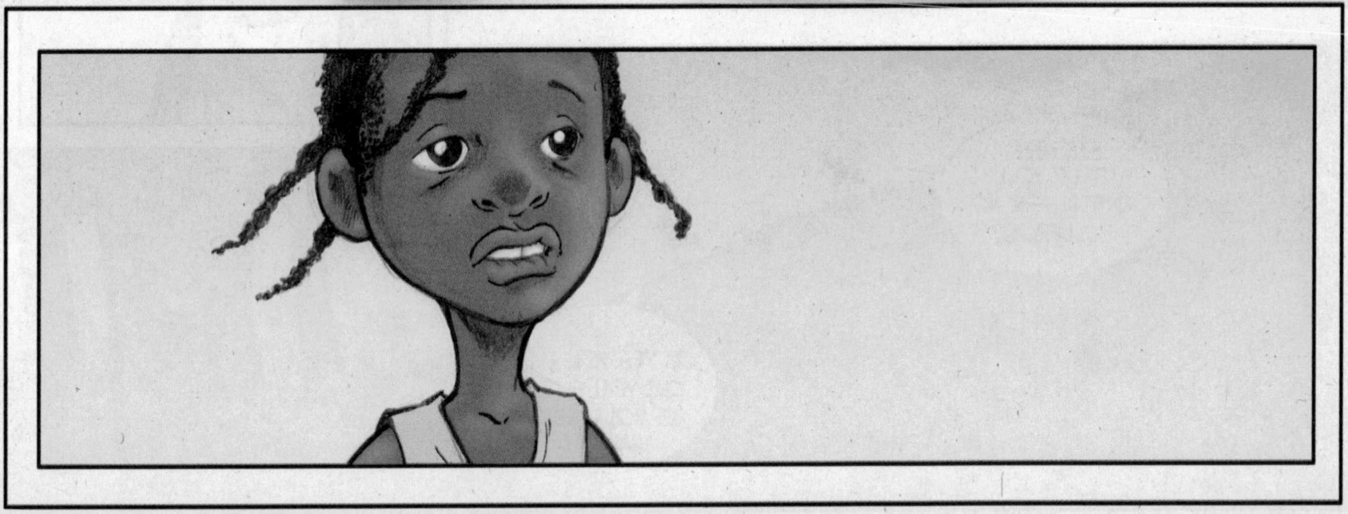

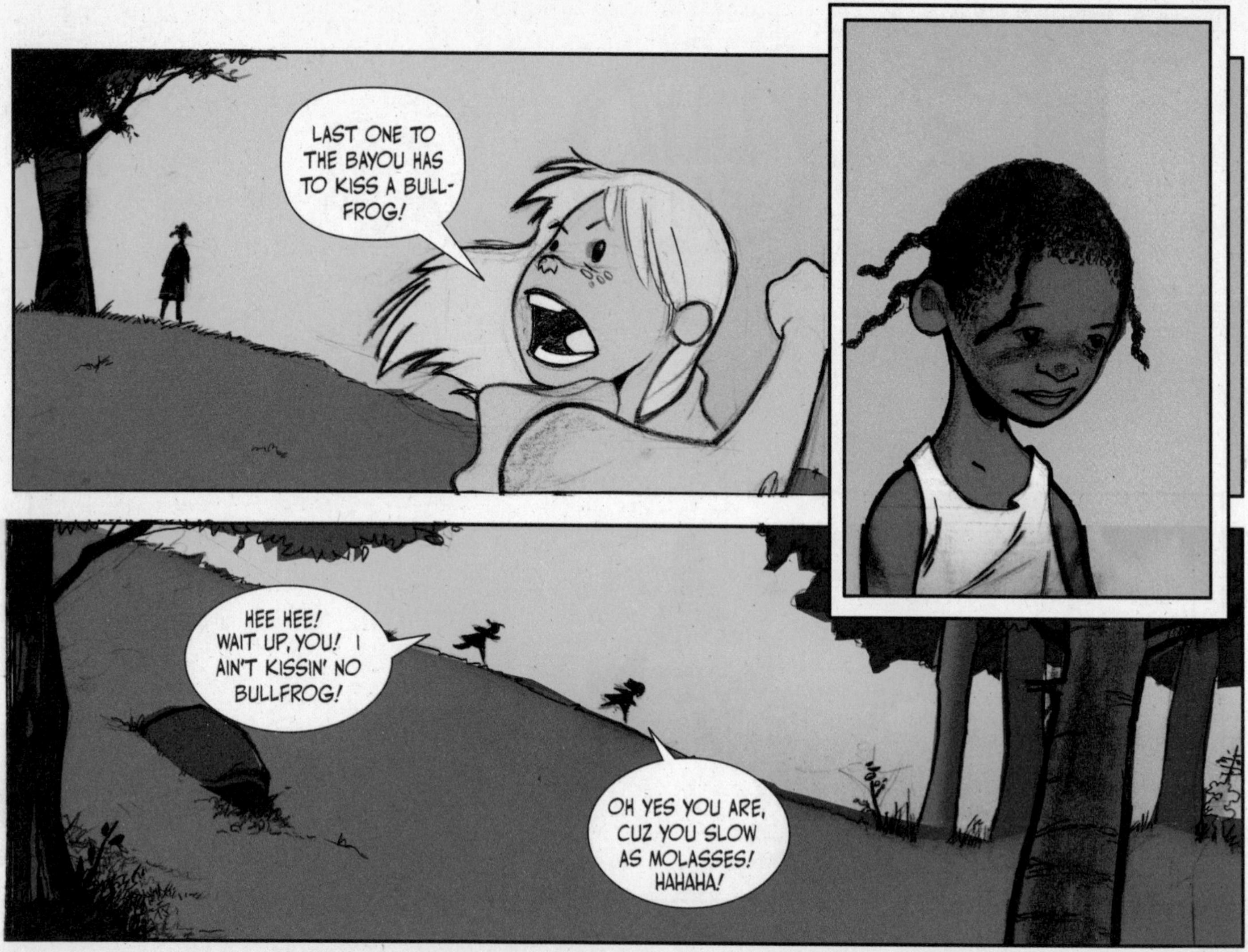
LAST ONE TO THE BAYOU HAS TO KISS A BULL-FROG!
HEE HEE! WAIT UP, YOU! I AIN'T KISSIN' NO BULLFROG!
OH YES YOU ARE, CUZ YOU SLOW AS MOLASSES! HAHAHA!

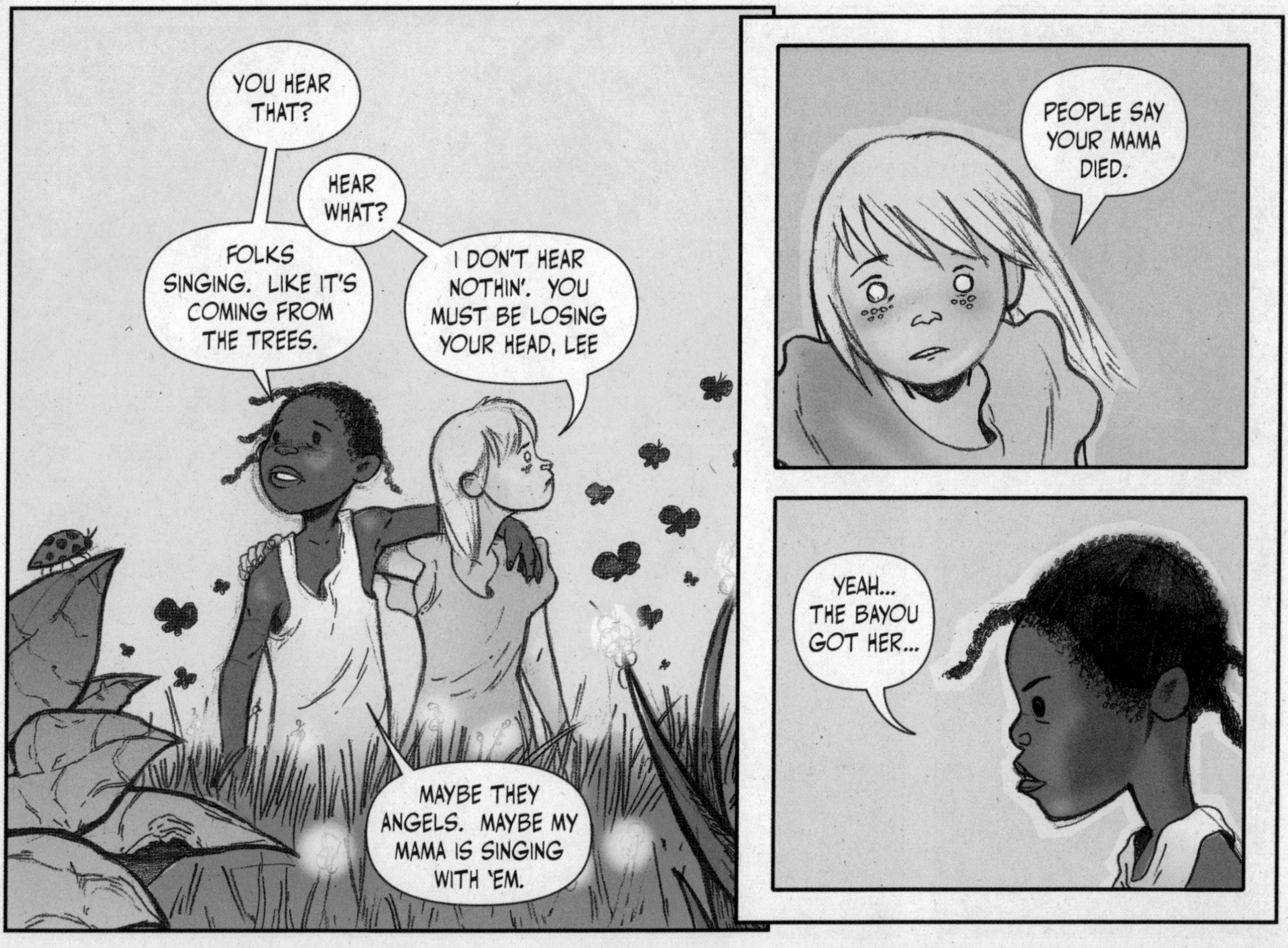
YOU HEAR THAT?
HEAR WHAT?
FOLKS SINGING. LIKE IT'S COMING FROM THE TREES.
I DON'T HEAR NOTHIN'. YOU MUST BE LOSING YOUR HEAD, LEE
MAYBE THEY ANGELS. MAYBE MY MAMA IS SINGING WITH 'EM.
PEOPLE SAY YOUR MAMA DIED.
YEAH... THE BAYOU GOT HER...

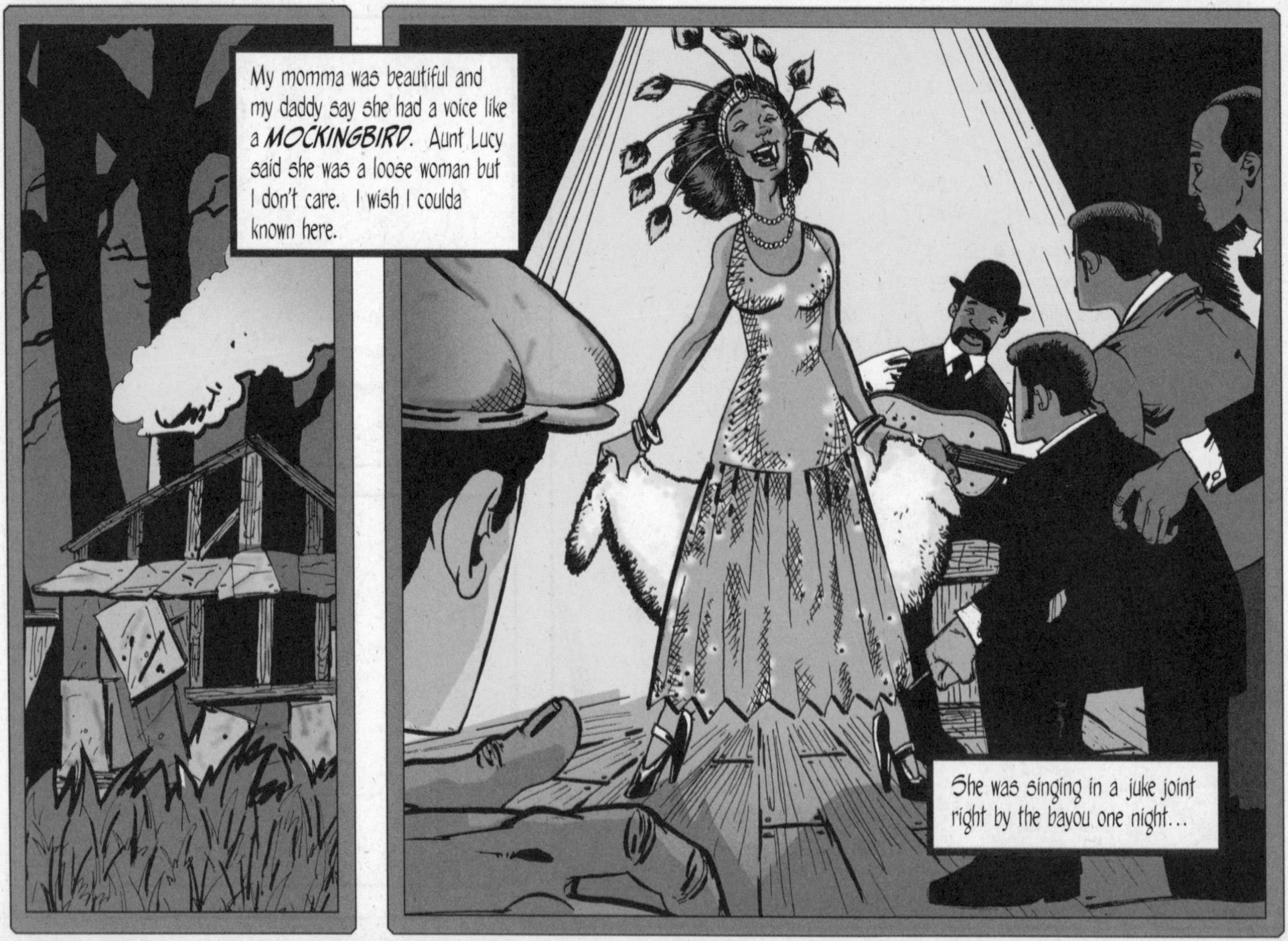
My momma was beautiful and my daddy say she had a voice like a MOCKINGBIRD. Aunt Lucy said she was a loose woman but I don't care. I wish I coulda known here.
She was singing in a juke joint right by the bayou one night...

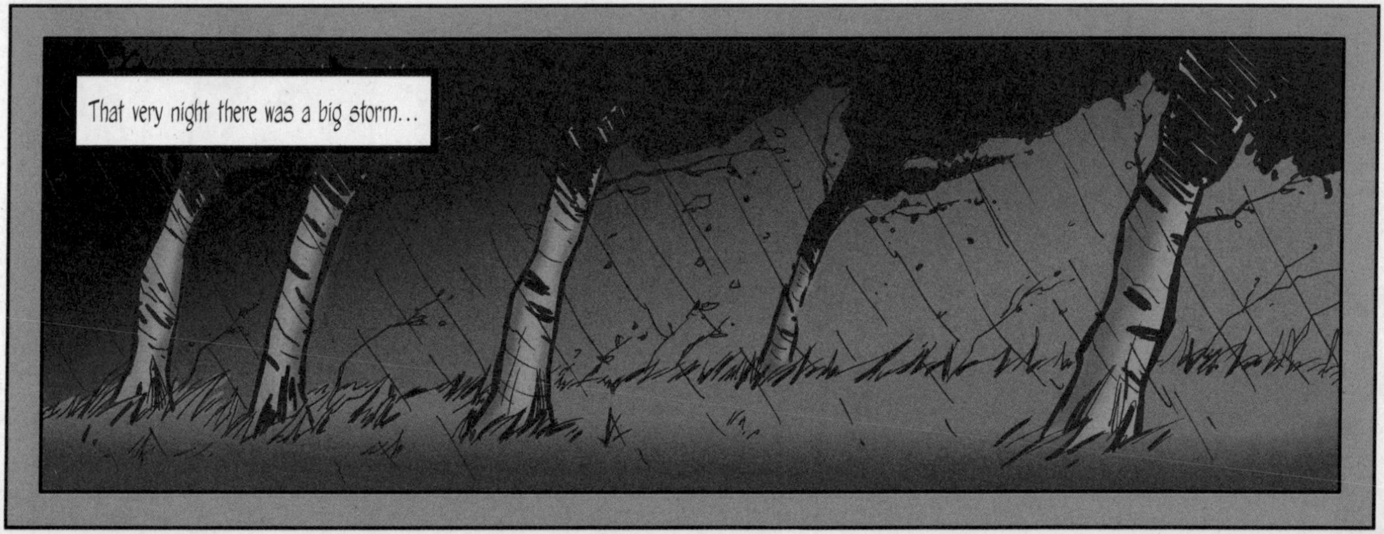
That very night there was a big storm...

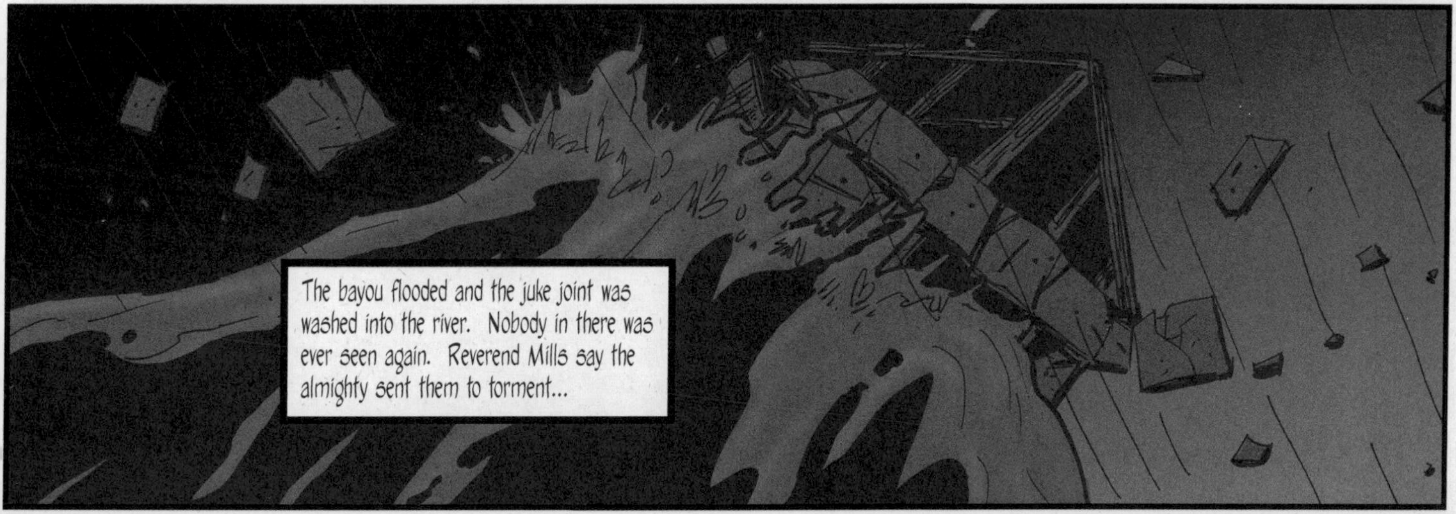
The bayou flooded and the juke joint was washed into the river. Nobody in there was ever seen again. Reverend Mills say the almighty sent them to torment...

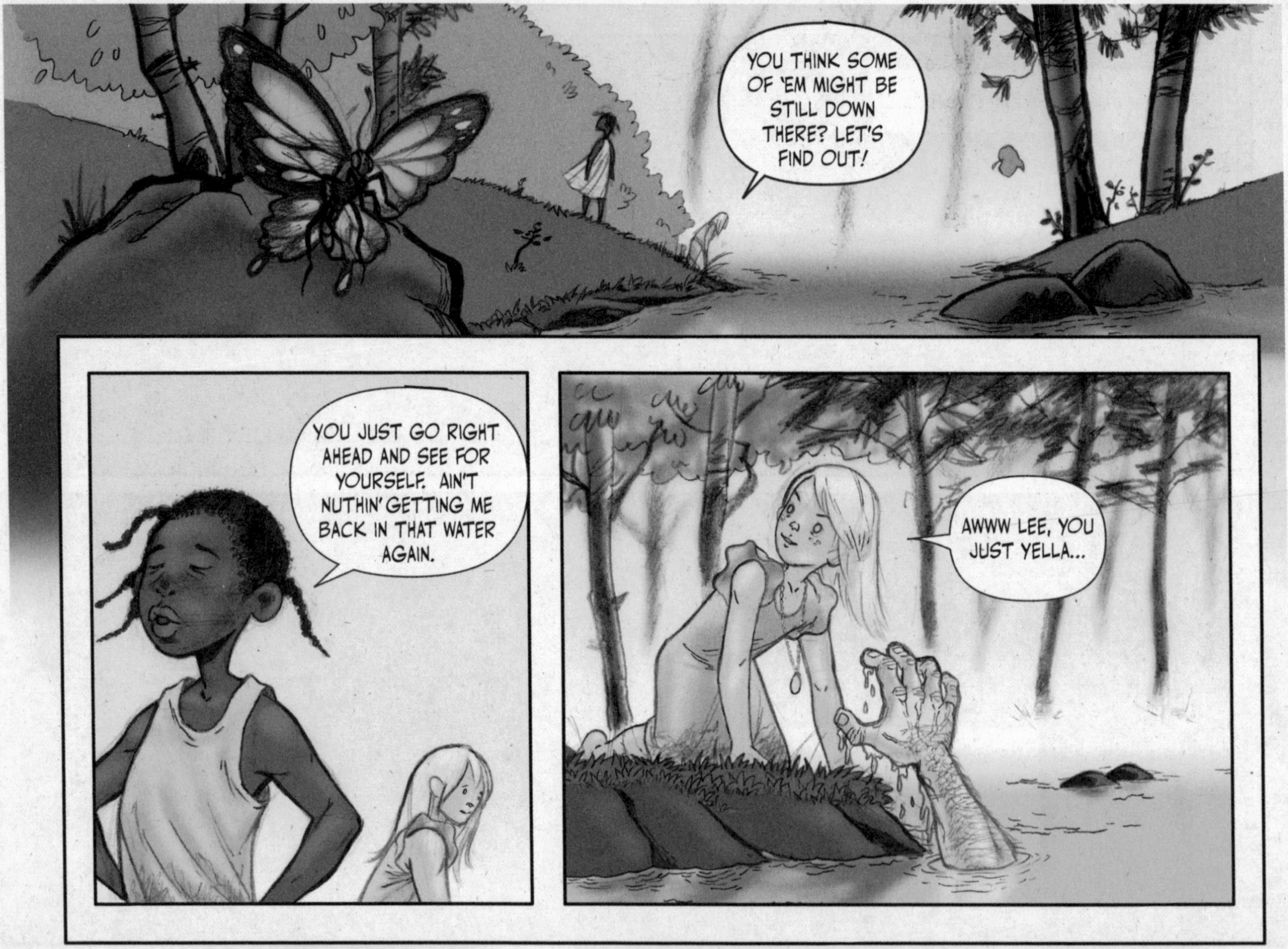
YOU THINK SOME OF 'EM MIGHT BE STILL DOWN THERE? LET'S FIND OUT!
YOU JUST GO RIGHT AHEAD AND SEE FOR YOURSELF. AIN'T NUTHIN' GETTING ME BACK IN THAT WATER AGAIN.
AWWW LEE, YOU JUST YELLA...

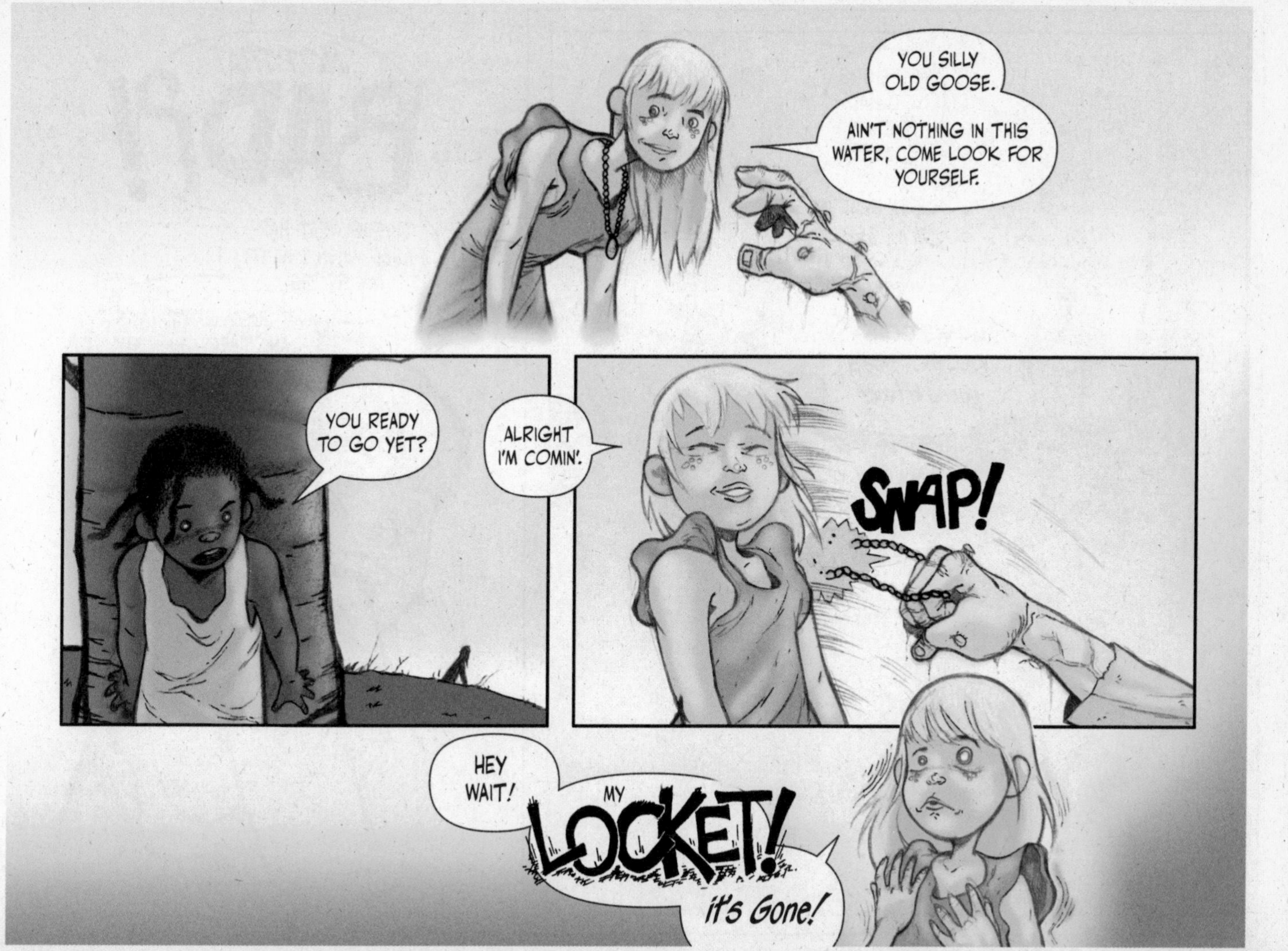
YOU SILLY OLD GOOSE.
AIN'T NOTHING IN THIS WATER, COME LOOK FOR YOURSELF.
YOU READY TO GO YET?
ALRIGHT I'M COMIN'.
SWAP!
HEY WAIT!
MY LOCKET!
it's Gone!

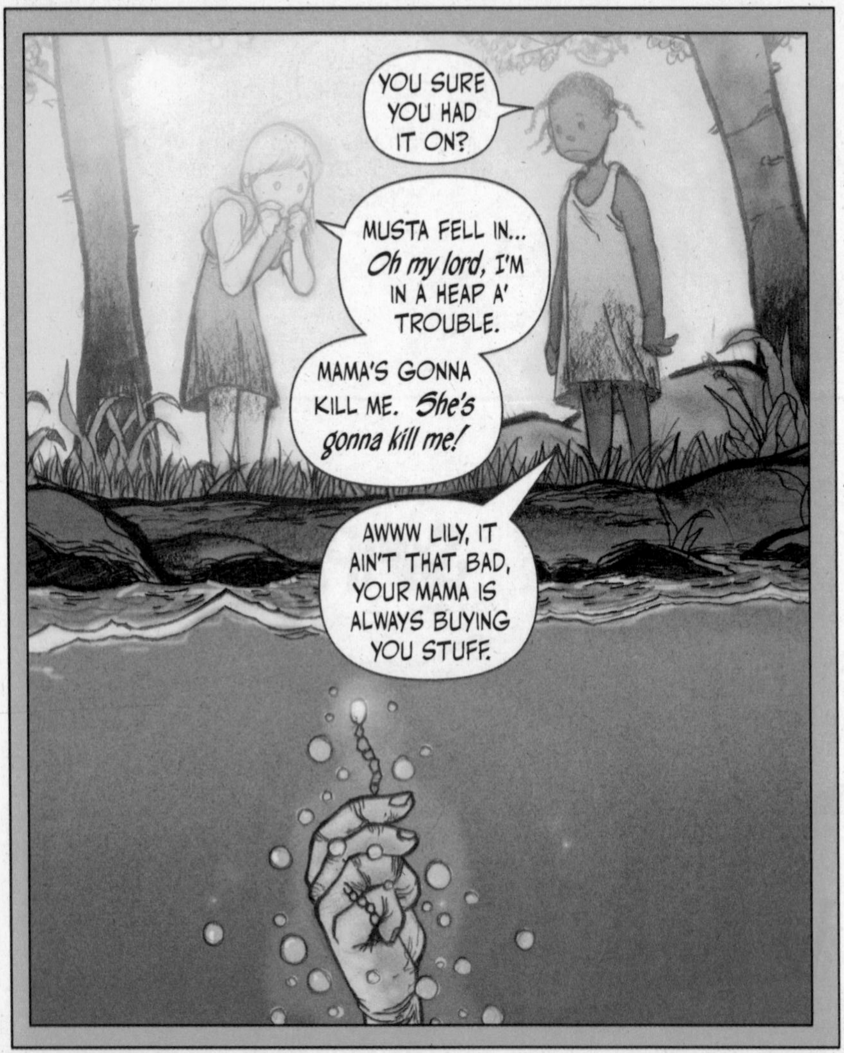
YOU SURE YOU HAD IT ON?
MUSTA FELL IN... *Oh my lord,* I'M IN A HEAP A' TROUBLE.
MAMA'S GONNA KILL ME. *She's gonna kill me!*
AWWW LILY, IT AIN'T THAT BAD, YOUR MAMA IS ALWAYS BUYING YOU STUFF.

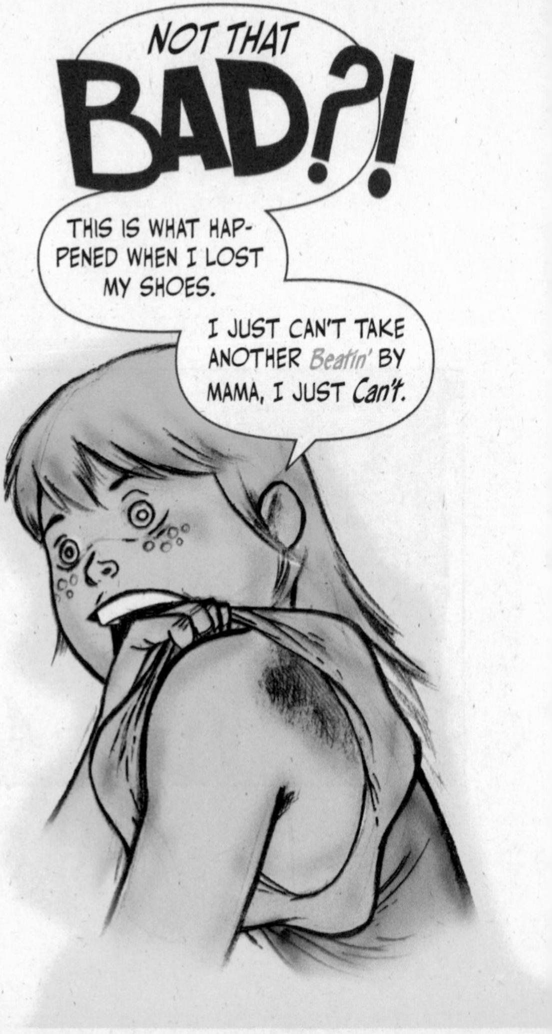
NOT THAT BAD?!
THIS IS WHAT HAPPENED WHEN I LOST MY SHOES.
I JUST CAN'T TAKE ANOTHER *Beatin'* BY MAMA, I JUST *Can't.*

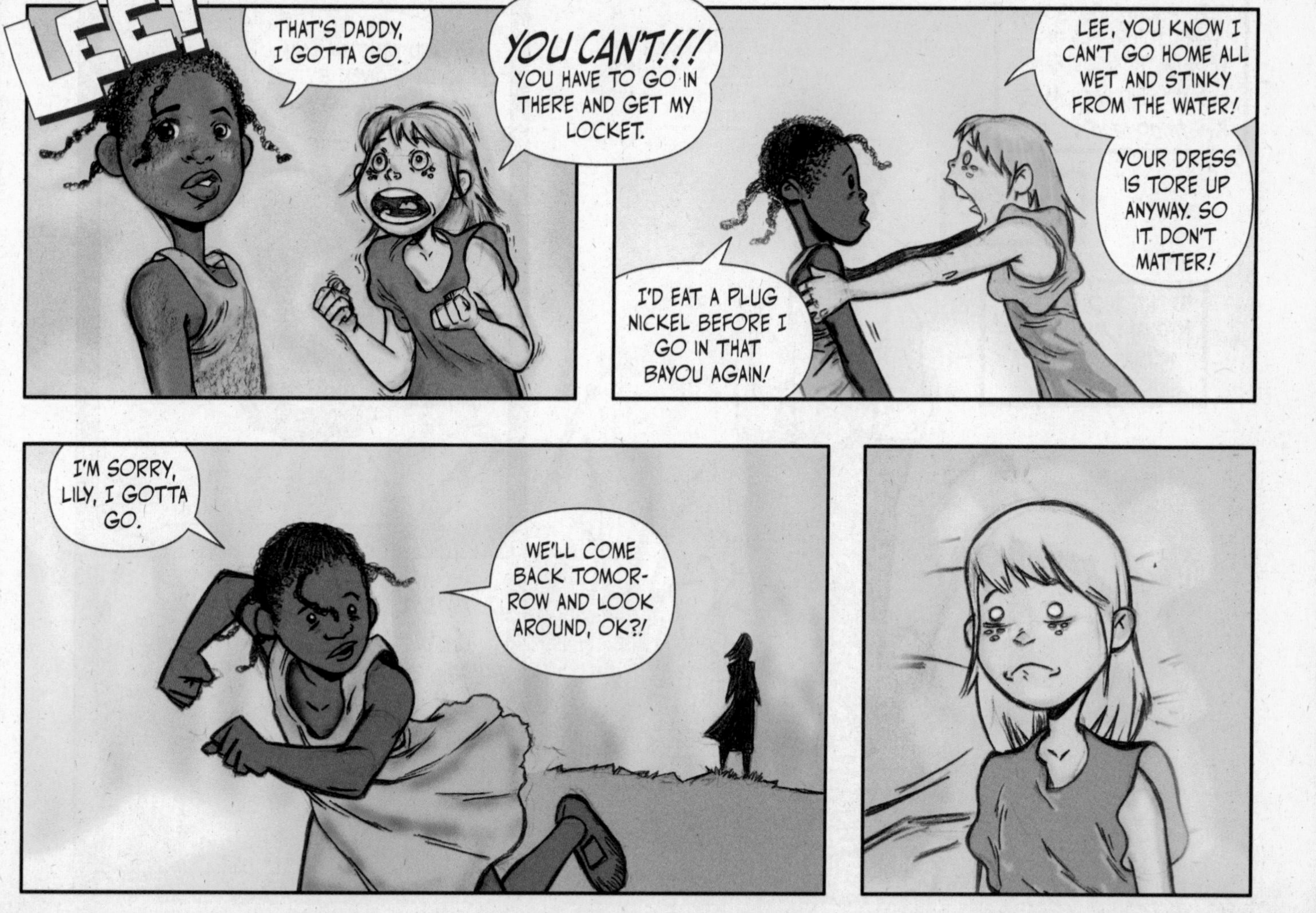
LEE!
THAT'S DADDY, I GOTTA GO.
YOU CAN'T!!! YOU HAVE TO GO IN THERE AND GET MY LOCKET.
LEE, YOU KNOW I CAN'T GO HOME ALL WET AND STINKY FROM THE WATER!
YOUR DRESS IS TORE UP ANYWAY. SO IT DON'T MATTER!
I'D EAT A PLUG NICKEL BEFORE I GO IN THAT BAYOU AGAIN!
I'M SORRY, LILY, I GOTTA GO.
WE'LL COME BACK TOMOR-ROW AND LOOK AROUND, OK?!

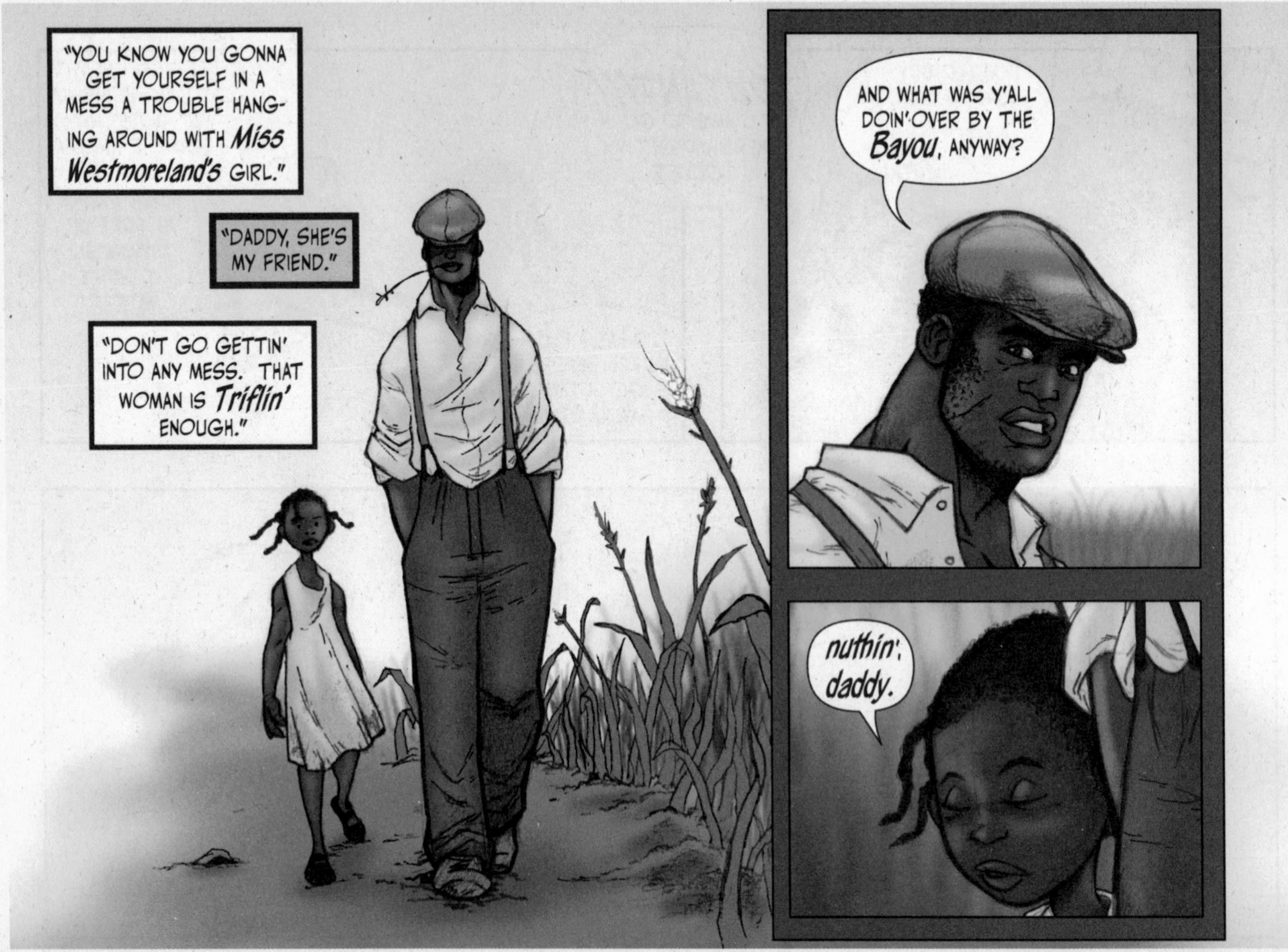
"YOU KNOW YOU GONNA GET YOURSELF IN A MESS A TROUBLE HANGING AROUND WITH Miss Westmoreland's GIRL."
"DADDY, SHE'S MY FRIEND."
"DON'T GO GETTIN' INTO ANY MESS. THAT WOMAN IS Triflin' ENOUGH."
AND WHAT WAS Y'ALL DOIN' OVER BY THE Bayou, ANYWAY?
nuthin', daddy.

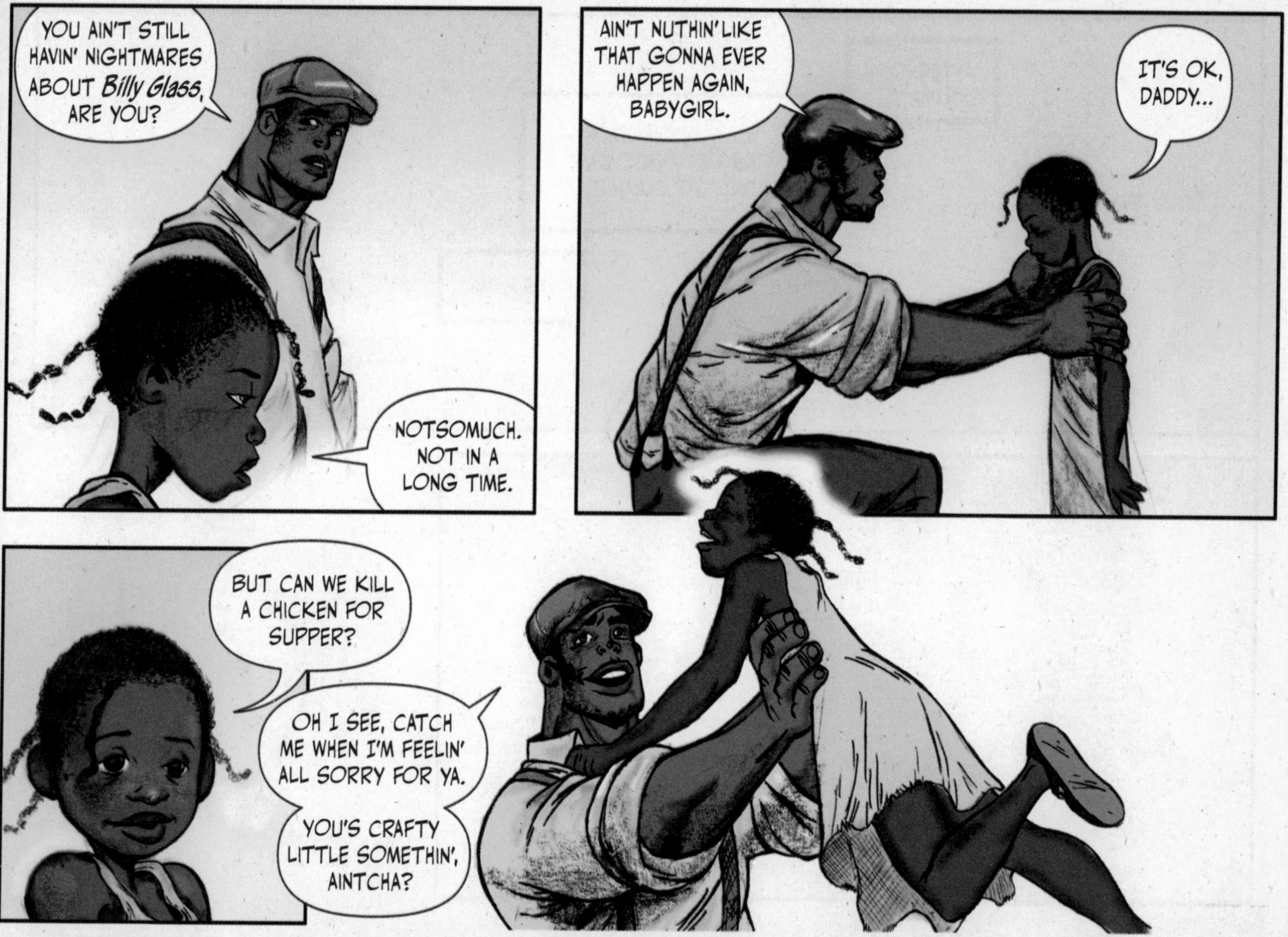
YOU AIN'T STILL HAVIN' NIGHTMARES ABOUT *Billy Glass*, ARE YOU?
NOTSOMUCH. NOT IN A LONG TIME.
AIN'T NUTHIN' LIKE THAT GONNA EVER HAPPEN AGAIN, BABYGIRL.
IT'S OK, DADDY...
BUT CAN WE KILL A CHICKEN FOR SUPPER?
OH I SEE, CATCH ME WHEN I'M FEELIN' ALL SORRY FOR YA.
YOU'S CRAFTY LITTLE SOMETHIN', AINTCHA?

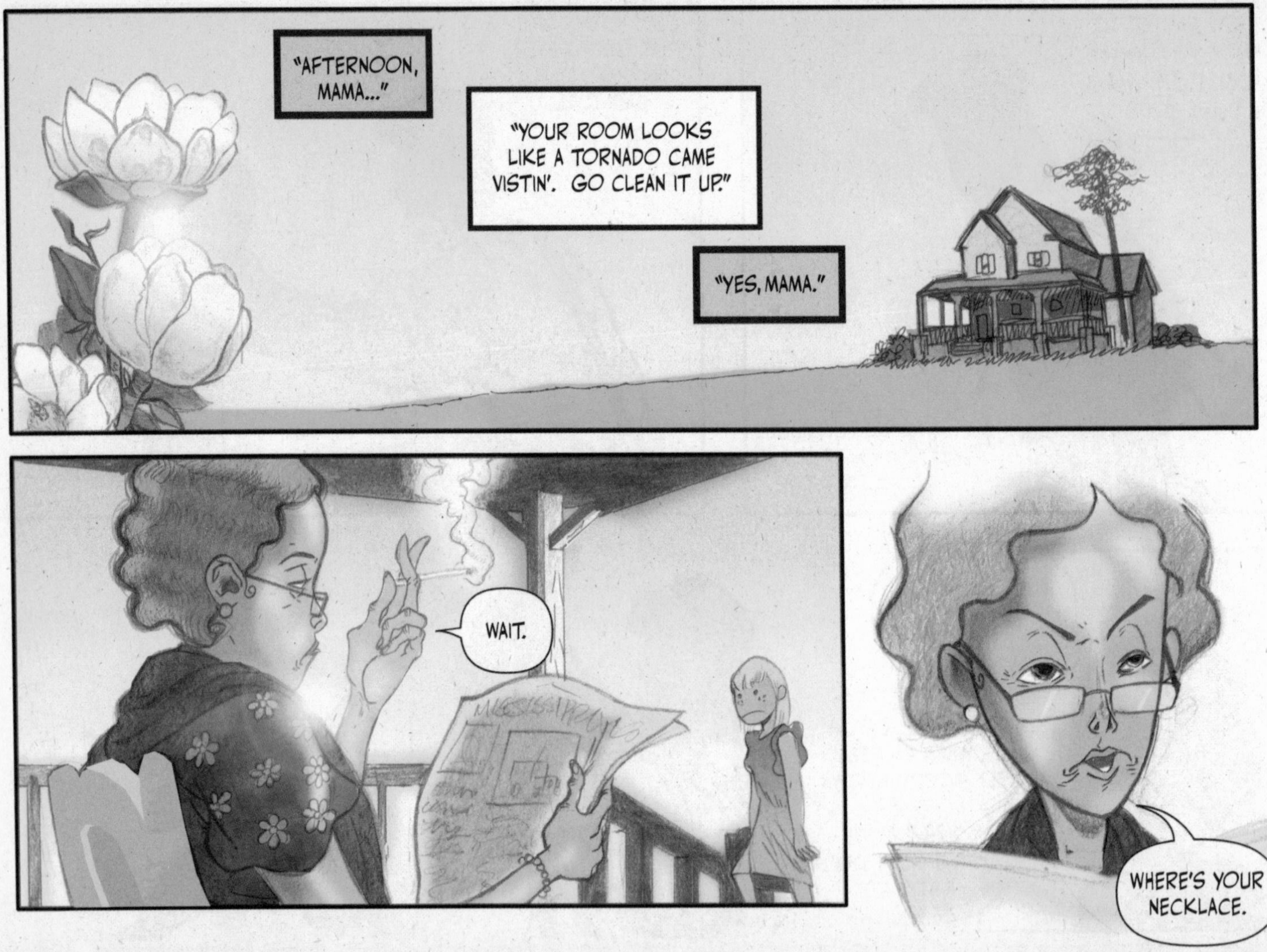
"AFTERNOON, MAMA..."
"YOUR ROOM LOOKS LIKE A TORNADO CAME VISTIN'. GO CLEAN IT UP."
"YES, MAMA."
WAIT.
WHERE'S YOUR NECKLACE.

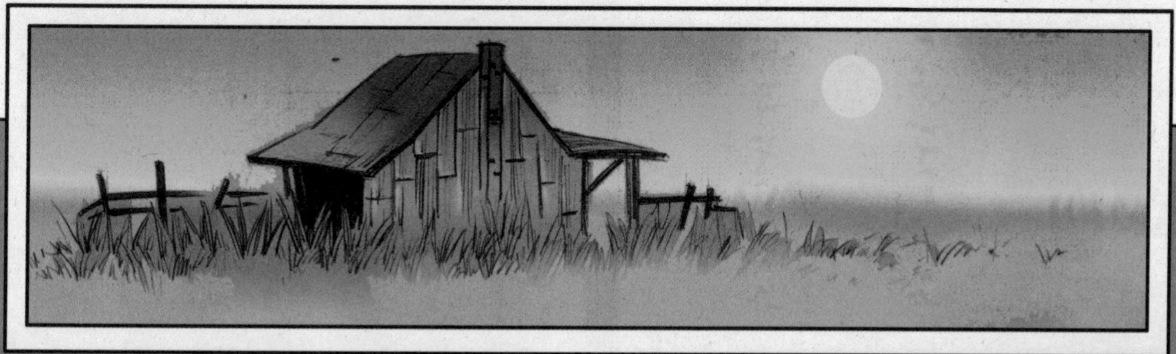
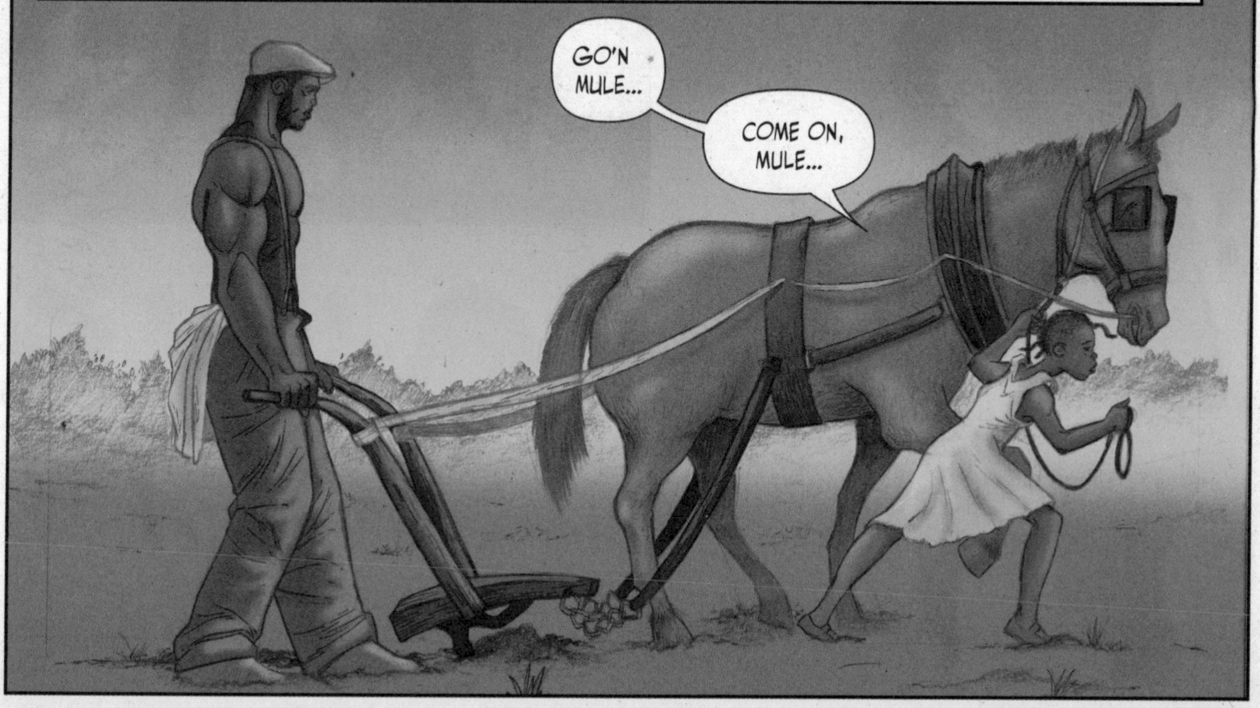
GO'N MULE...
COME ON, MULE...

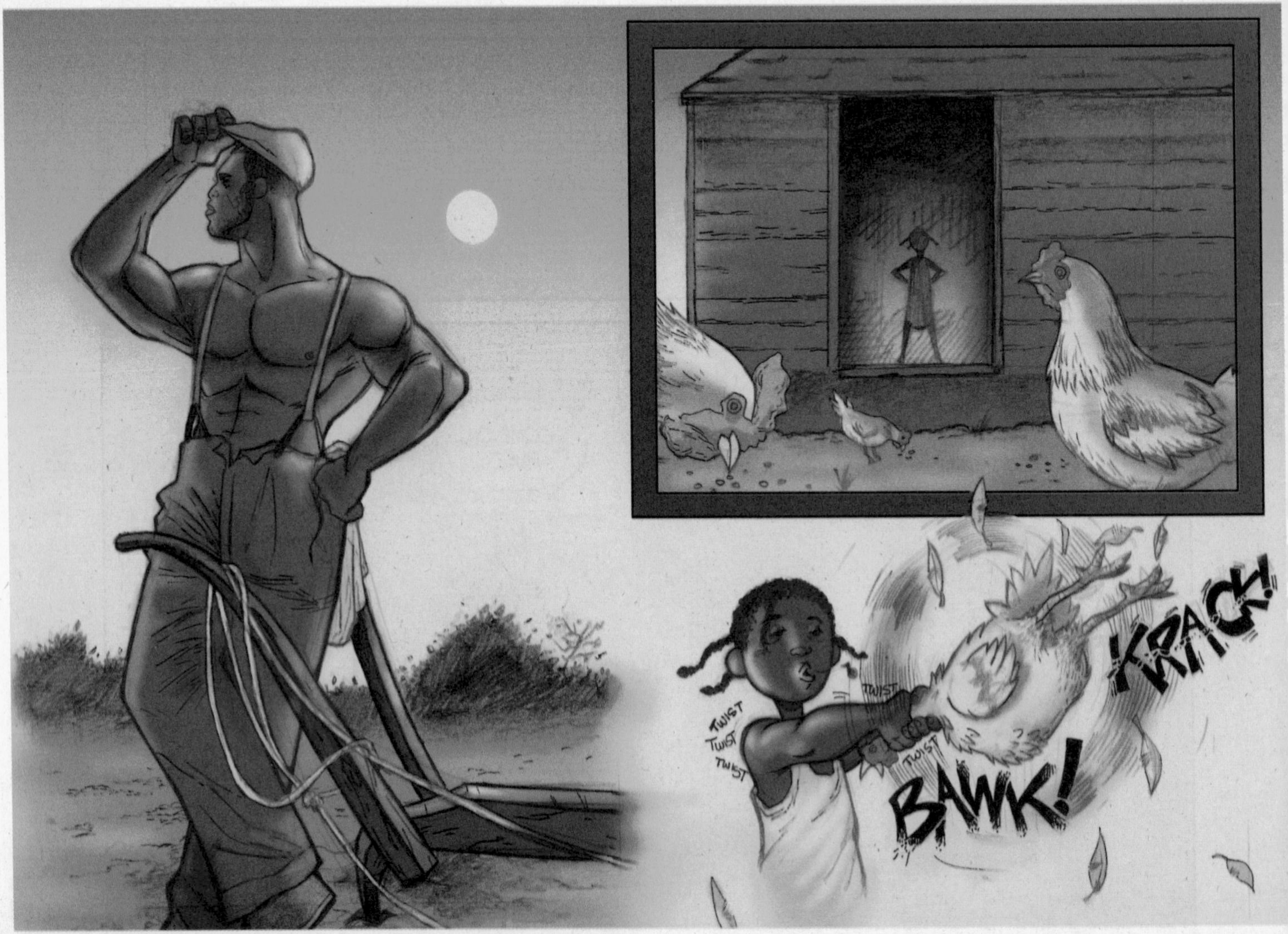
TWIST
TWIST
TWIST
TWIST
TWIST
TWIST
BAWK!
KRACK!

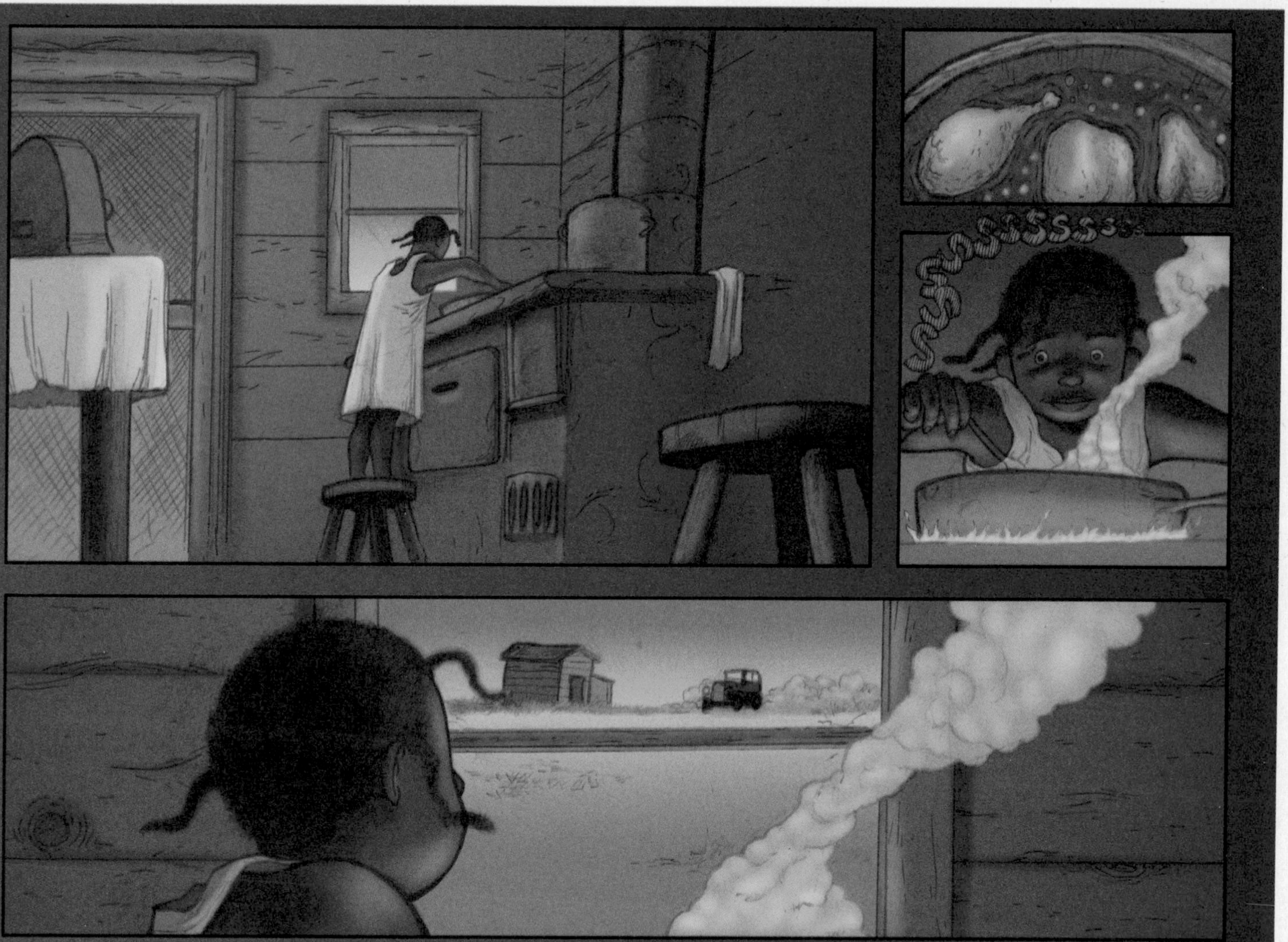
SSSSSSSSSSSsss

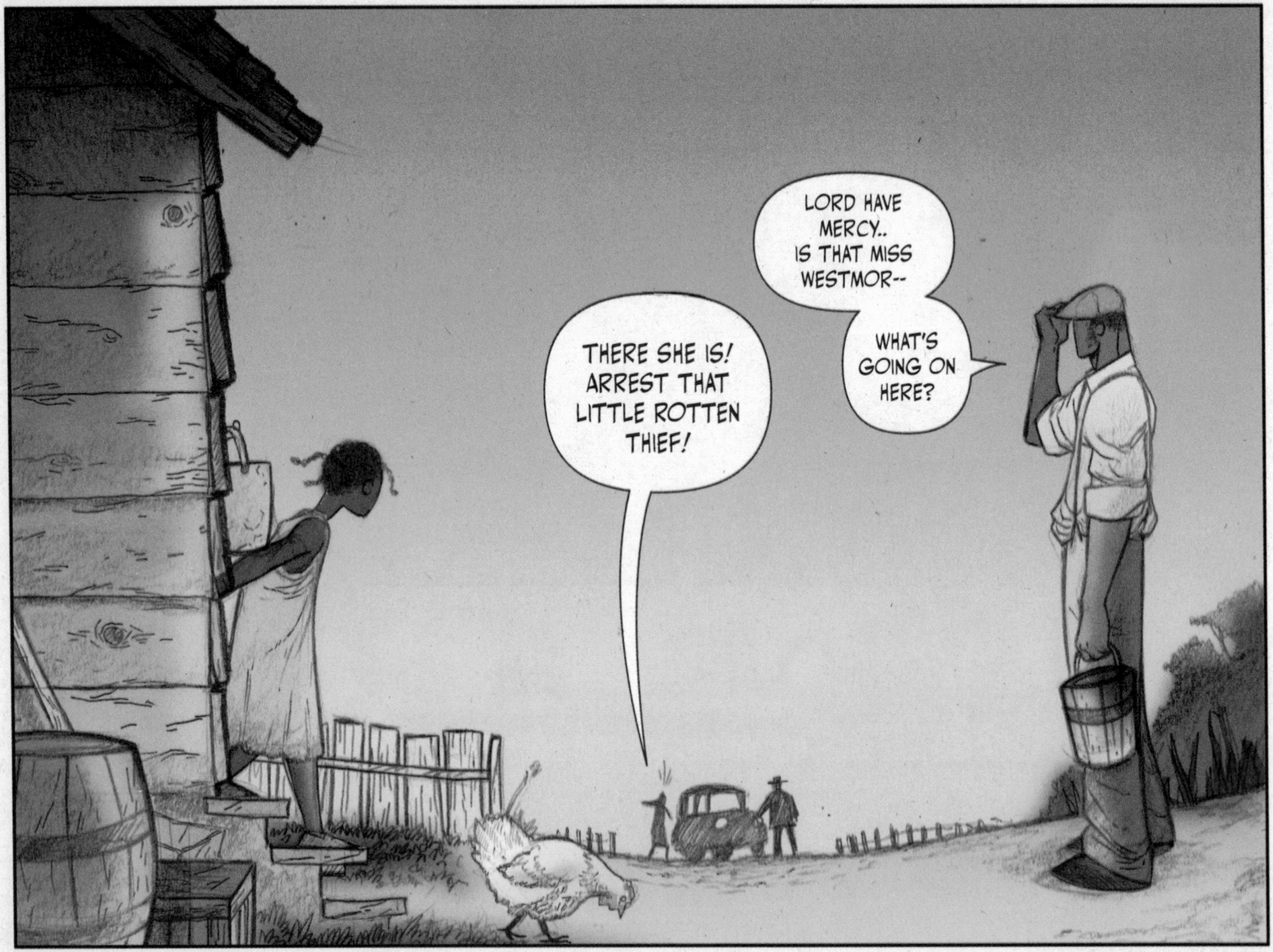
LORD HAVE MERCY.. IS THAT MISS WESTMOR--
WHAT'S GOING ON HERE?
THERE SHE IS! ARREST THAT LITTLE ROTTEN THIEF!

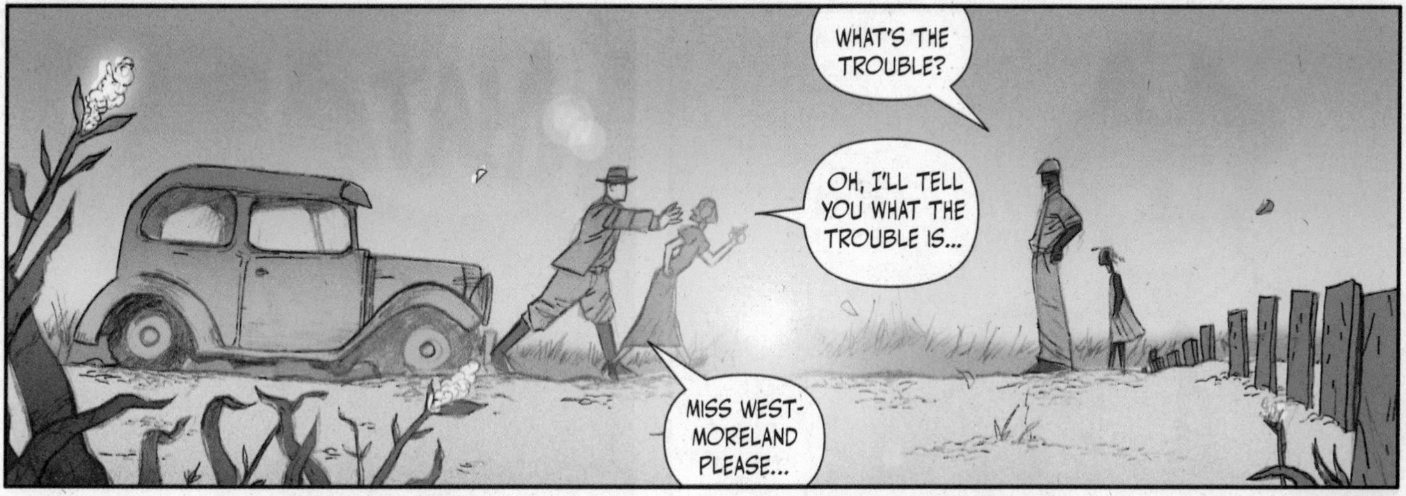
WHAT'S THE TROUBLE?
OH, I'LL TELL YOU WHAT THE TROUBLE IS...
MISS WEST-MORELAND PLEASE...

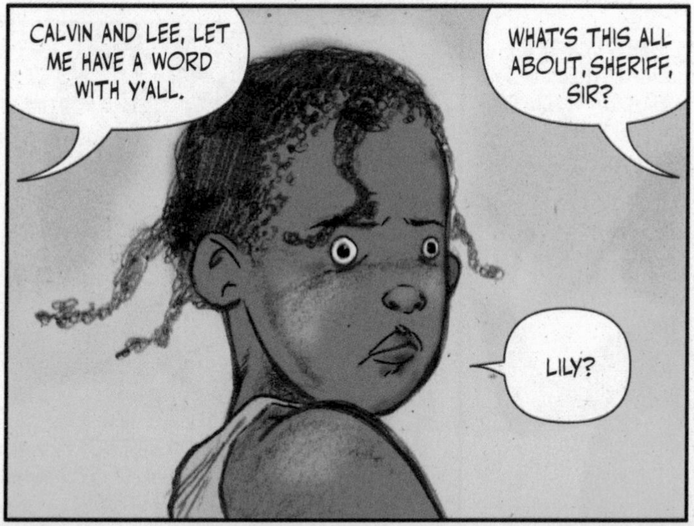
CALVIN AND LEE, LET ME HAVE A WORD WITH Y'ALL.
WHAT'S THIS ALL ABOUT, SHERIFF, SIR?
LILY?

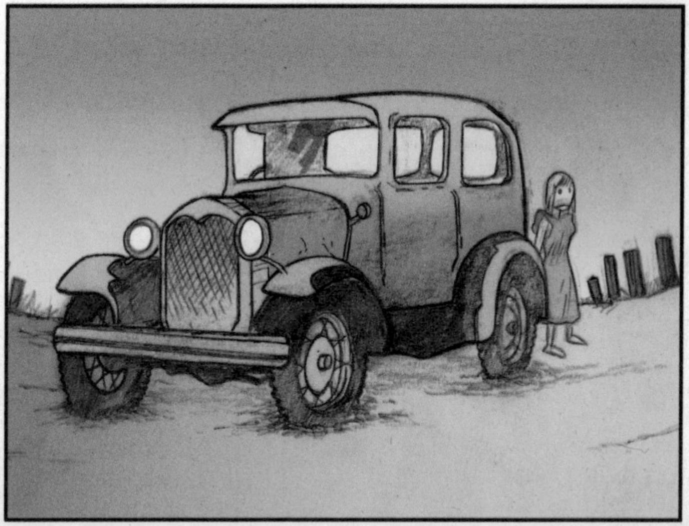

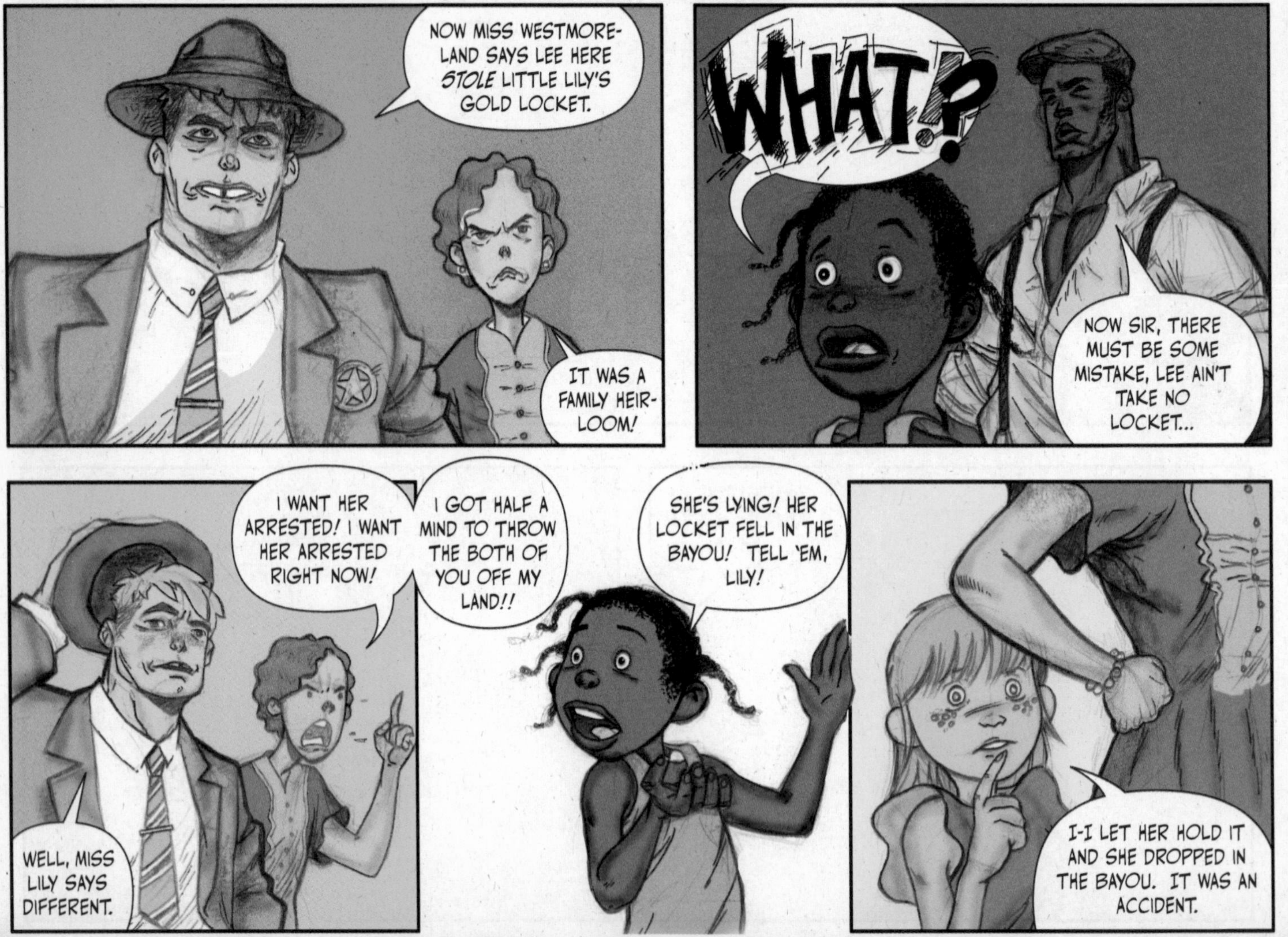
NOW MISS WESTMORE-LAND SAYS LEE HERE *STOLE* LITTLE LILY'S GOLD LOCKET.
IT WAS A FAMILY HEIR-LOOM!
WHAT!?
NOW SIR, THERE MUST BE SOME MISTAKE, LEE AIN'T TAKE NO LOCKET...
I WANT HER ARRESTED! I WANT HER ARRESTED RIGHT NOW!
I GOT HALF A MIND TO THROW THE BOTH OF YOU OFF MY LAND!!
WELL, MISS LILY SAYS DIFFERENT.
SHE'S LYING! HER LOCKET FELL IN THE BAYOU! TELL 'EM, LILY!
I-I LET HER HOLD IT AND SHE DROPPED IN THE BAYOU. IT WAS AN ACCIDENT.

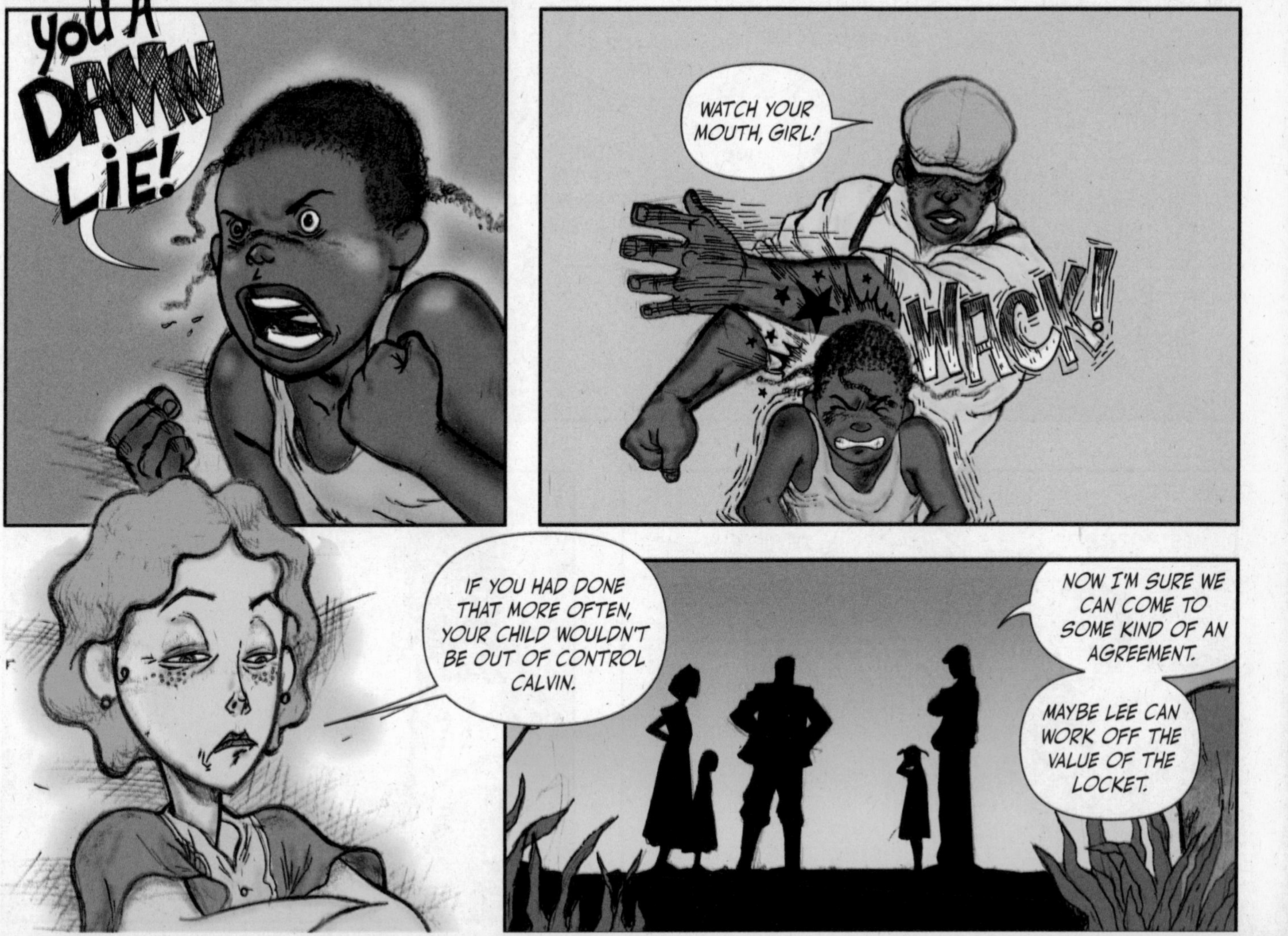
YOU A DAMN LIE!
WATCH YOUR MOUTH, GIRL!
WACK!
IF YOU HAD DONE THAT MORE OFTEN, YOUR CHILD WOULDN'T BE OUT OF CONTROL CALVIN.
NOW I'M SURE WE CAN COME TO SOME KIND OF AN AGREEMENT.
MAYBE LEE CAN WORK OFF THE VALUE OF THE LOCKET.

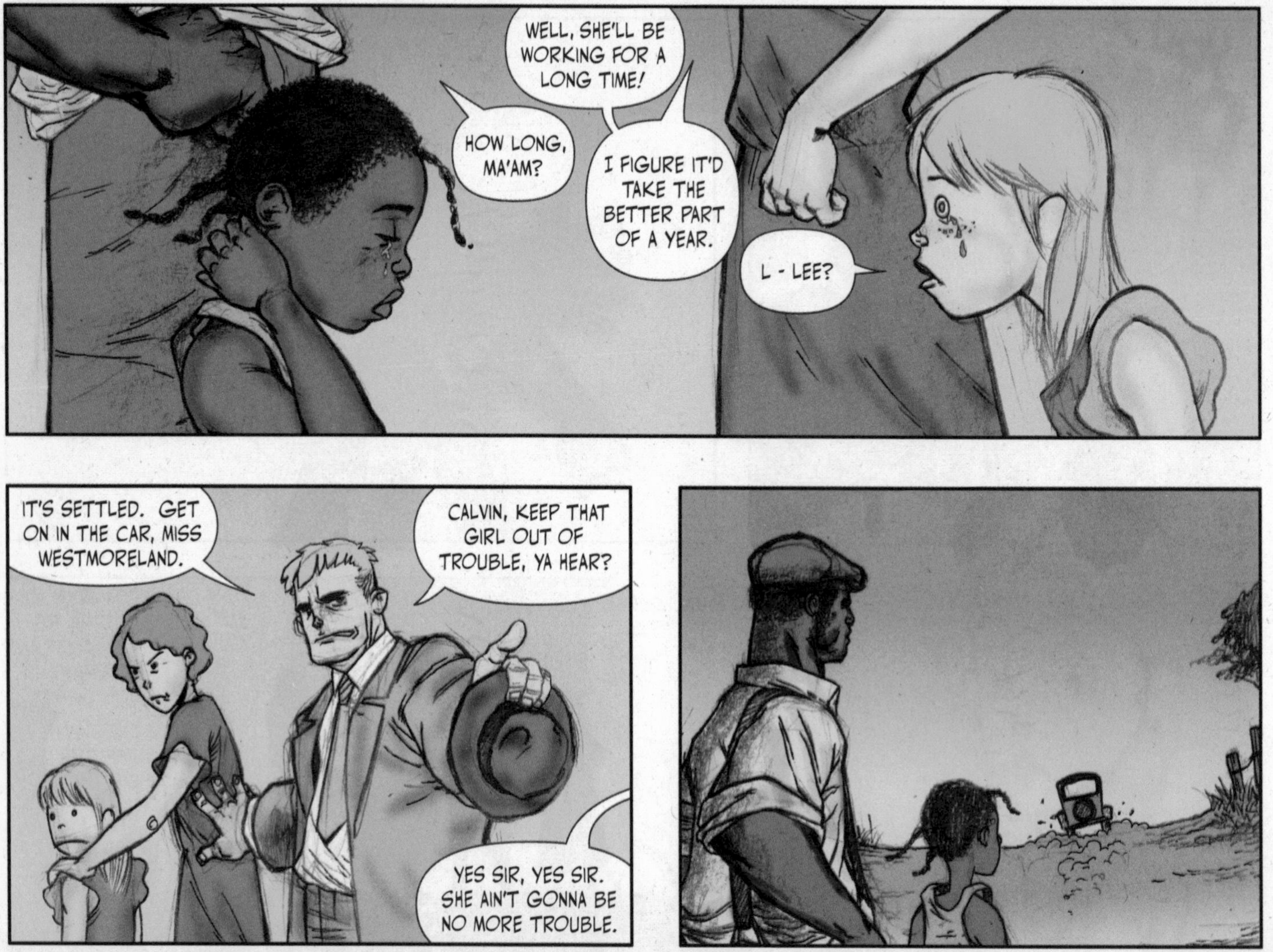
HOW LONG, MA'AM?
WELL, SHE'LL BE WORKING FOR A LONG TIME!
I FIGURE IT'D TAKE THE BETTER PART OF A YEAR.
L - LEE?
IT'S SETTLED. GET ON IN THE CAR, MISS WESTMORELAND.
CALVIN, KEEP THAT GIRL OUT OF TROUBLE, YA HEAR?
YES SIR, YES SIR. SHE AIN'T GONNA BE NO MORE TROUBLE.

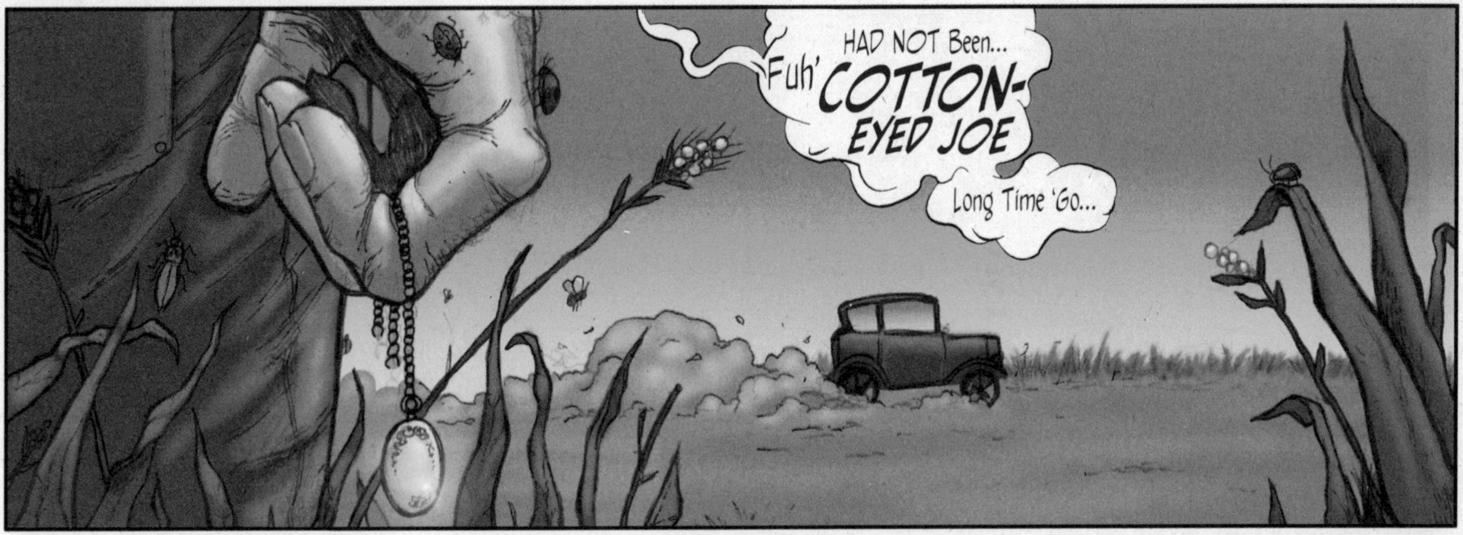
HAD NOT Been... Fuh' COTTON-EYED JOE
Long Time 'Go...
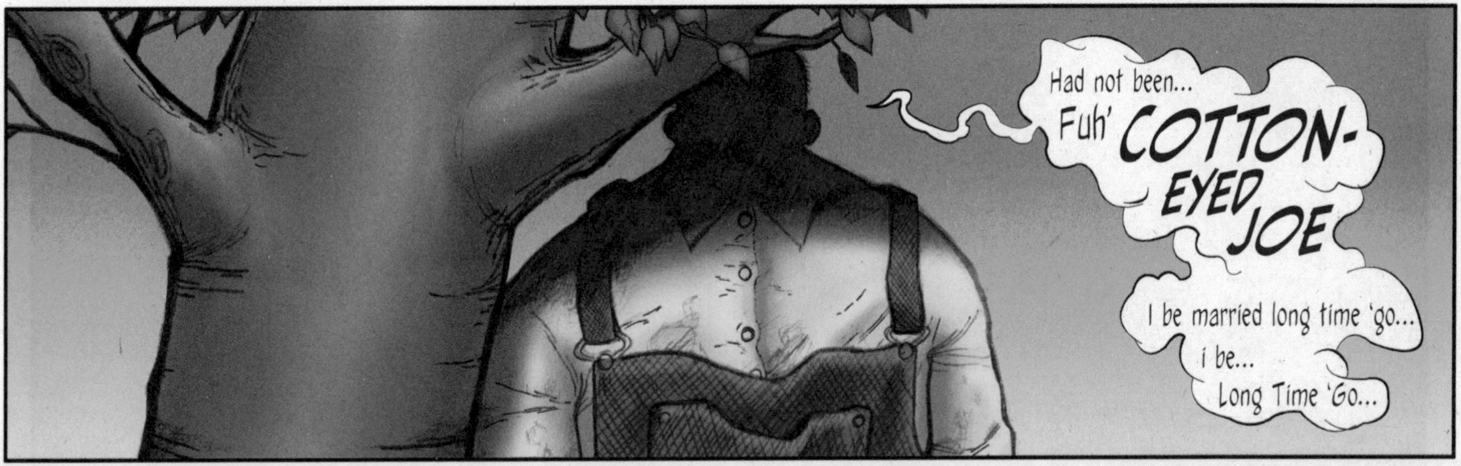
Had not been... Fuh' COTTON-EYED JOE
I be married long time 'go... i be... Long Time 'Go...

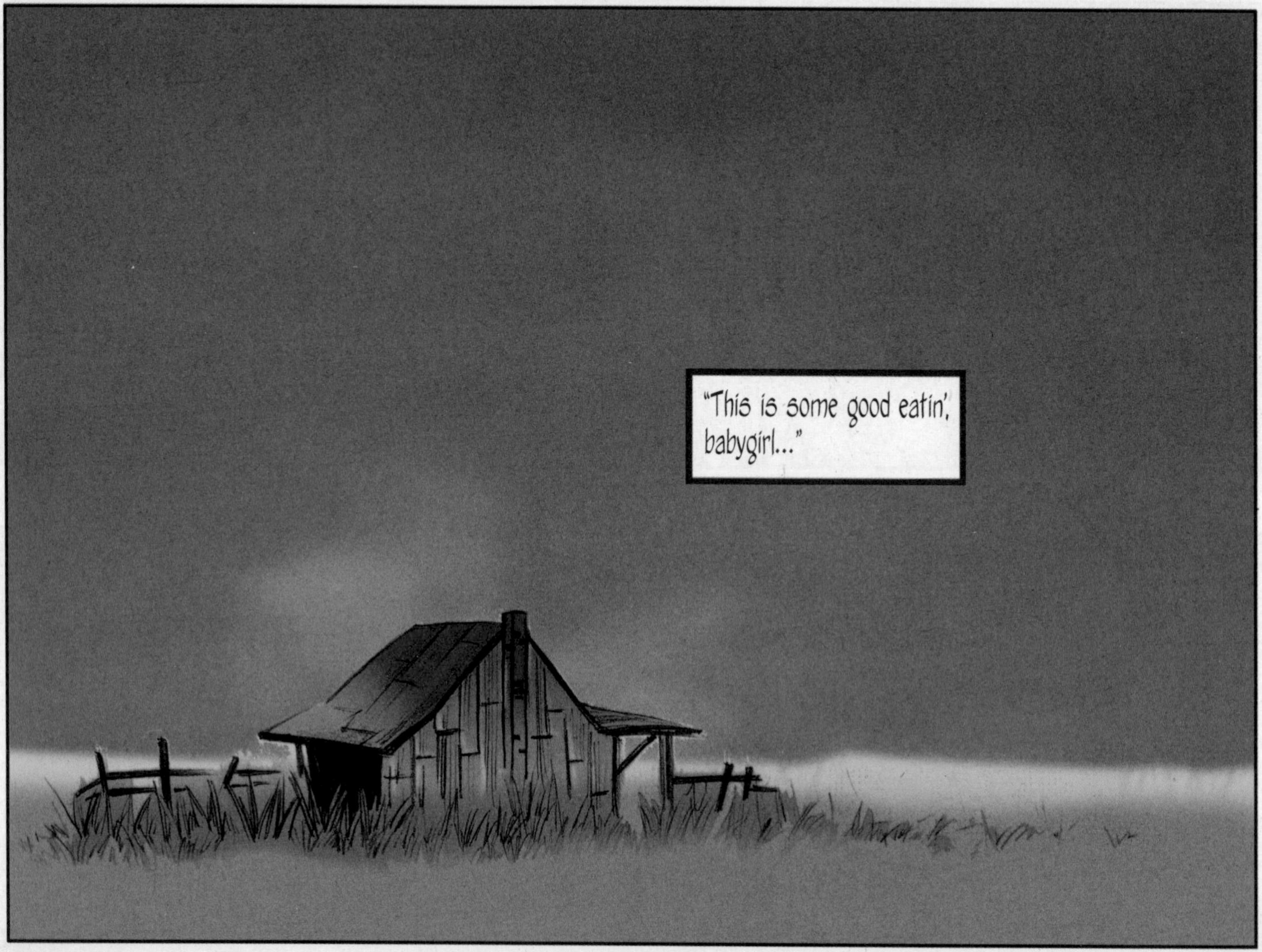
"This is some good eatin', babygirl..."

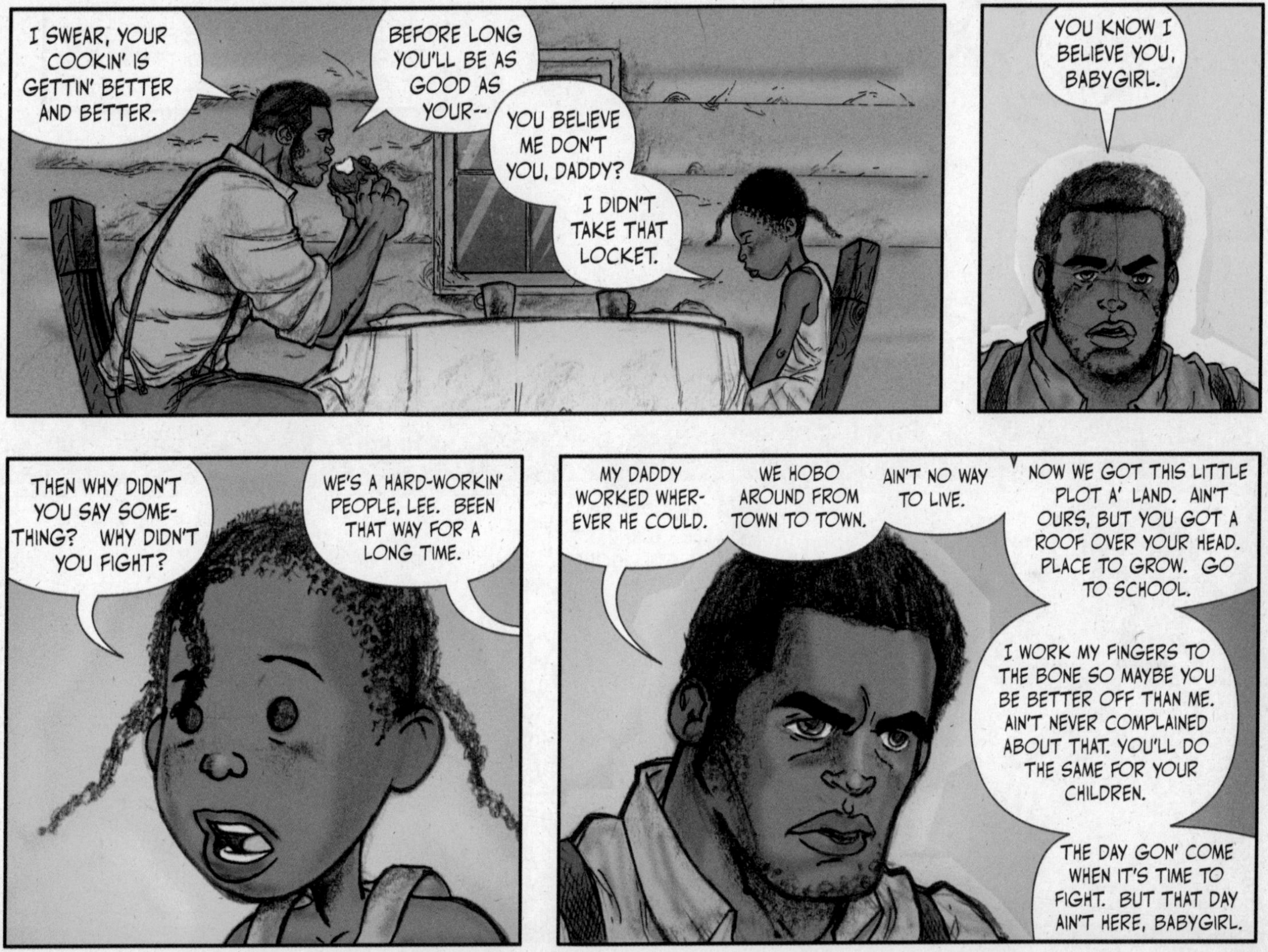
I SWEAR, YOUR COOKIN' IS GETTIN' BETTER AND BETTER.
BEFORE LONG YOU'LL BE AS GOOD AS YOUR--
YOU BELIEVE ME DON'T YOU, DADDY?
I DIDN'T TAKE THAT LOCKET.
YOU KNOW I BELIEVE YOU, BABYGIRL.
THEN WHY DIDN'T YOU SAY SOME-THING? WHY DIDN'T YOU FIGHT?
WE'S A HARD-WORKIN' PEOPLE, LEE. BEEN THAT WAY FOR A LONG TIME.
MY DADDY WORKED WHER-EVER HE COULD.
WE HOBO AROUND FROM TOWN TO TOWN.
AIN'T NO WAY TO LIVE.
NOW WE GOT THIS LITTLE PLOT A' LAND. AIN'T OURS, BUT YOU GOT A ROOF OVER YOUR HEAD. PLACE TO GROW. GO TO SCHOOL.
I WORK MY FINGERS TO THE BONE SO MAYBE YOU BE BETTER OFF THAN ME. AIN'T NEVER COMPLAINED ABOUT THAT. YOU'LL DO THE SAME FOR YOUR CHILDREN.
THE DAY GON' COME WHEN IT'S TIME TO FIGHT. BUT THAT DAY AIN'T HERE, BABYGIRL.

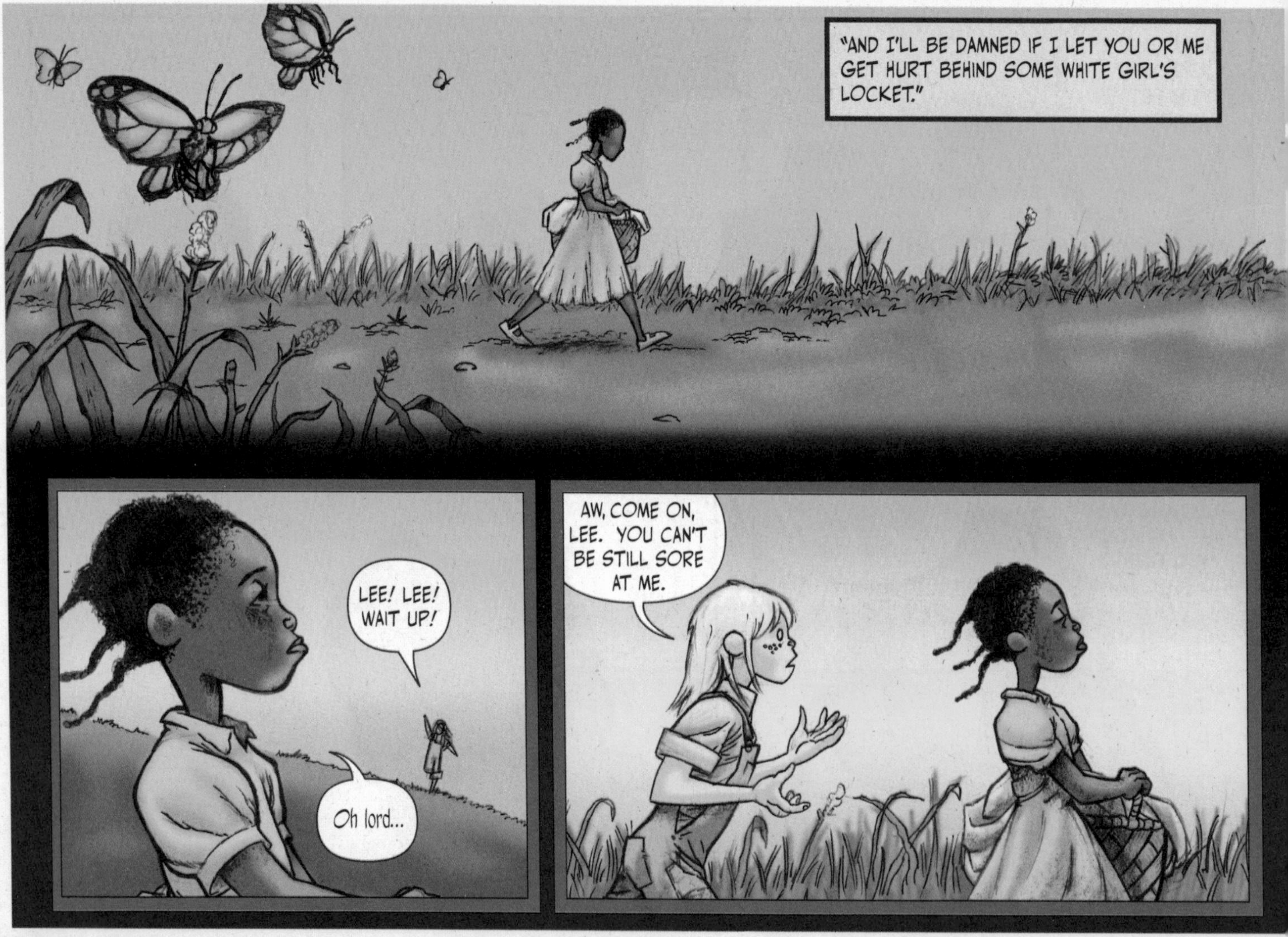
"AND I'LL BE DAMNED IF I LET YOU OR ME GET HURT BEHIND SOME WHITE GIRL'S LOCKET."
LEE! LEE! WAIT UP!
Oh lord...
AW, COME ON, LEE. YOU CAN'T BE STILL SORE AT ME.

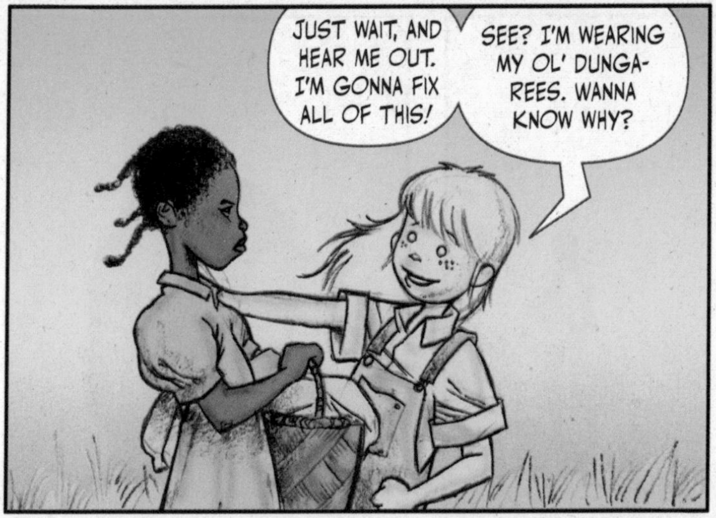
JUST WAIT, AND HEAR ME OUT. I'M GONNA FIX ALL OF THIS!
SEE? I'M WEARING MY OL' DUNGA-REES. WANNA KNOW WHY?

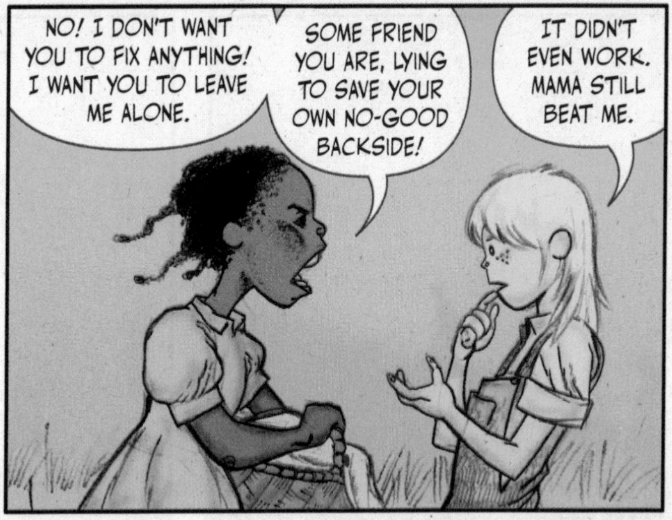
NO! I DON'T WANT YOU TO FIX ANYTHING! I WANT YOU TO LEAVE ME ALONE.
SOME FRIEND YOU ARE, LYING TO SAVE YOUR OWN NO-GOOD BACKSIDE!
IT DIDN'T EVEN WORK. MAMA STILL BEAT ME.

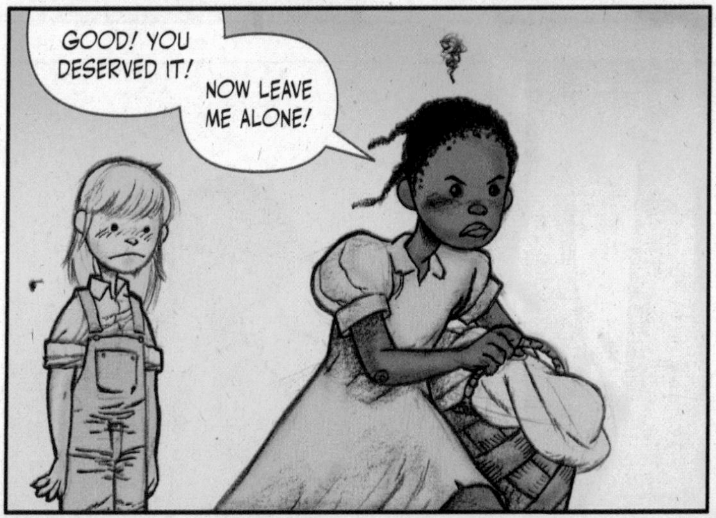
GOOD! YOU DESERVED IT!
NOW LEAVE ME ALONE!

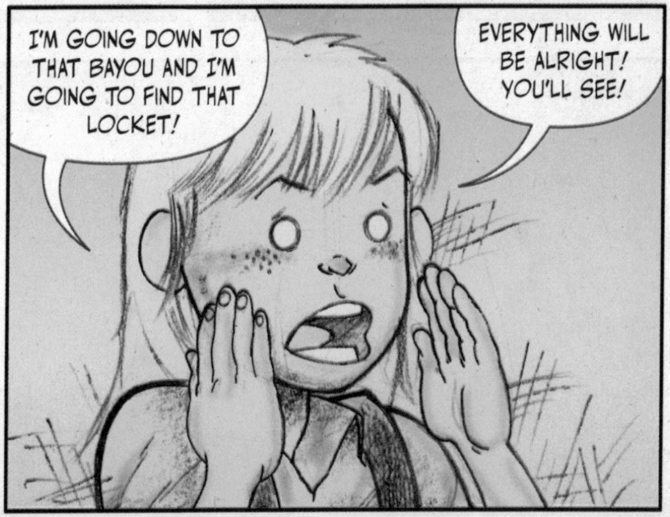
I'M GOING DOWN TO THAT BAYOU AND I'M GOING TO FIND THAT LOCKET!
EVERYTHING WILL BE ALRIGHT! YOU'LL SEE!

Go Down...
Go Down...
Go Down...

Down to the Bayou...
Down to the Bayou...
Down to the Bayou...

Lily...
Lily... Lily... Lily...
Lily...

Down to the Bayou...
Down to the Bayou...
Go Down...
Go Down...
Go Down...
Go Down...

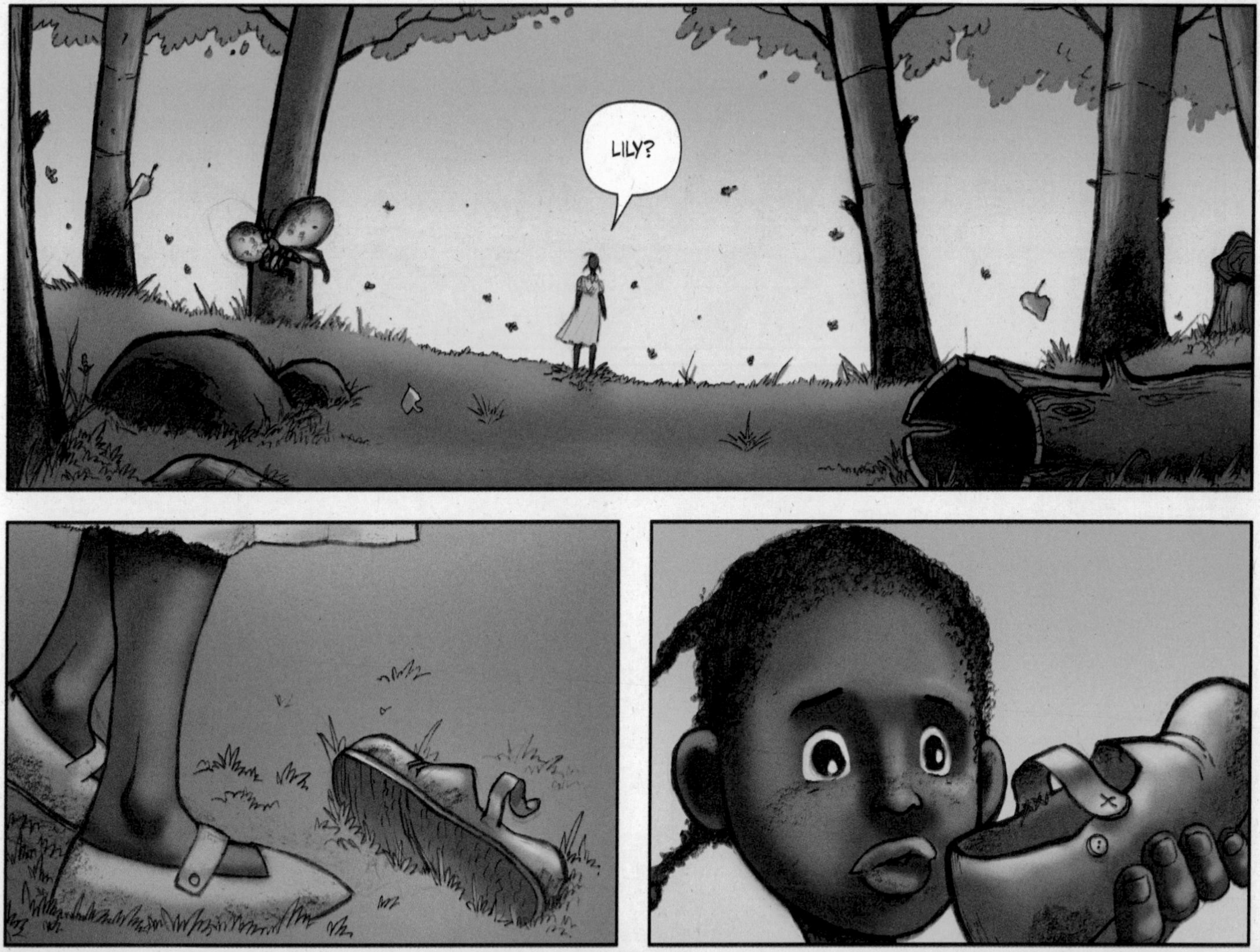
LILY?

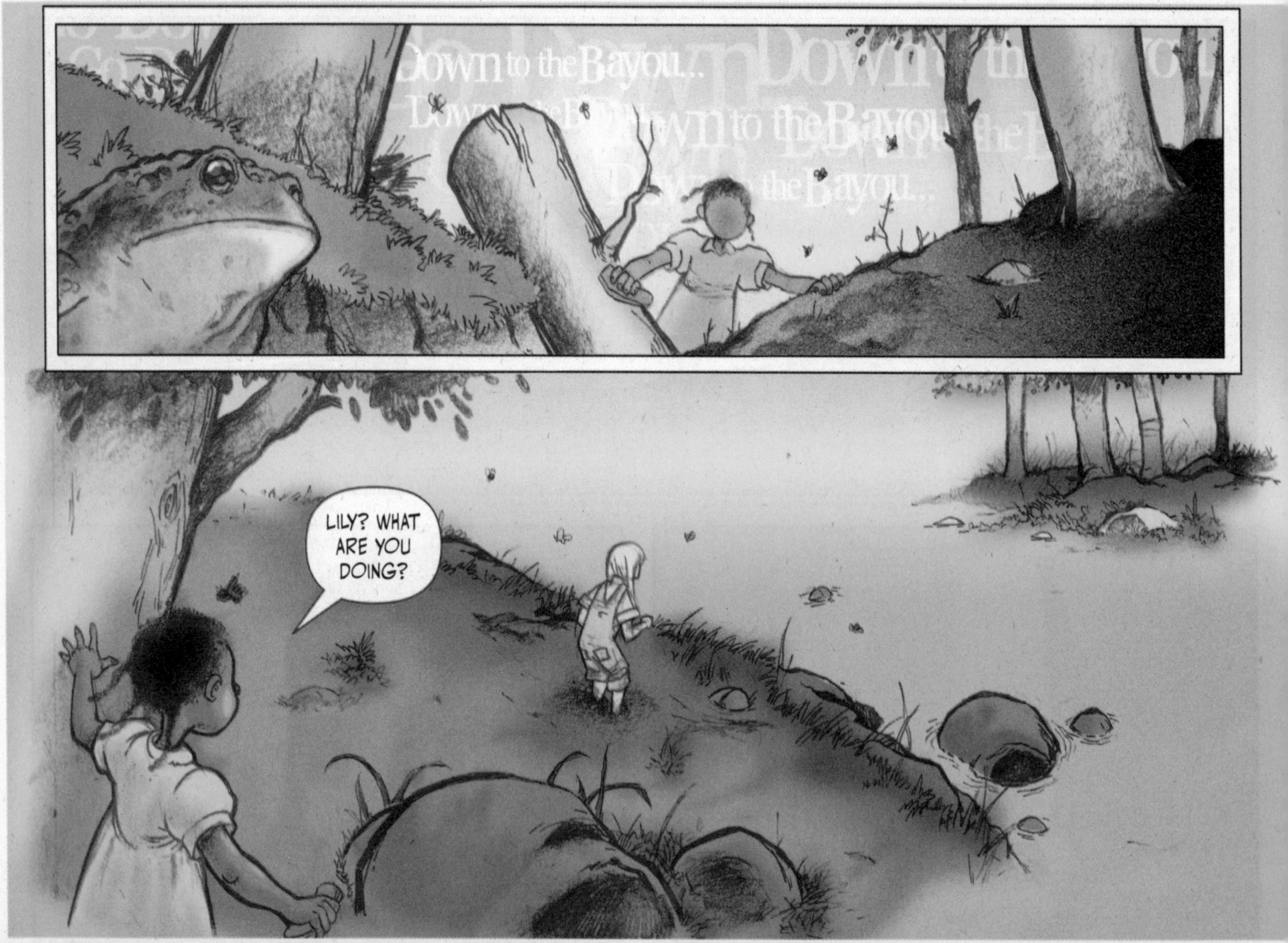
Down to the Bayou...
Down to the Bayou...
LILY? WHAT ARE YOU DOING?

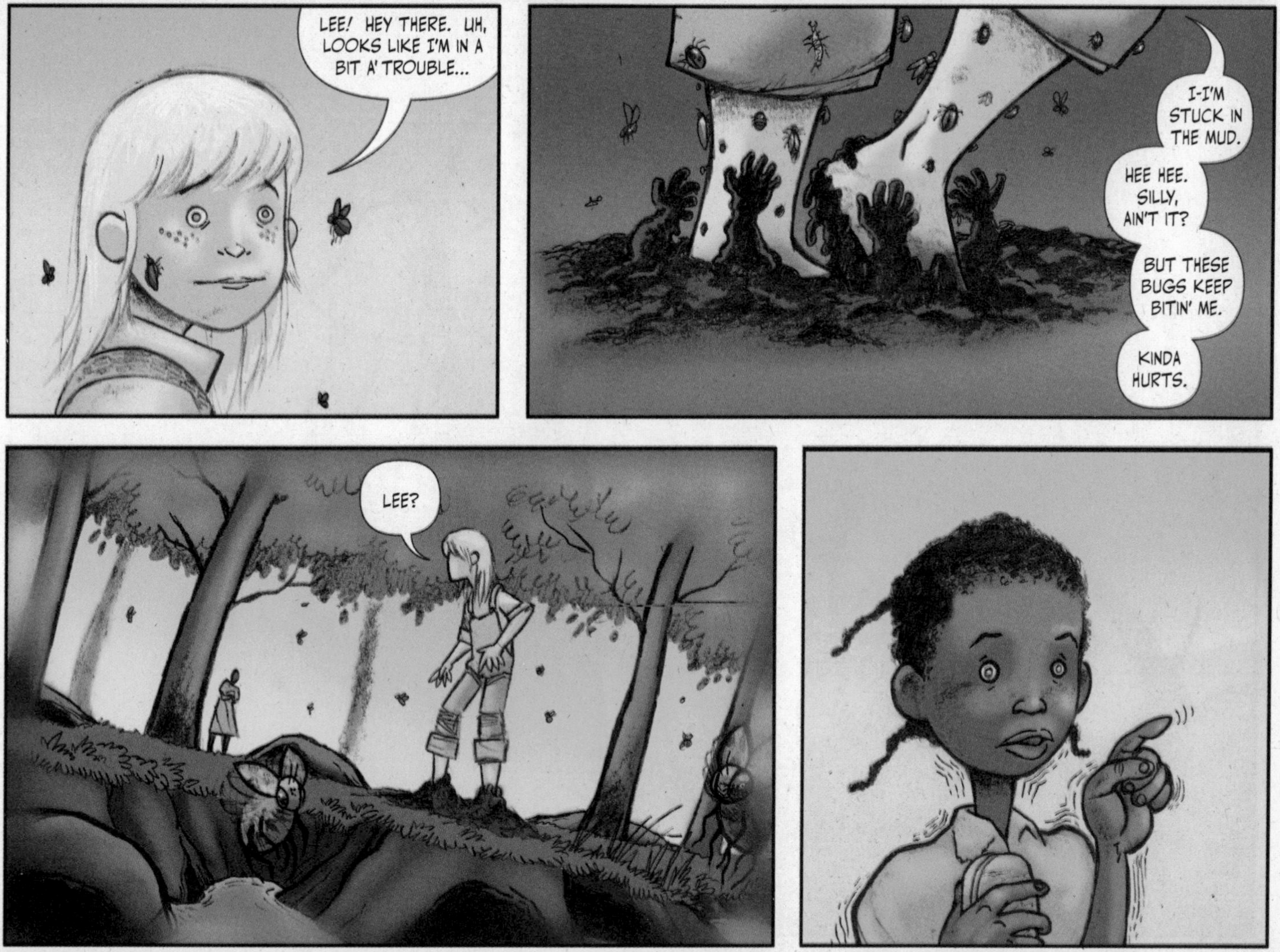
LEE! HEY THERE. UH, LOOKS LIKE I'M IN A BIT A' TROUBLE...
I-I'M STUCK IN THE MUD.
HEE HEE. SILLY, AIN'T IT?
BUT THESE BUGS KEEP BITIN' ME.
KINDA HURTS.
LEE?

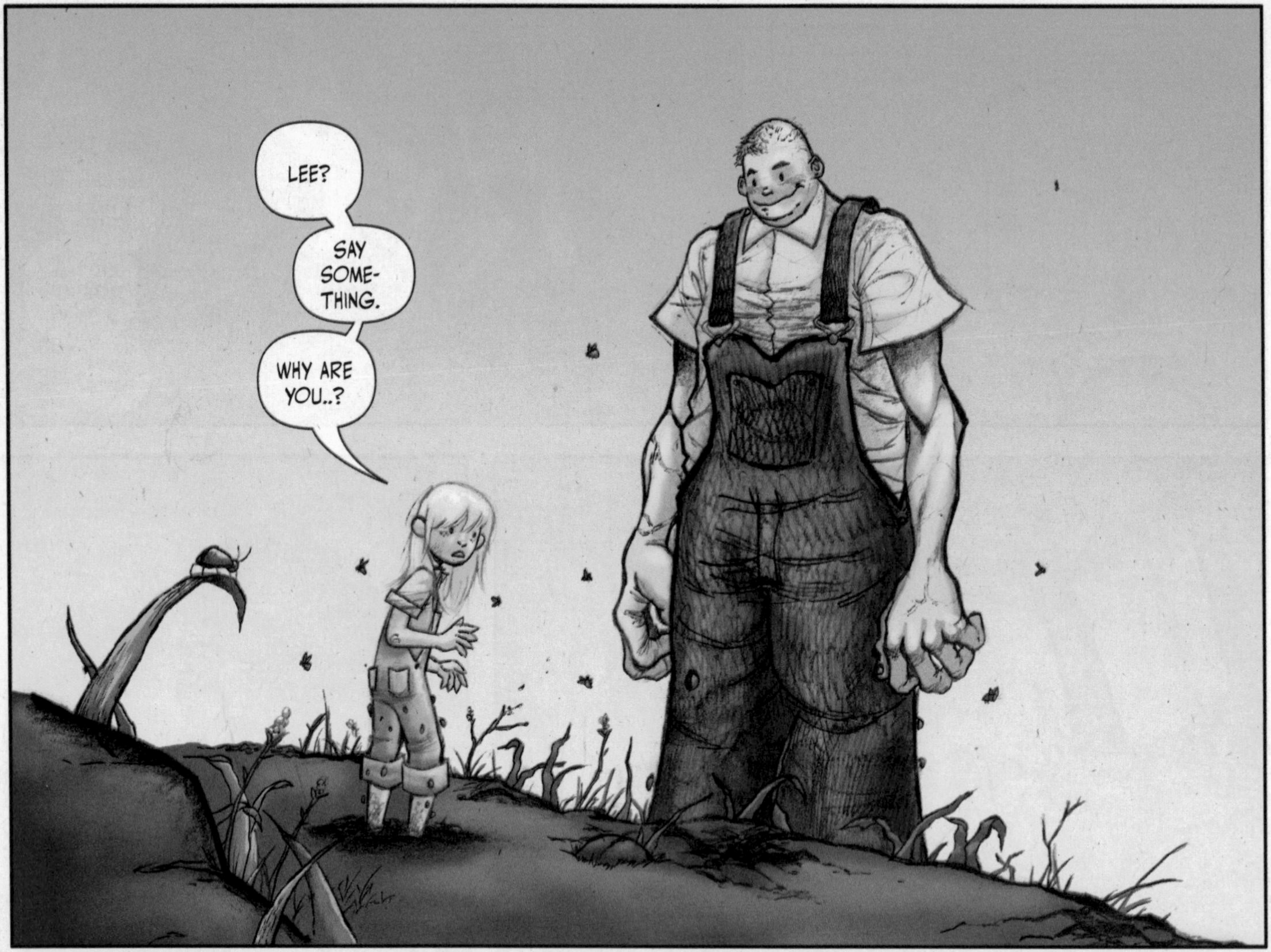
LEE?
SAY SOME-THING.
WHY ARE YOU..?

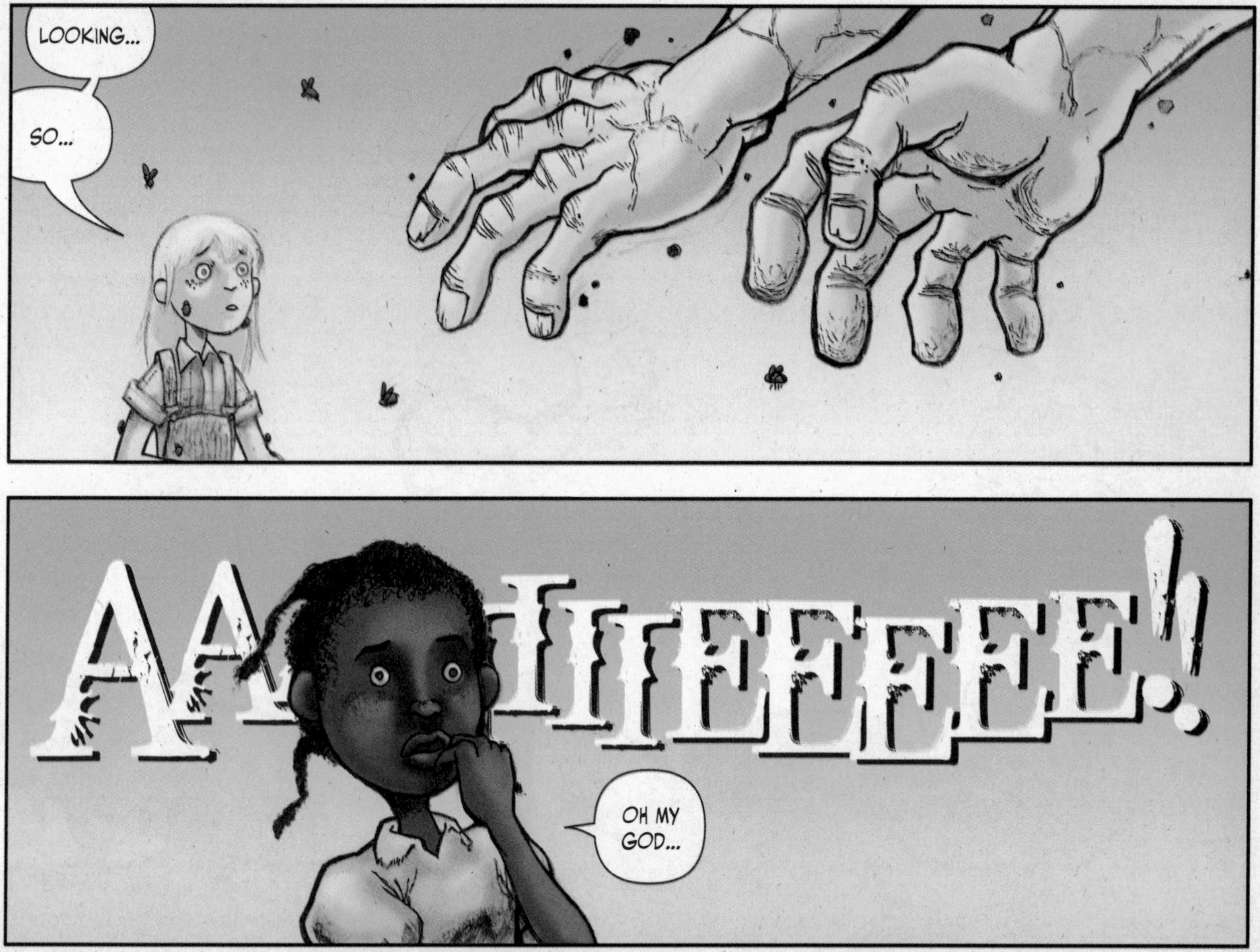
LOOKING...
SO...
AAAHIIEEEEE!
OH MY GOD...

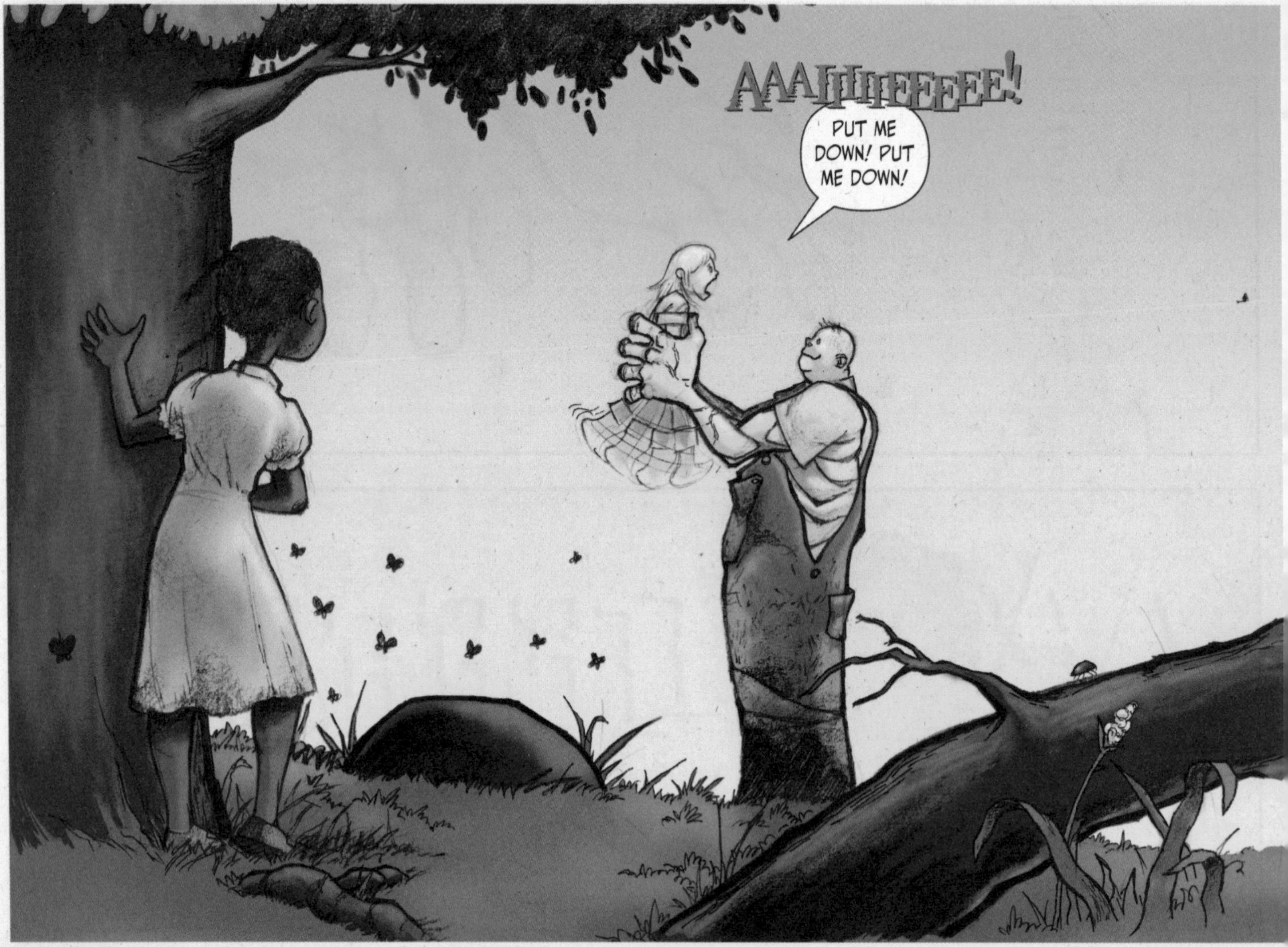
AAAIIIIIEEEEEE!
PUT ME DOWN! PUT ME DOWN!

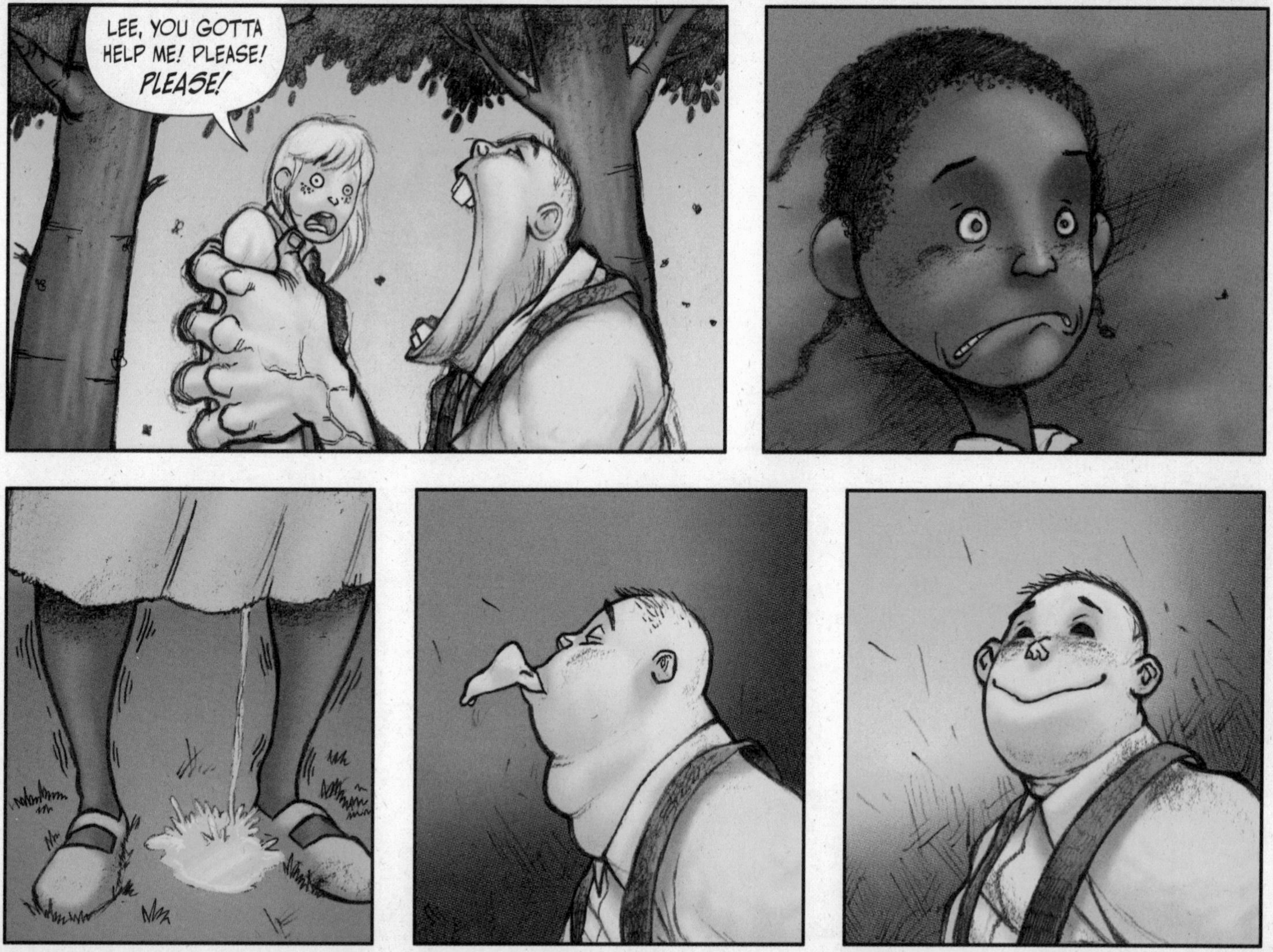
LEE, YOU GOTTA HELP ME! PLEASE! PLEASE!

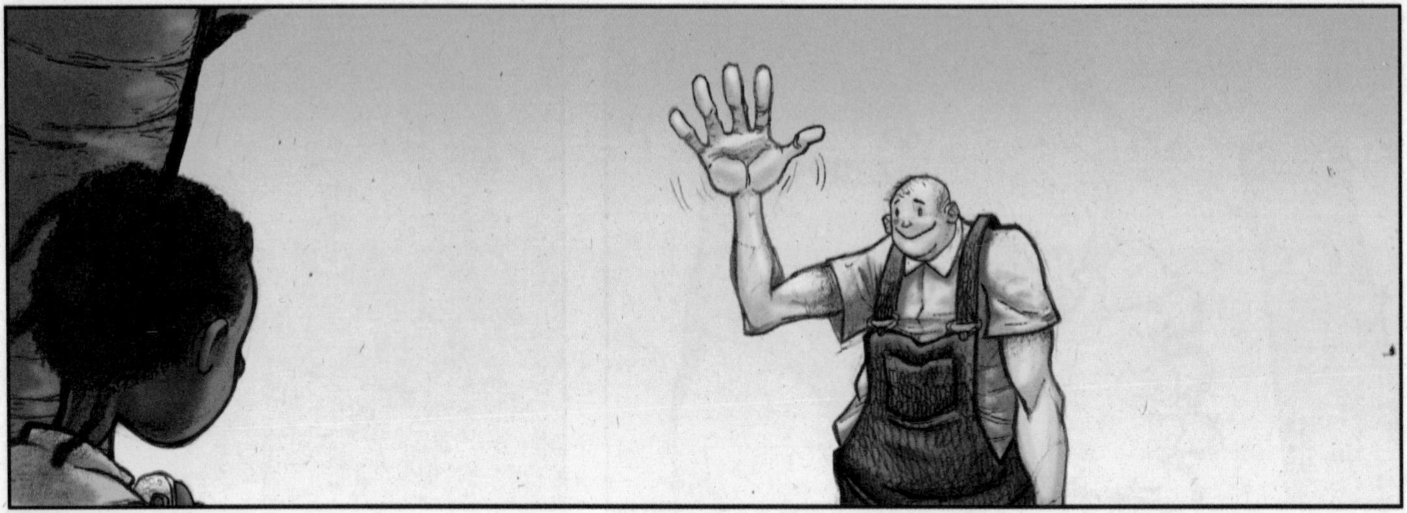

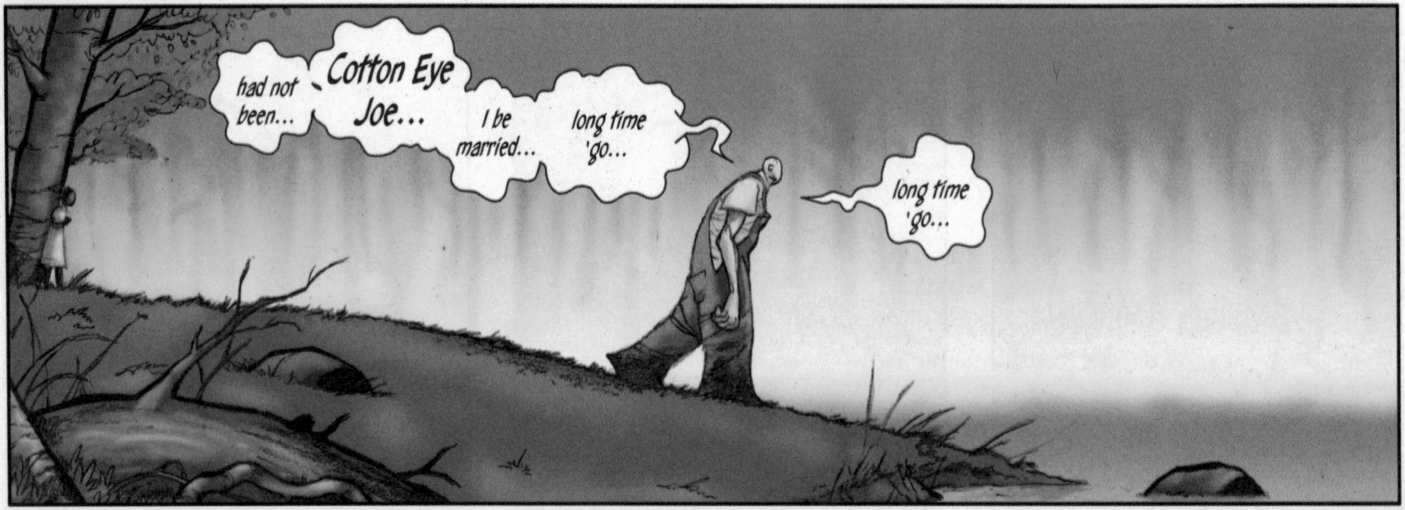

had not been...
Cotton Eye Joe...
I be married...
long time 'go...
long time 'go...

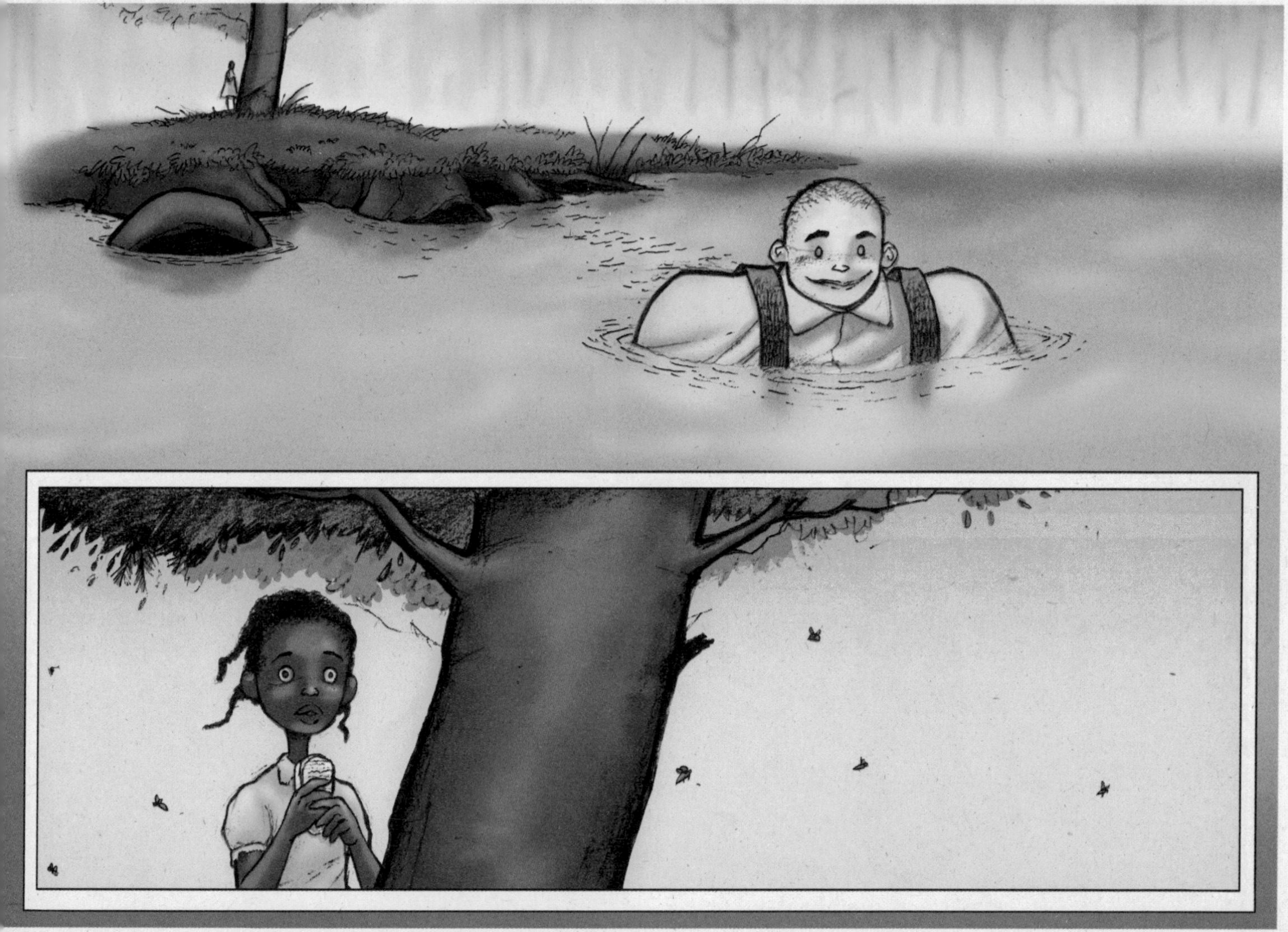

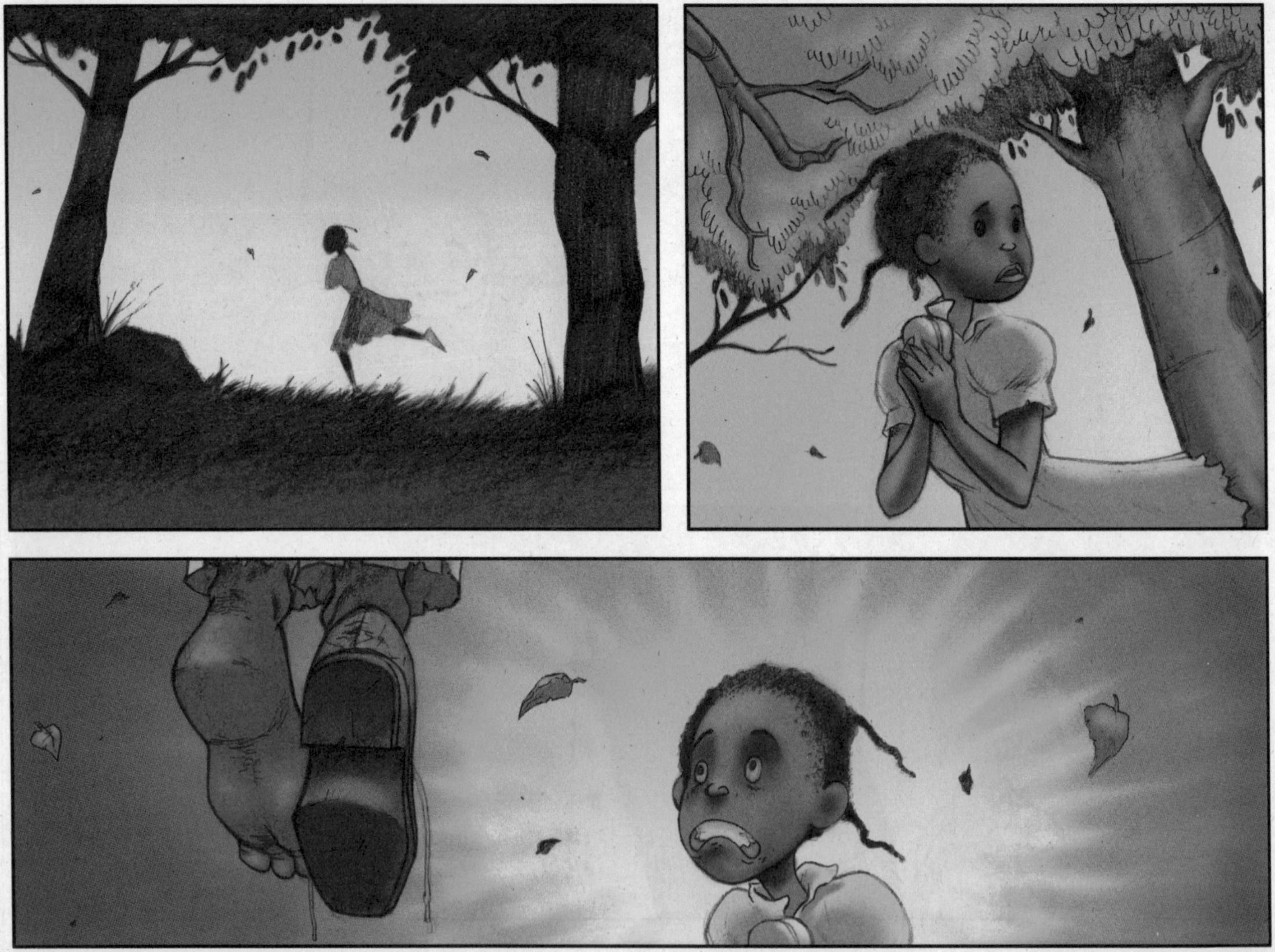

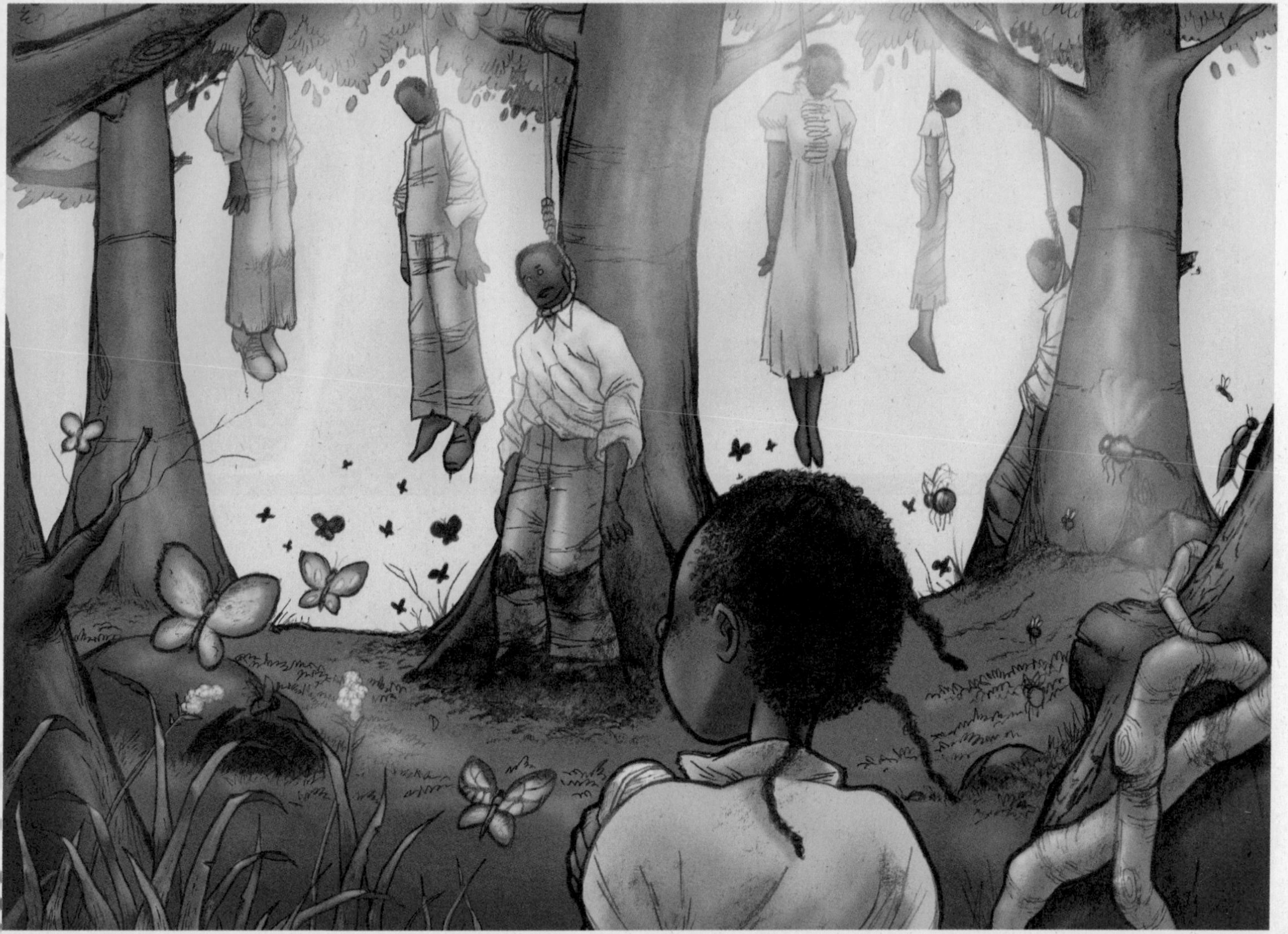

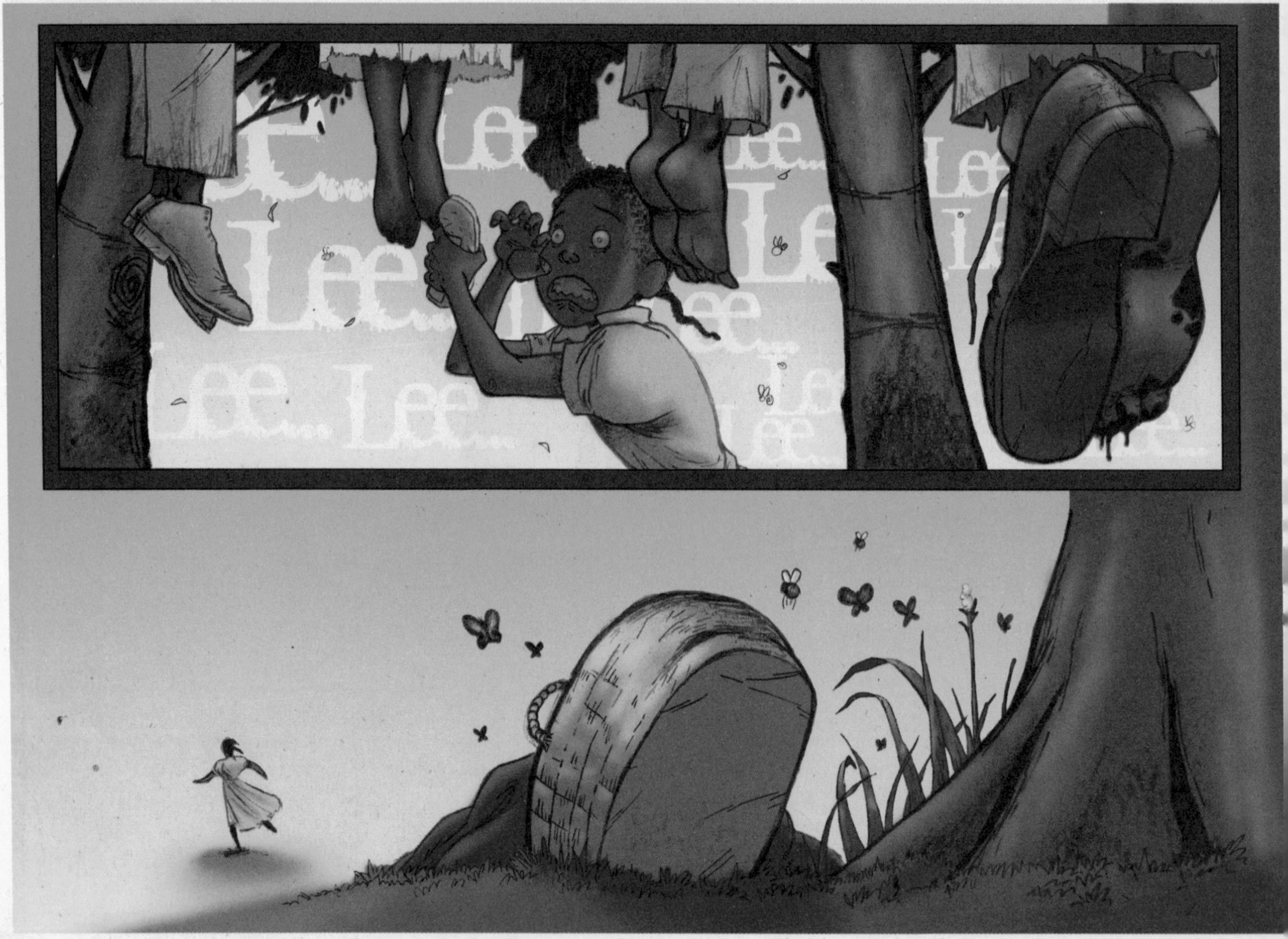

Lee...
Lee...
Lee...
Lee...
Lee...

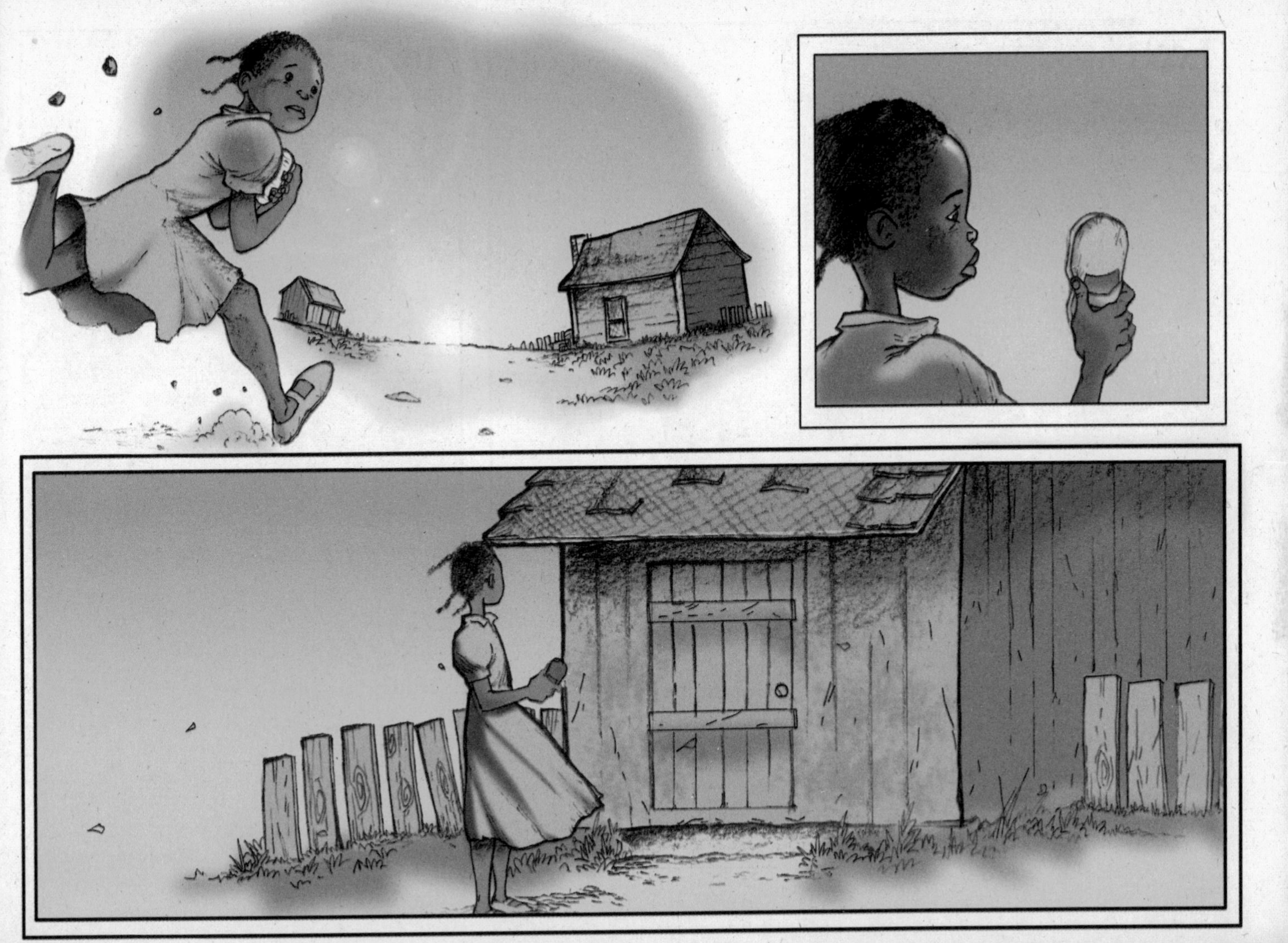

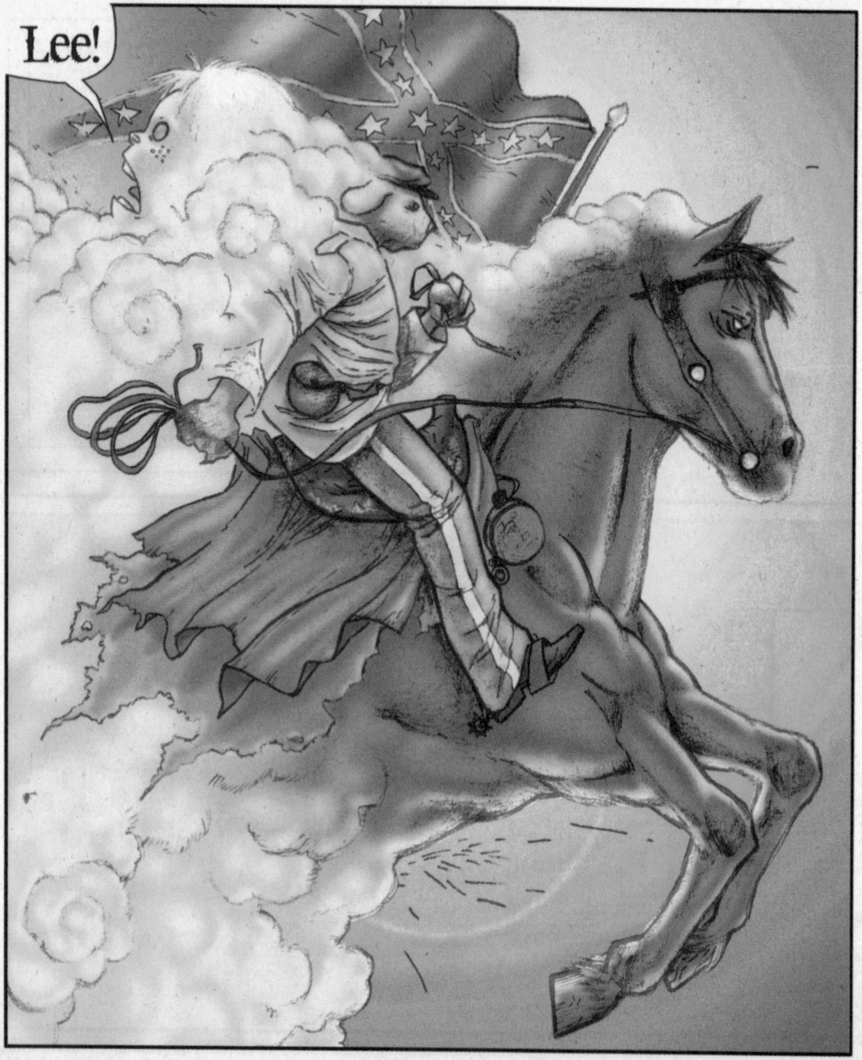
Lee!

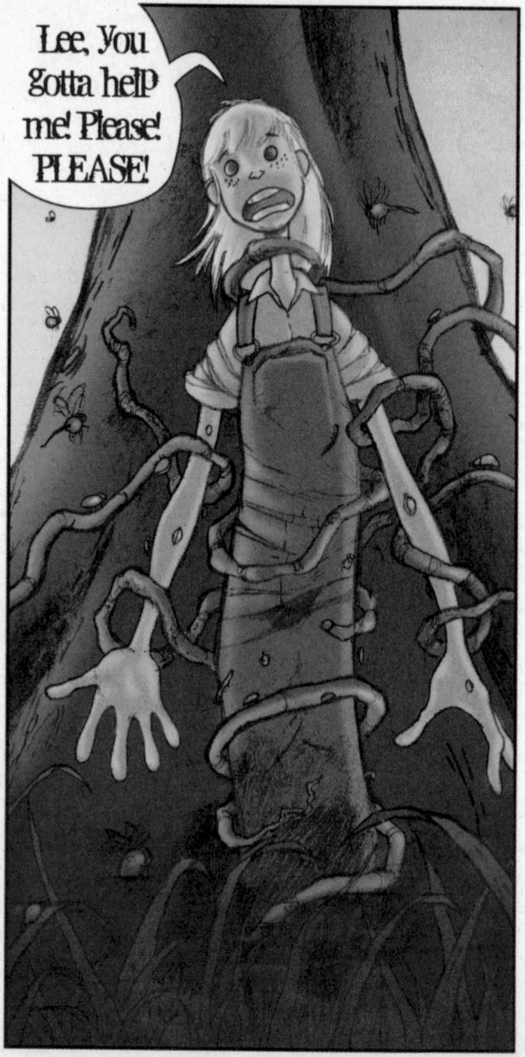
Lee, You gotta help me! Please! PLEASE!

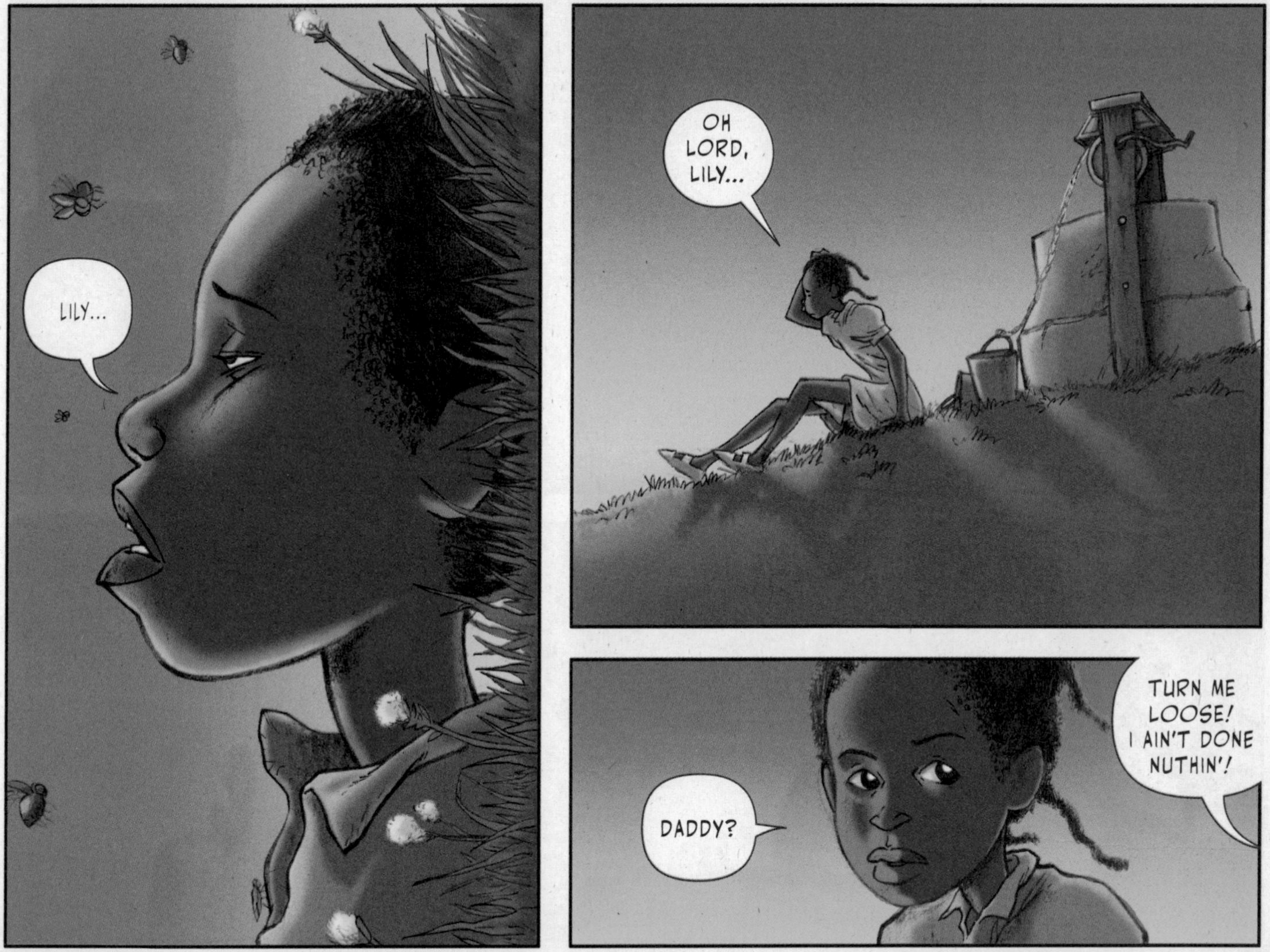
LILY...
OH LORD, LILY...
DADDY?
TURN ME LOOSE! I AIN'T DONE NUTHIN'!

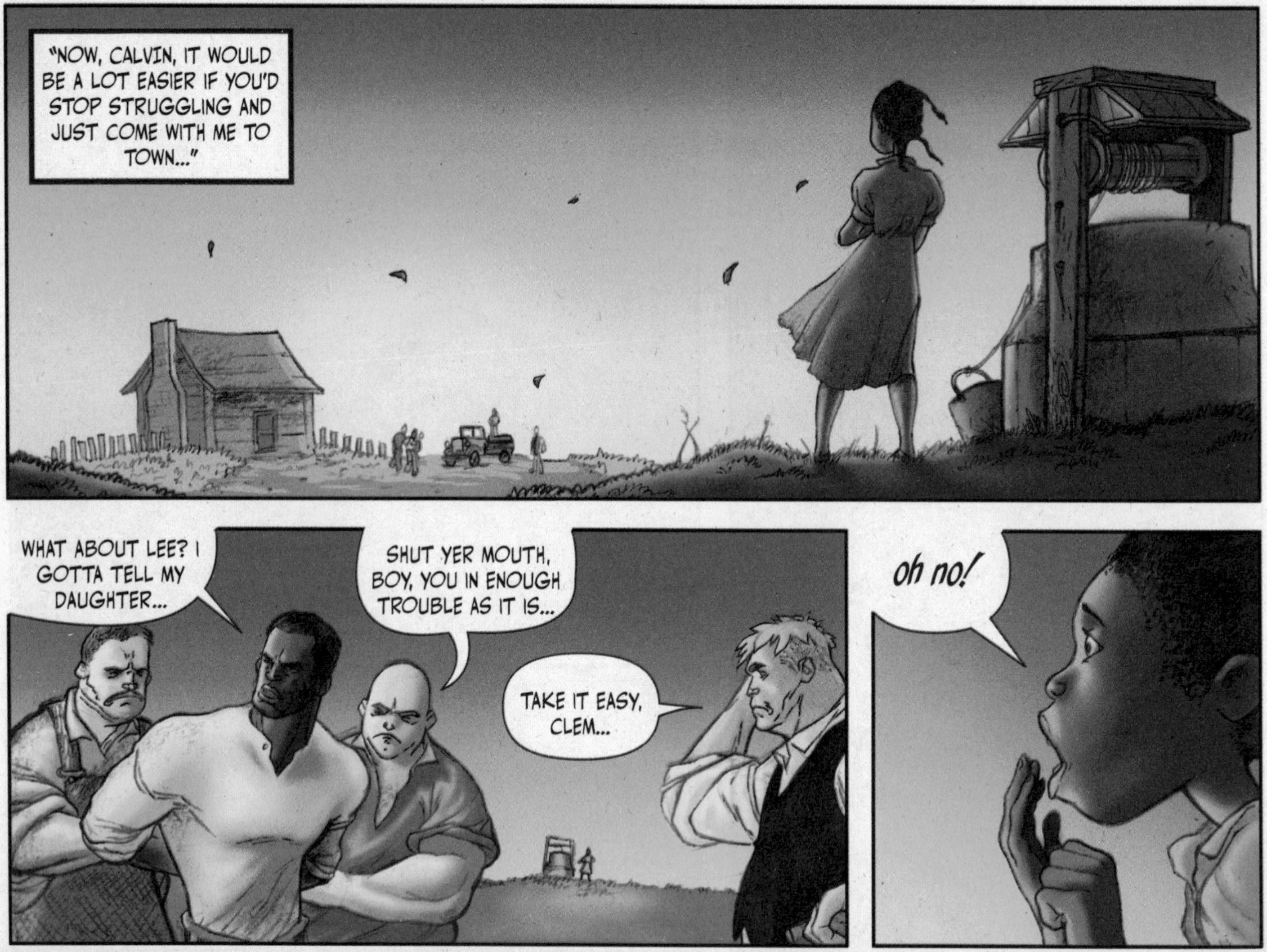
"NOW, CALVIN, IT WOULD BE A LOT EASIER IF YOU'D STOP STRUGGLING AND JUST COME WITH ME TO TOWN..."
WHAT ABOUT LEE? I GOTTA TELL MY DAUGHTER...
SHUT YER MOUTH, BOY, YOU IN ENOUGH TROUBLE AS IT IS...
TAKE IT EASY, CLEM...
oh no!

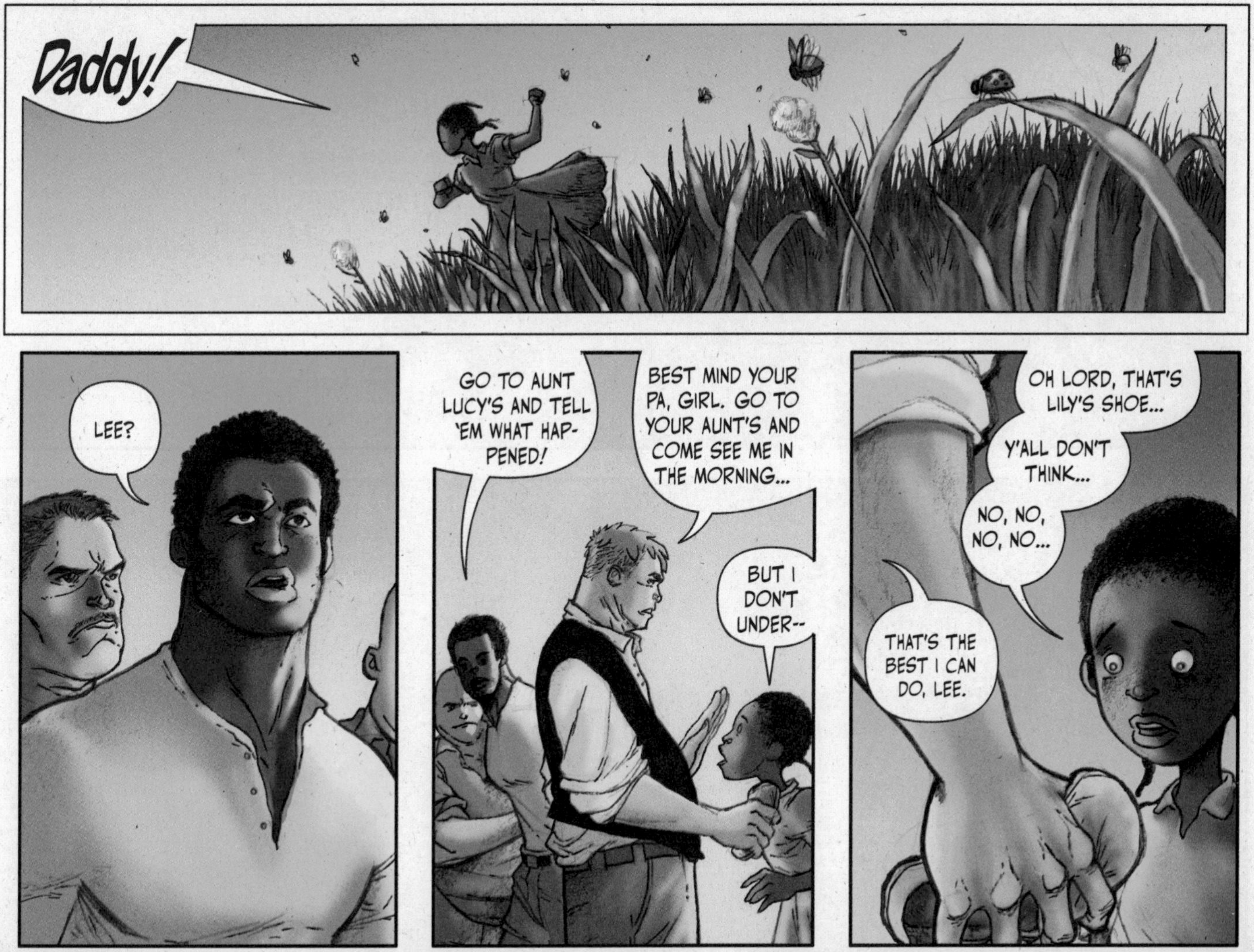
Daddy!
LEE?
GO TO AUNT LUCY'S AND TELL 'EM WHAT HAP-PENED!
BEST MIND YOUR PA, GIRL. GO TO YOUR AUNT'S AND COME SEE ME IN THE MORNING...
BUT I DON'T UNDER--
OH LORD, THAT'S LILY'S SHOE...
Y'ALL DON'T THINK...
NO, NO, NO, NO...
THAT'S THE BEST I CAN DO, LEE.

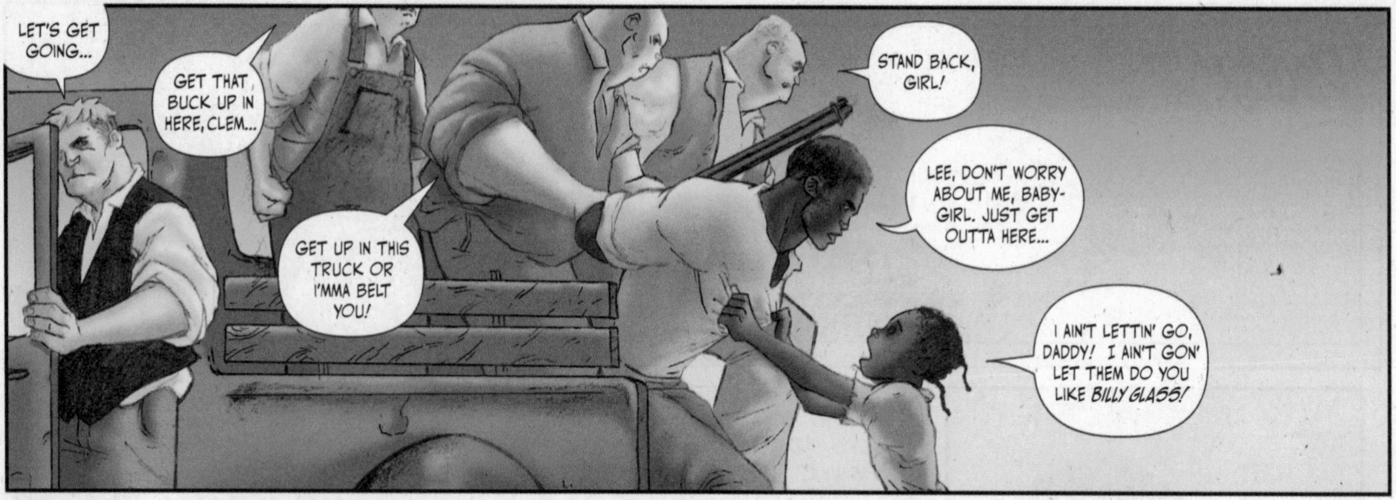
LET'S GET GOING...
GET THAT BUCK UP IN HERE, CLEM...
GET UP IN THIS TRUCK OR I'MMA BELT YOU!
STAND BACK, GIRL!
LEE, DON'T WORRY ABOUT ME, BABY-GIRL. JUST GET OUTTA HERE...
I AIN'T LETTIN' GO, DADDY! I AIN'T GON' LET THEM DO YOU LIKE *BILLY GLASS!*

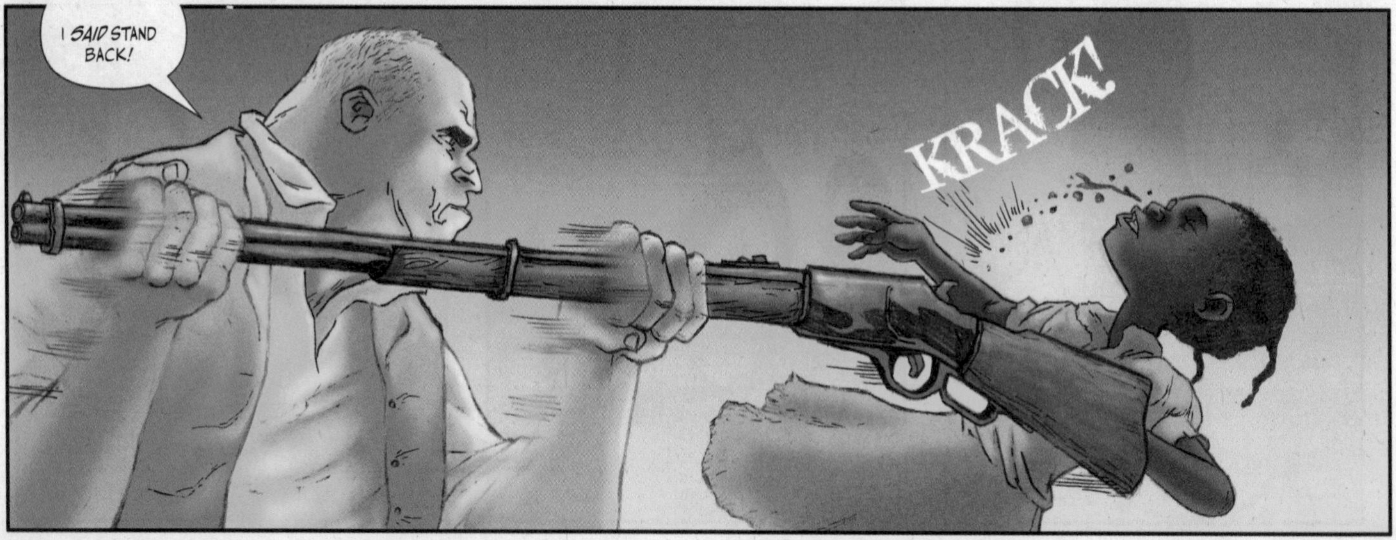
I *SAID* STAND BACK!
KRACK!

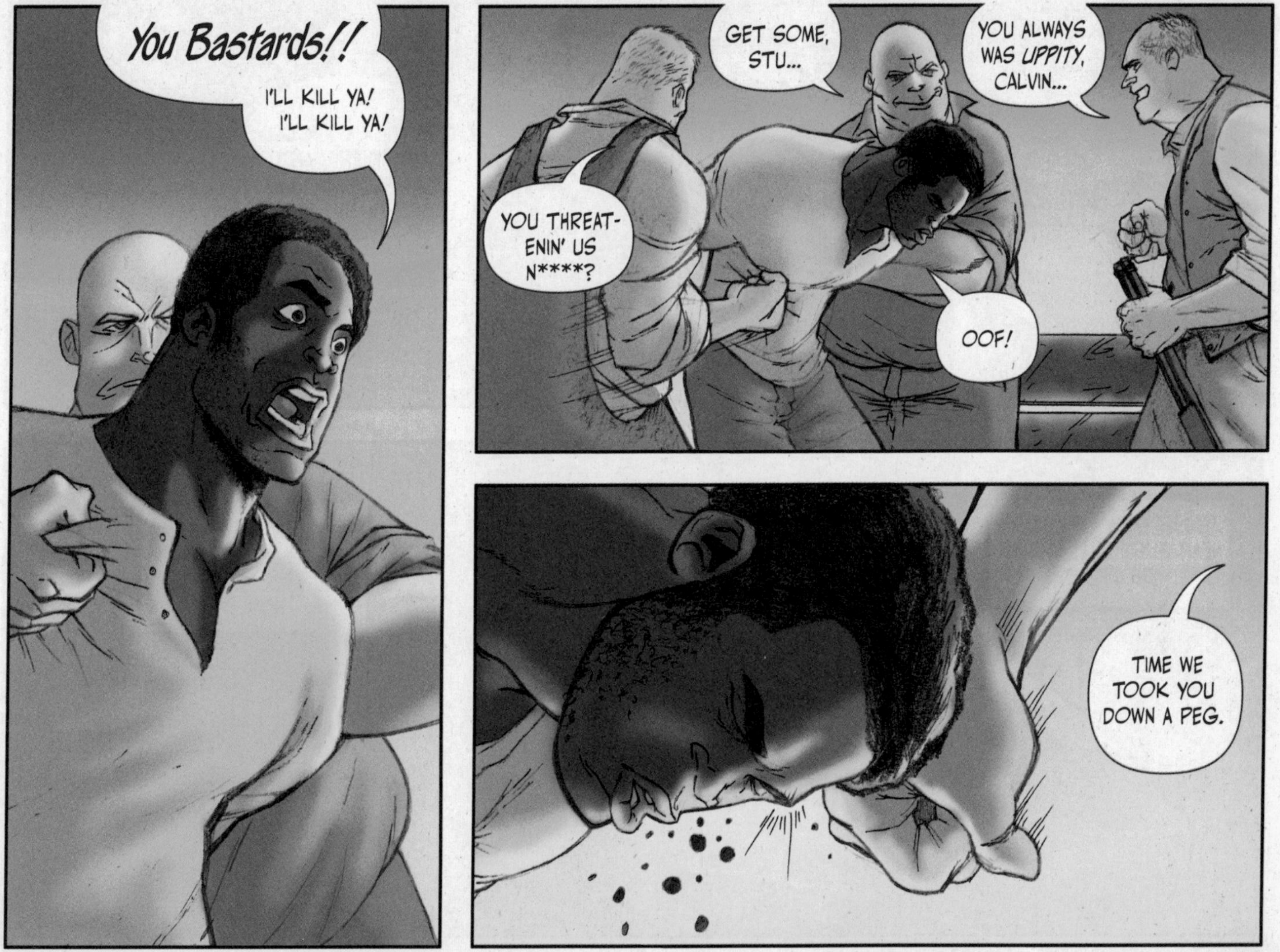
You Bastards!!
I'LL KILL YA! I'LL KILL YA!
GET SOME, STU...
YOU ALWAYS WAS UPPITY, CALVIN...
YOU THREAT-ENIN' US N****?
OOF!
TIME WE TOOK YOU DOWN A PEG.

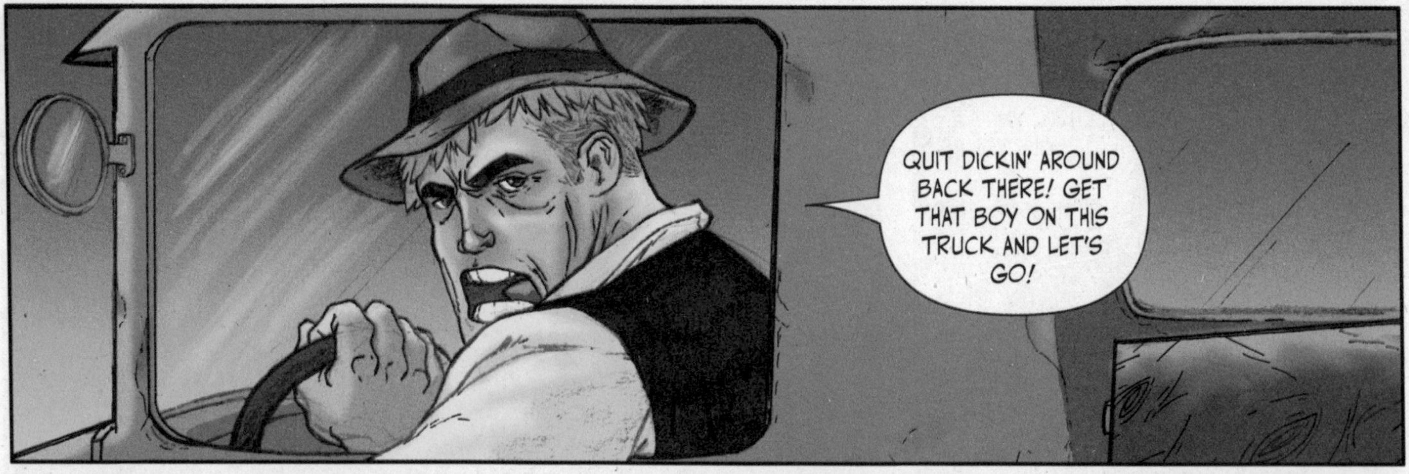
QUIT DICKIN' AROUND BACK THERE! GET THAT BOY ON THIS TRUCK AND LET'S GO!

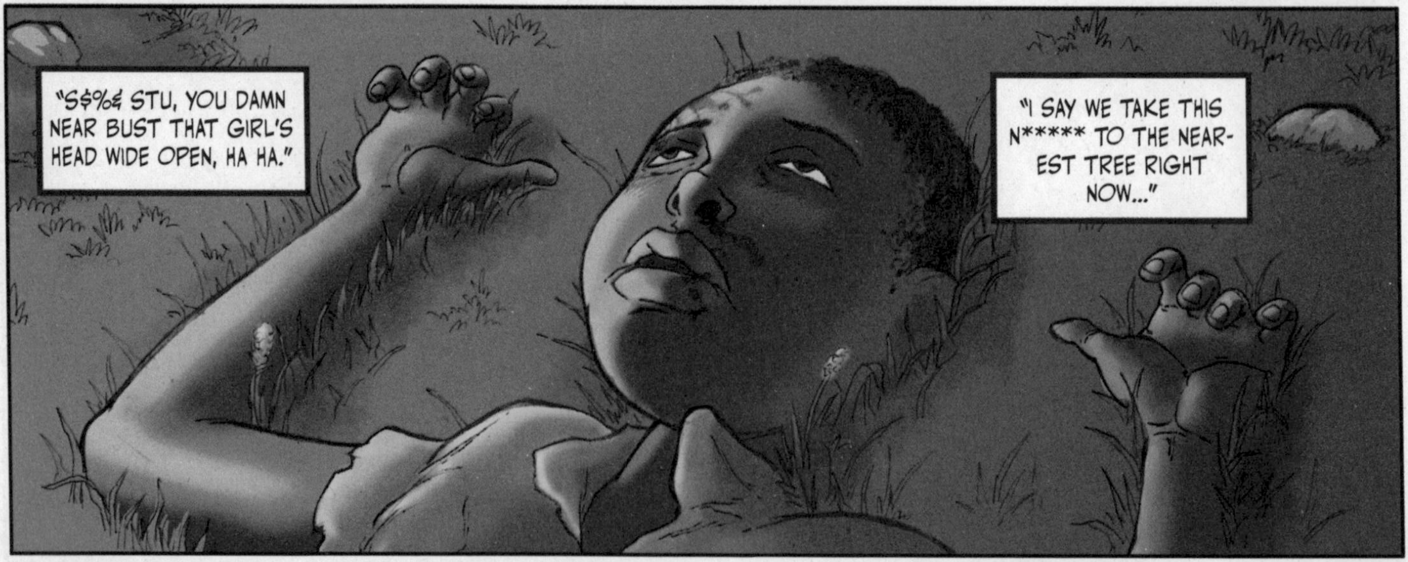
"S$%& STU, YOU DAMN NEAR BUST THAT GIRL'S HEAD WIDE OPEN, HA HA."
"I SAY WE TAKE THIS N***** TO THE NEAR-EST TREE RIGHT NOW..."

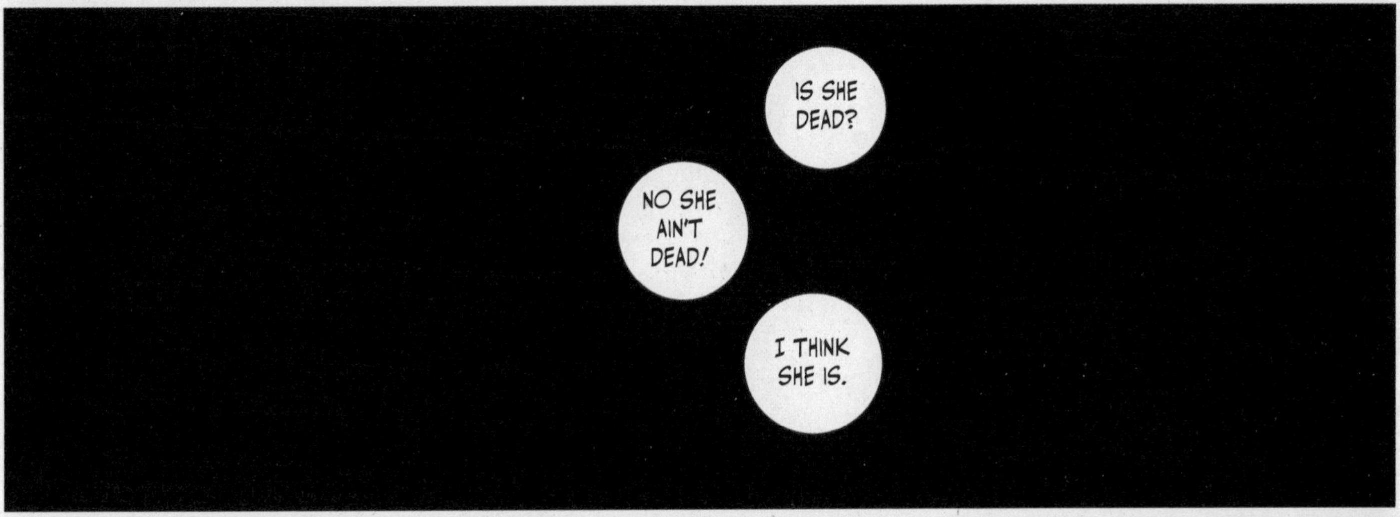
IS SHE DEAD?
NO SHE AIN'T DEAD!
I THINK SHE IS.

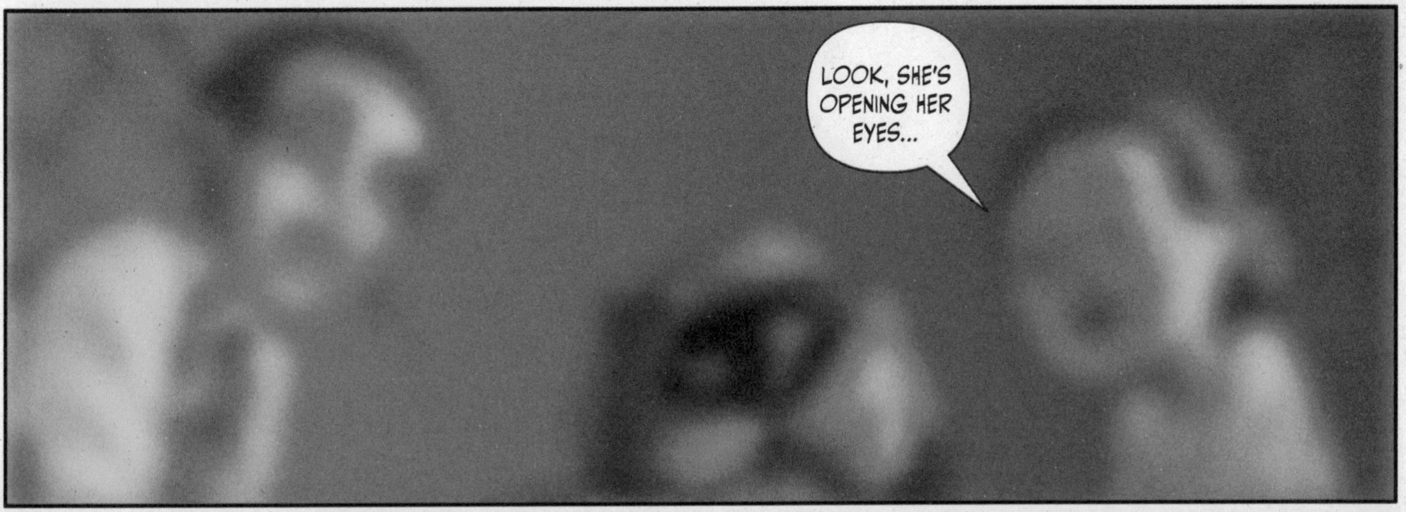
LOOK, SHE'S OPENING HER EYES...

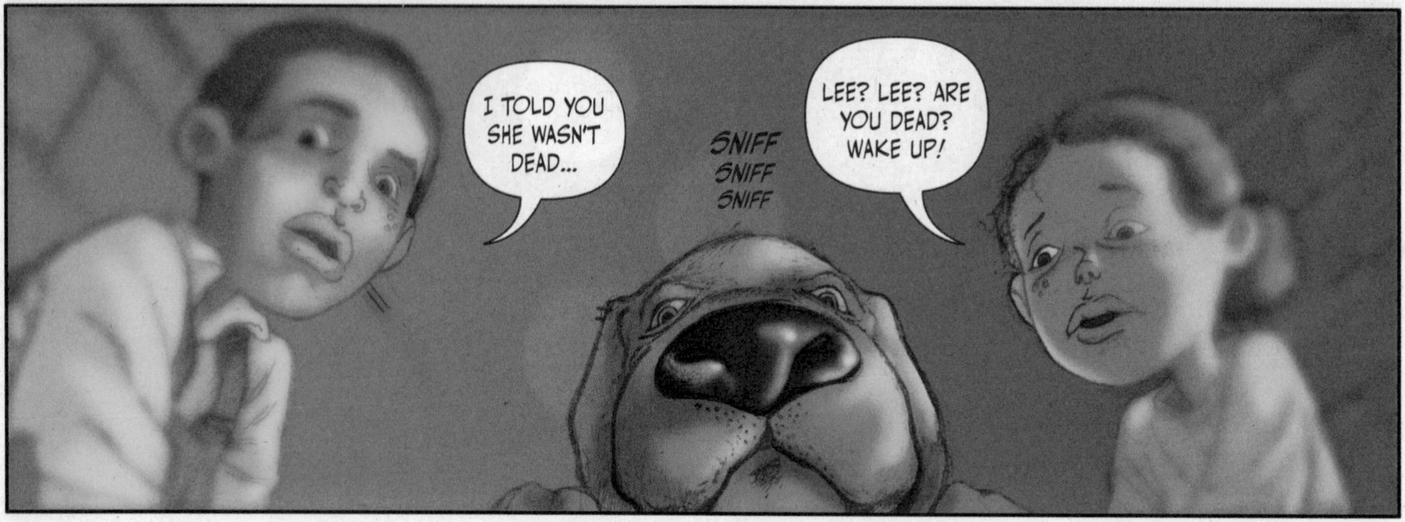
I TOLD YOU SHE WASN'T DEAD...
SNIFF SNIFF SNIFF
LEE? LEE? ARE YOU DEAD? WAKE UP!

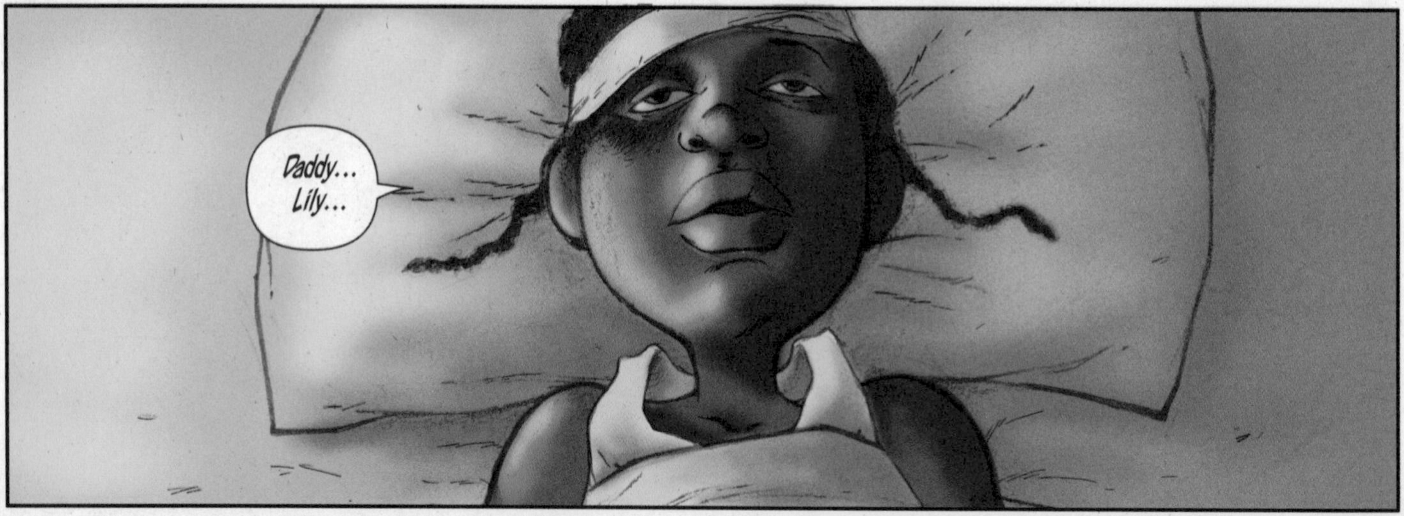
Daddy... Lily...

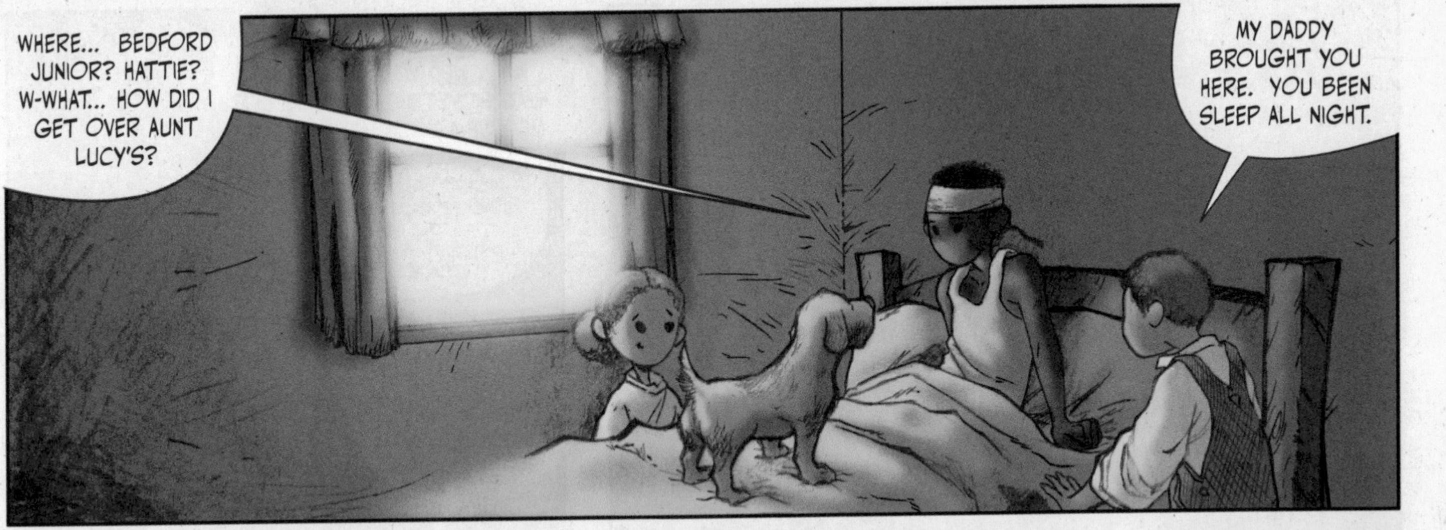
WHERE... BEDFORD JUNIOR? HATTIE? W-WHAT... HOW DID I GET OVER AUNT LUCY'S?
MY DADDY BROUGHT YOU HERE. YOU BEEN SLEEP ALL NIGHT.

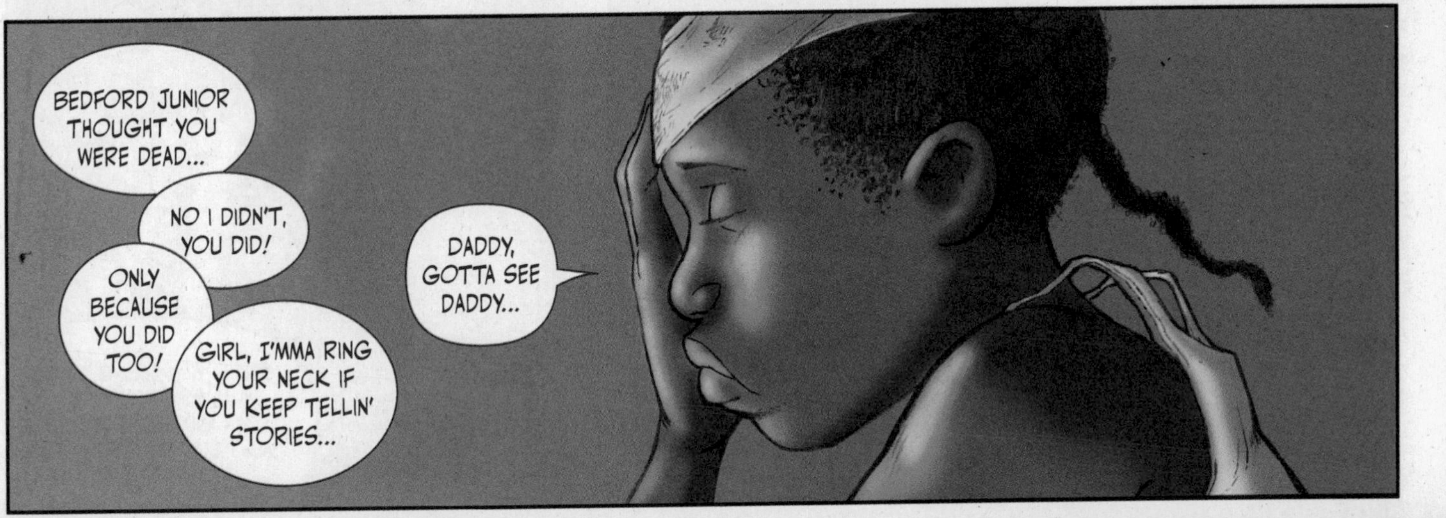
BEDFORD JUNIOR THOUGHT YOU WERE DEAD...
NO I DIDN'T, YOU DID!
ONLY BECAUSE YOU DID TOO!
GIRL, I'MMA RING YOUR NECK IF YOU KEEP TELLIN' STORIES...
DADDY, GOTTA SEE DADDY...

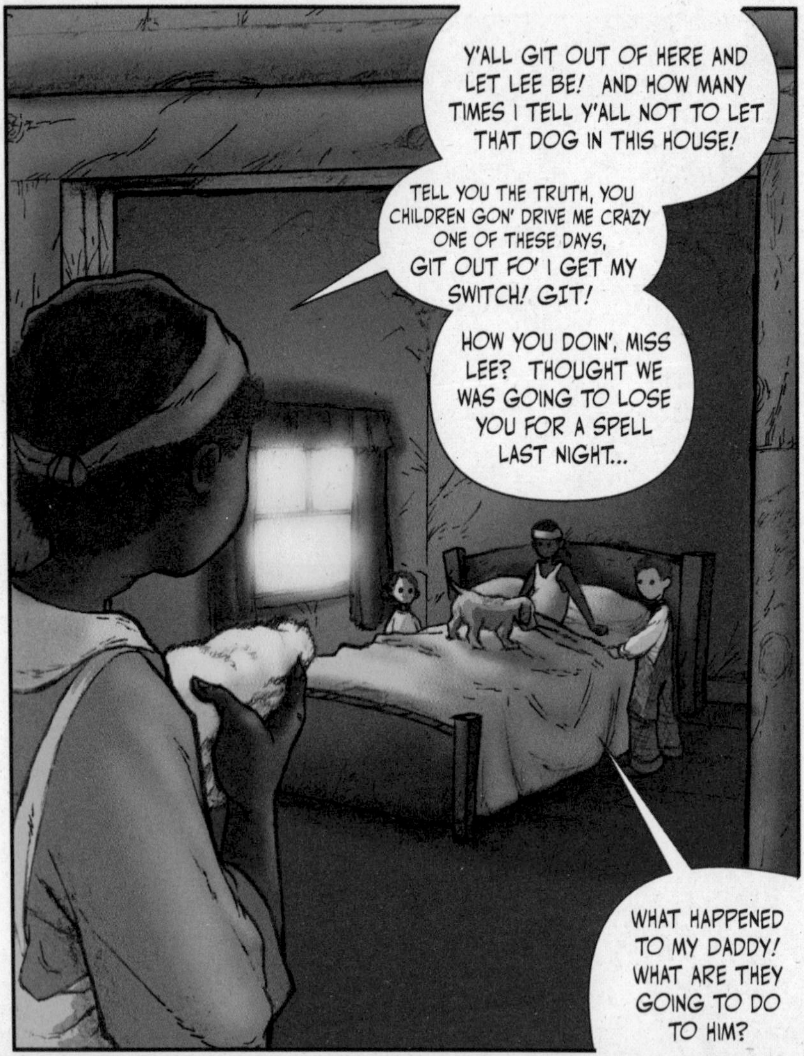
Y'ALL GIT OUT OF HERE AND LET LEE BE! AND HOW MANY TIMES I TELL Y'ALL NOT TO LET THAT DOG IN THIS HOUSE!
TELL YOU THE TRUTH, YOU CHILDREN GON' DRIVE ME CRAZY ONE OF THESE DAYS, GIT OUT FO' I GET MY SWITCH! GIT!
HOW YOU DOIN', MISS LEE? THOUGHT WE WAS GOING TO LOSE YOU FOR A SPELL LAST NIGHT...
WHAT HAPPENED TO MY DADDY! WHAT ARE THEY GOING TO DO TO HIM?

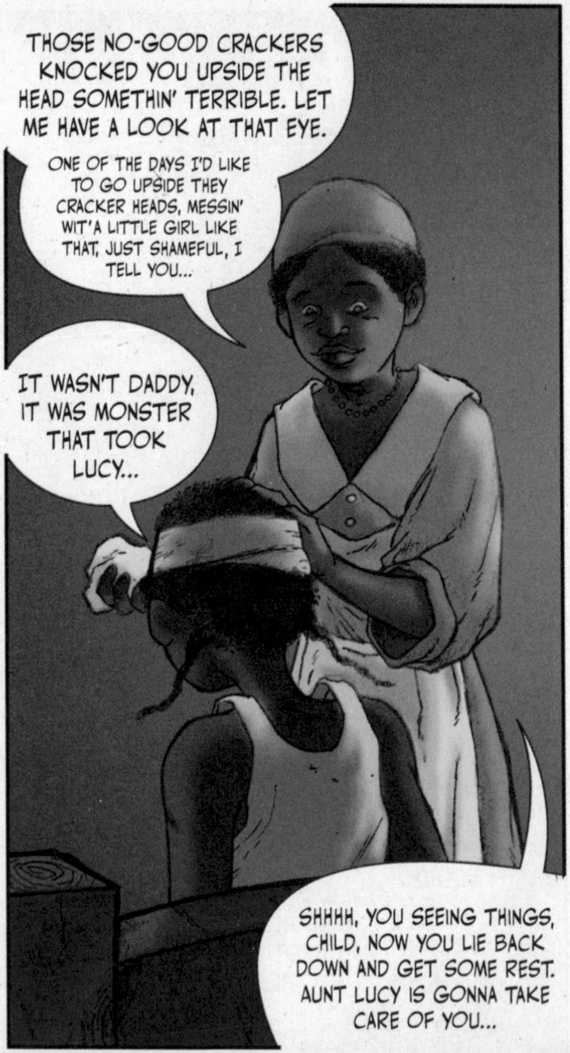
THOSE NO-GOOD CRACKERS KNOCKED YOU UPSIDE THE HEAD SOMETHIN' TERRIBLE. LET ME HAVE A LOOK AT THAT EYE.
ONE OF THE DAYS I'D LIKE TO GO UPSIDE THEY CRACKER HEADS, MESSIN' WIT'A LITTLE GIRL LIKE THAT, JUST SHAMEFUL, I TELL YOU...
IT WASN'T DADDY, IT WAS MONSTER THAT TOOK LUCY...
SHHHH, YOU SEEING THINGS, CHILD, NOW YOU LIE BACK DOWN AND GET SOME REST. AUNT LUCY IS GONNA TAKE CARE OF YOU...

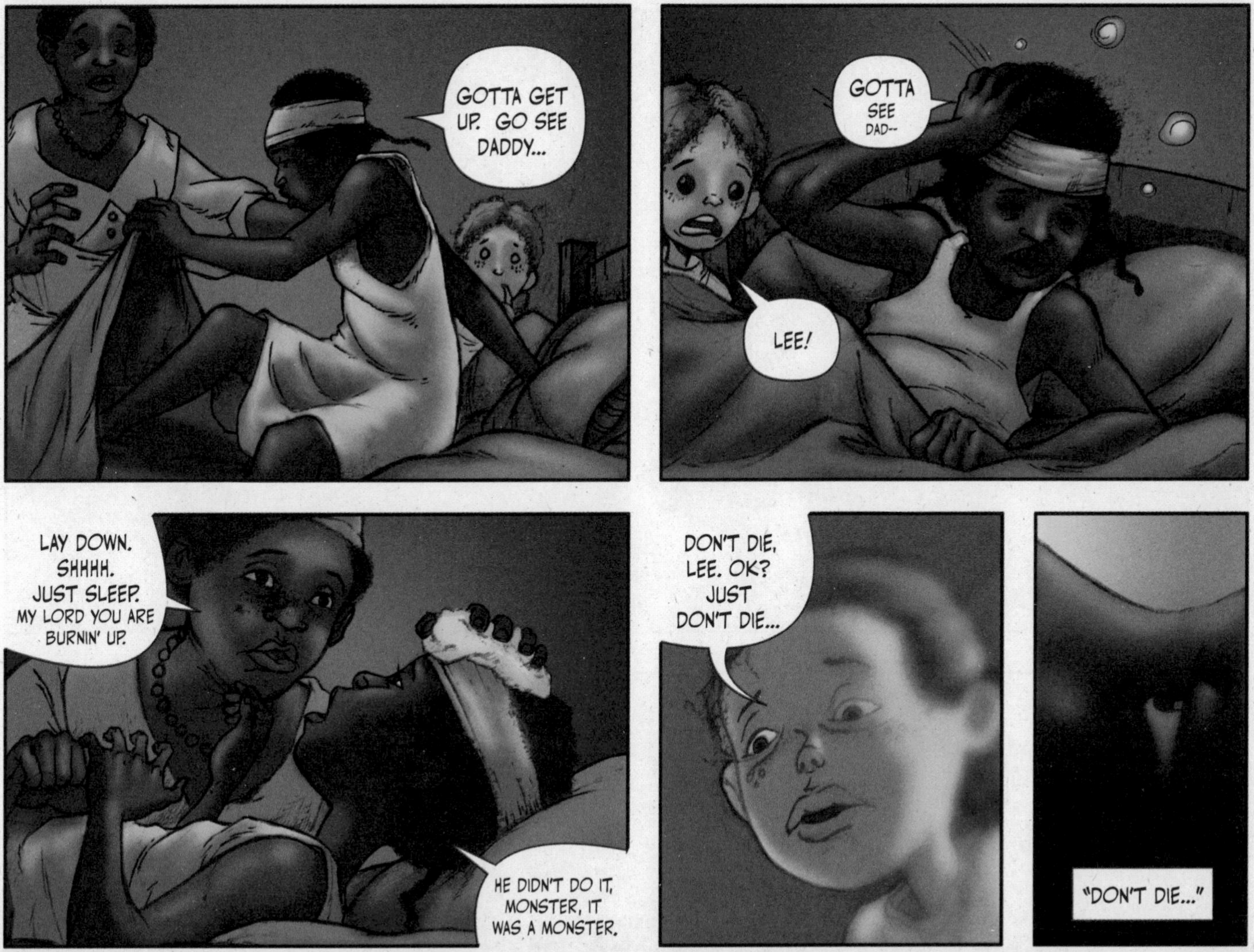
GOTTA GET UP. GO SEE DADDY...
GOTTA SEE DAD--
LEE!
LAY DOWN. SHHHH. JUST SLEEP. MY LORD YOU ARE BURNIN' UP.
HE DIDN'T DO IT, MONSTER, IT WAS A MONSTER.
DON'T DIE, LEE. OK? JUST DON'T DIE...
"DON'T DIE..."

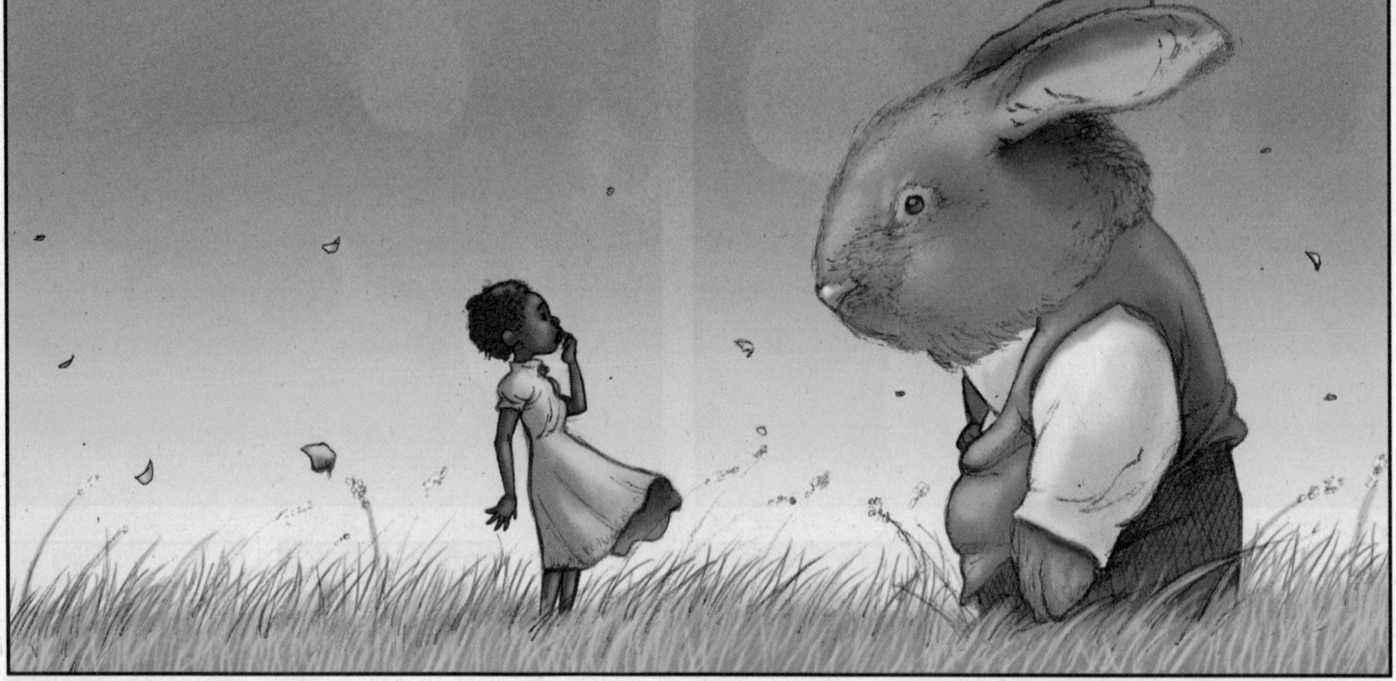

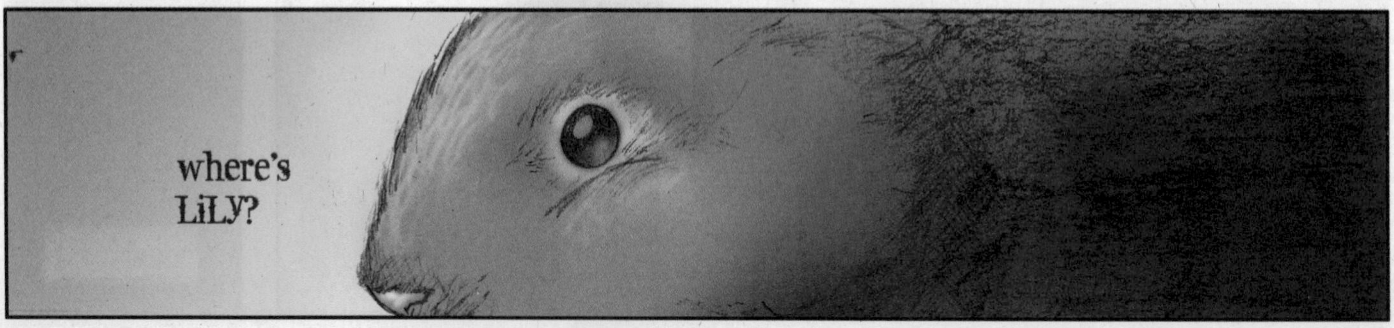
where's
LiLY?

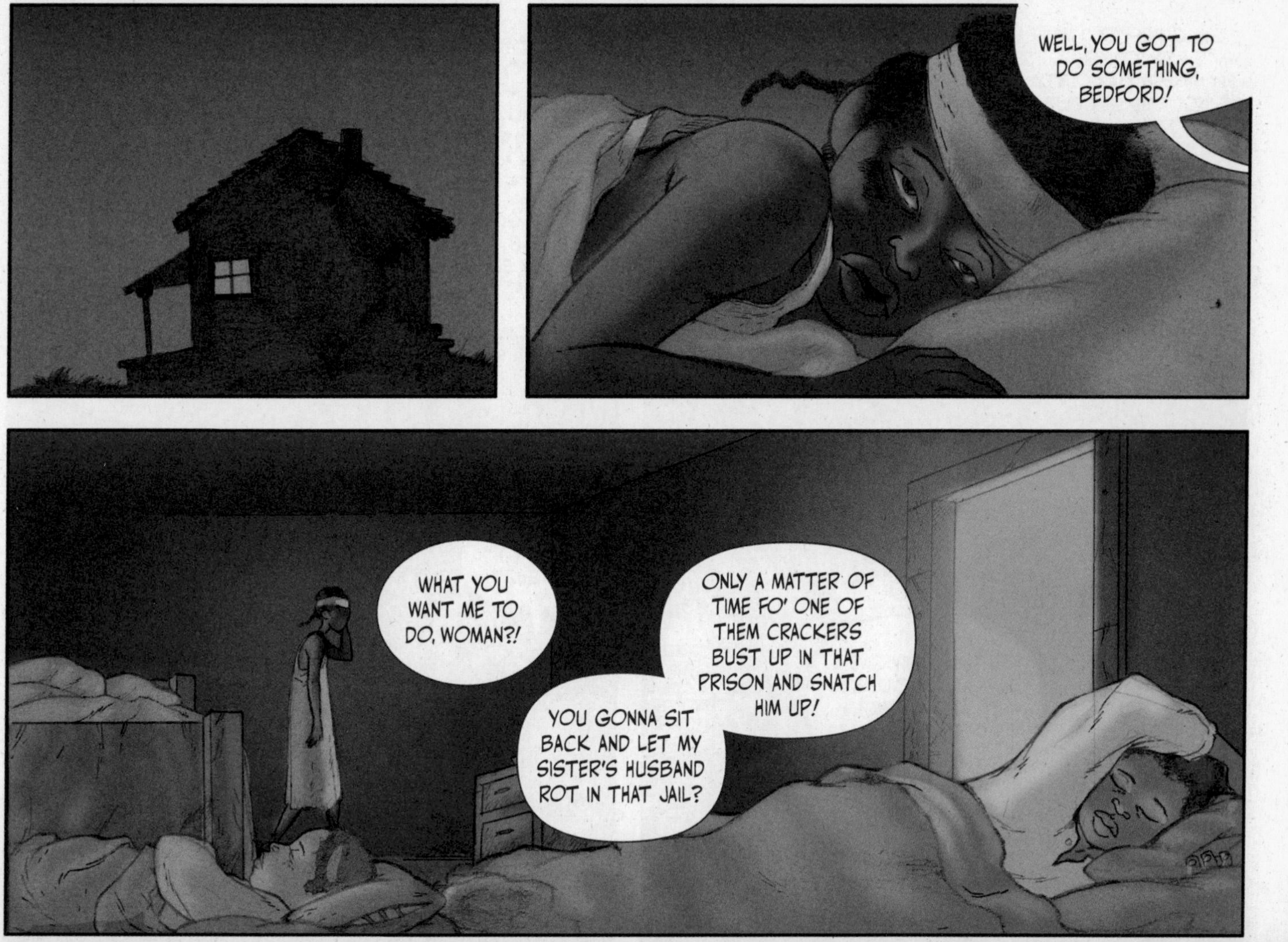
WELL, YOU GOT TO DO SOMETHING, BEDFORD!
WHAT YOU WANT ME TO DO, WOMAN?!
ONLY A MATTER OF TIME FO' ONE OF THEM CRACKERS BUST UP IN THAT PRISON AND SNATCH HIM UP!
YOU GONNA SIT BACK AND LET MY SISTER'S HUSBAND ROT IN THAT JAIL?

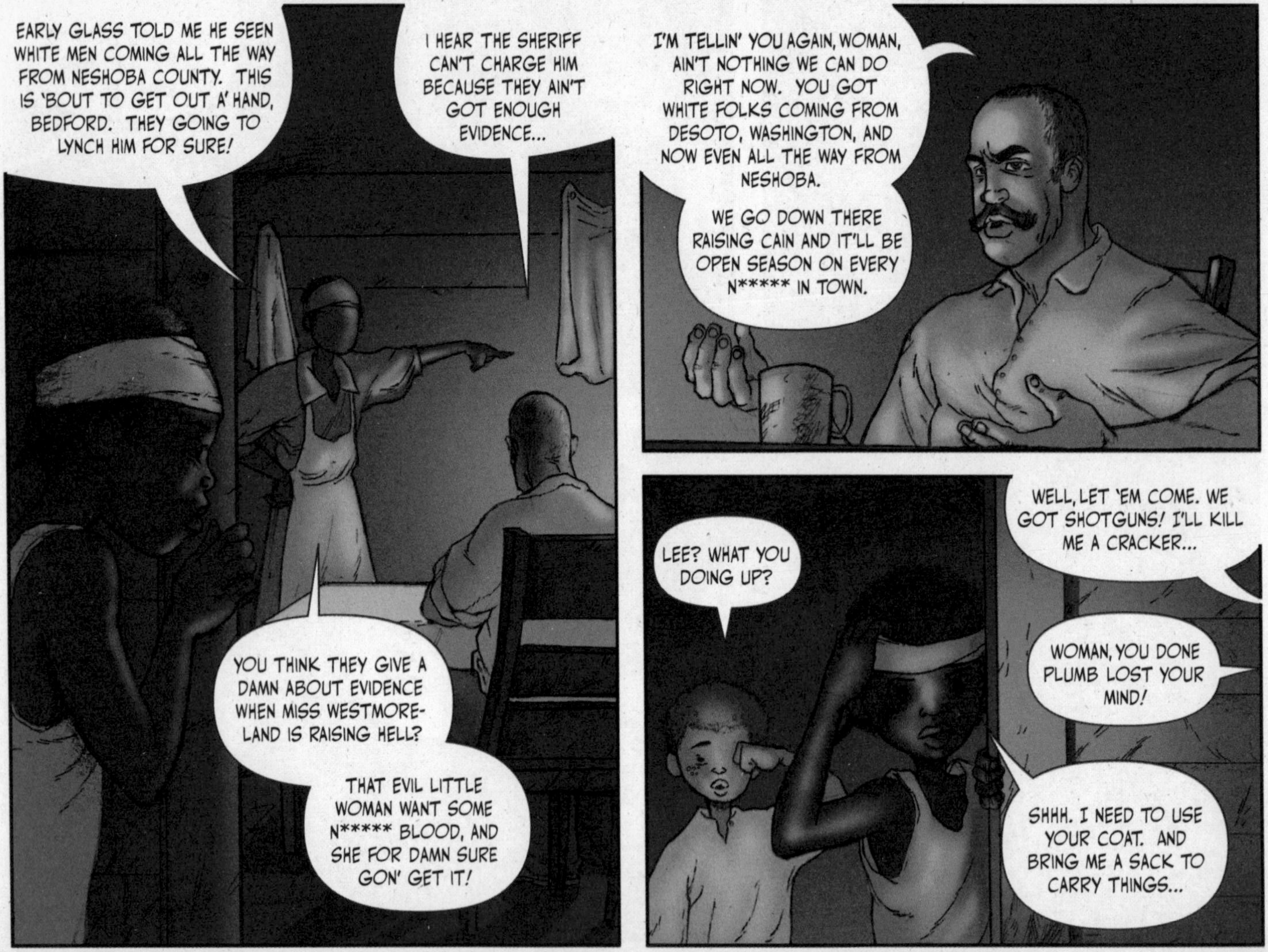
EARLY GLASS TOLD ME HE SEEN WHITE MEN COMING ALL THE WAY FROM NESHOBA COUNTY. THIS IS 'BOUT TO GET OUT A' HAND, BEDFORD. THEY GOING TO LYNCH HIM FOR SURE!
I HEAR THE SHERIFF CAN'T CHARGE HIM BECAUSE THEY AIN'T GOT ENOUGH EVIDENCE...
YOU THINK THEY GIVE A DAMN ABOUT EVIDENCE WHEN MISS WESTMORE-LAND IS RAISING HELL?
THAT EVIL LITTLE WOMAN WANT SOME N***** BLOOD, AND SHE FOR DAMN SURE GON' GET IT!
I'M TELLIN' YOU AGAIN, WOMAN, AIN'T NOTHING WE CAN DO RIGHT NOW. YOU GOT WHITE FOLKS COMING FROM DESOTO, WASHINGTON, AND NOW EVEN ALL THE WAY FROM NESHOBA.
WE GO DOWN THERE RAISING CAIN AND IT'LL BE OPEN SEASON ON EVERY N***** IN TOWN.
WELL, LET 'EM COME. WE GOT SHOTGUNS! I'LL KILL ME A CRACKER...
LEE? WHAT YOU DOING UP?
WOMAN, YOU DONE PLUMB LOST YOUR MIND!
SHHH. I NEED TO USE YOUR COAT. AND BRING ME A SACK TO CARRY THINGS...

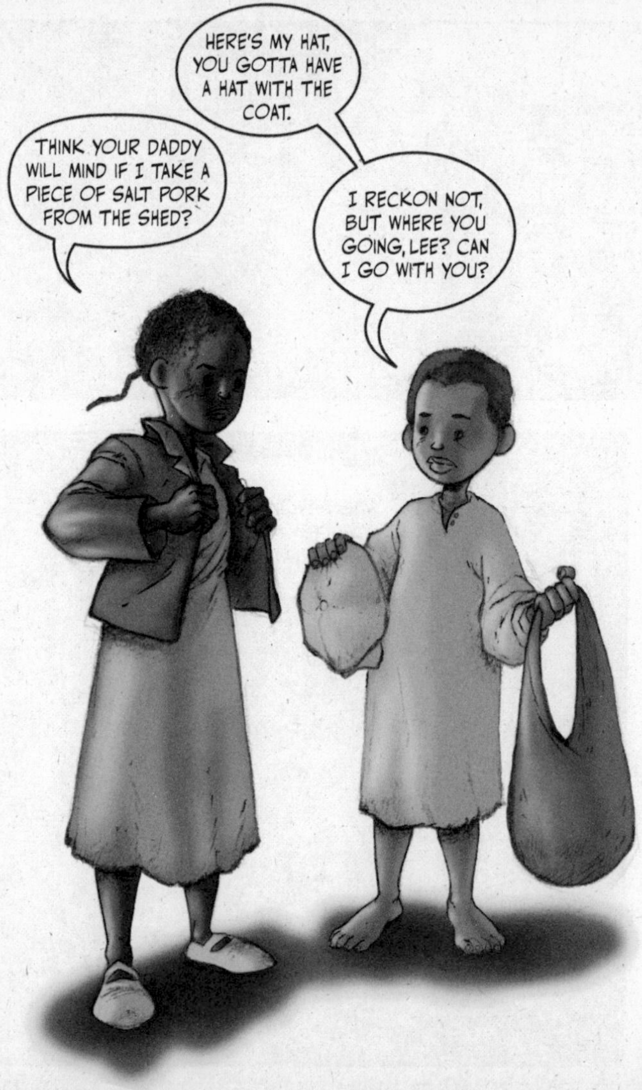
THINK YOUR DADDY WILL MIND IF I TAKE A PIECE OF SALT PORK FROM THE SHED?
HERE'S MY HAT, YOU GOTTA HAVE A HAT WITH THE COAT.
I RECKON NOT, BUT WHERE YOU GOING, LEE? CAN I GO WITH YOU?

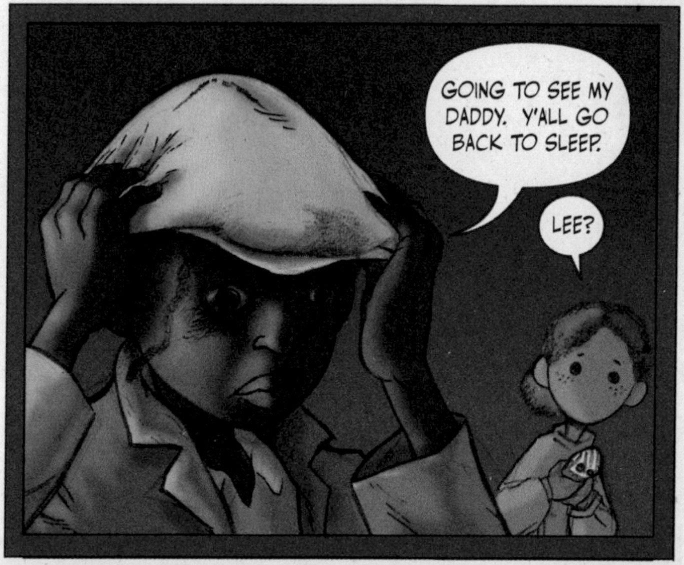
GOING TO SEE MY DADDY. Y'ALL GO BACK TO SLEEP.
LEE?

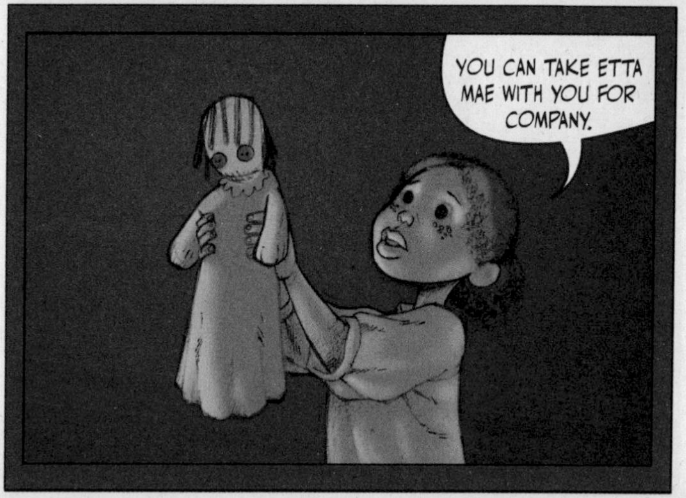
YOU CAN TAKE ETTA MAE WITH YOU FOR COMPANY.

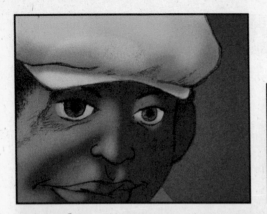

THANK YOU, HATTIE. I'LL BRING IT BACK TO YOU, I PROMISE. NOW GO BACK TO BED, OK?

WHERE YOU RUNNIN' OFF TO THIS TIME OF NIGHT?

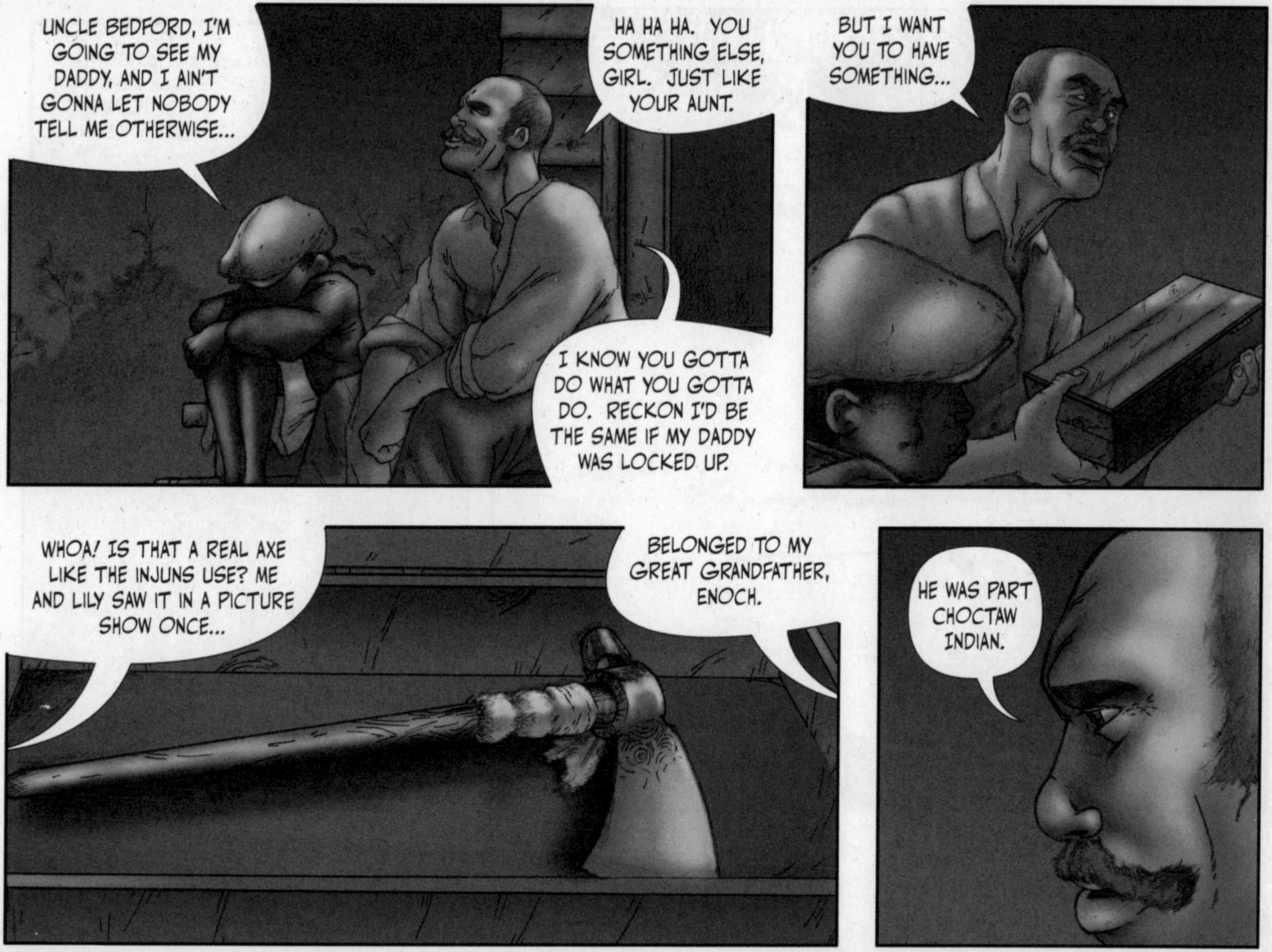
UNCLE BEDFORD, I'M GOING TO SEE MY DADDY, AND I AIN'T GONNA LET NOBODY TELL ME OTHERWISE...
HA HA HA. YOU SOMETHING ELSE, GIRL. JUST LIKE YOUR AUNT.
I KNOW YOU GOTTA DO WHAT YOU GOTTA DO. RECKON I'D BE THE SAME IF MY DADDY WAS LOCKED UP.
BUT I WANT YOU TO HAVE SOMETHING...
WHOA! IS THAT A REAL AXE LIKE THE INJUNS USE? ME AND LILY SAW IT IN A PICTURE SHOW ONCE...
BELONGED TO MY GREAT GRANDFATHER, ENOCH.
HE WAS PART CHOCTAW INDIAN.

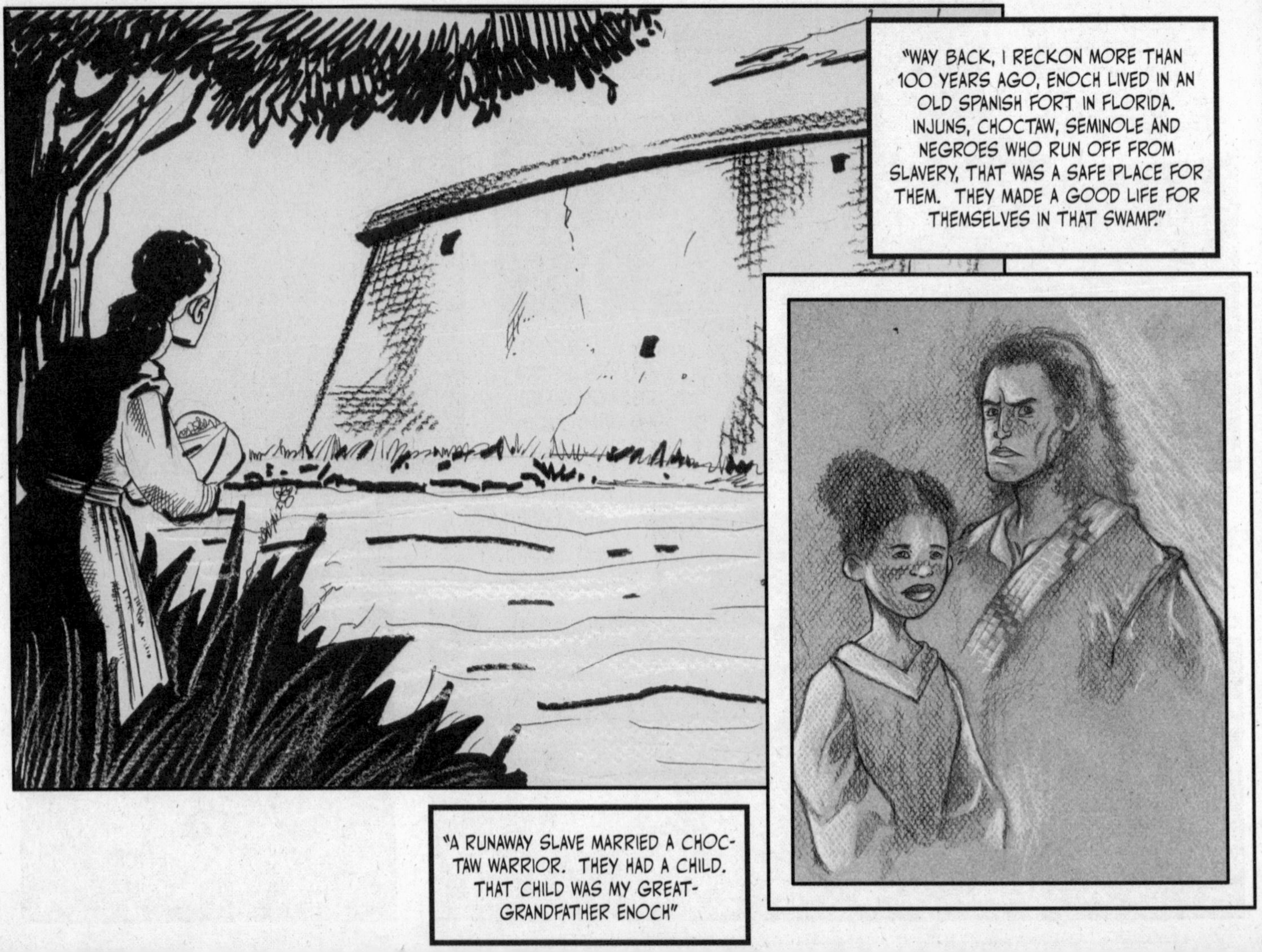
"WAY BACK, I RECKON MORE THAN 100 YEARS AGO, ENOCH LIVED IN AN OLD SPANISH FORT IN FLORIDA. INJUNS, CHOCTAW, SEMINOLE AND NEGROES WHO RUN OFF FROM SLAVERY, THAT WAS A SAFE PLACE FOR THEM. THEY MADE A GOOD LIFE FOR THEMSELVES IN THAT SWAMP."
"A RUNAWAY SLAVE MARRIED A CHOCTAW WARRIOR. THEY HAD A CHILD. THAT CHILD WAS MY GREAT-GRANDFATHER ENOCH"

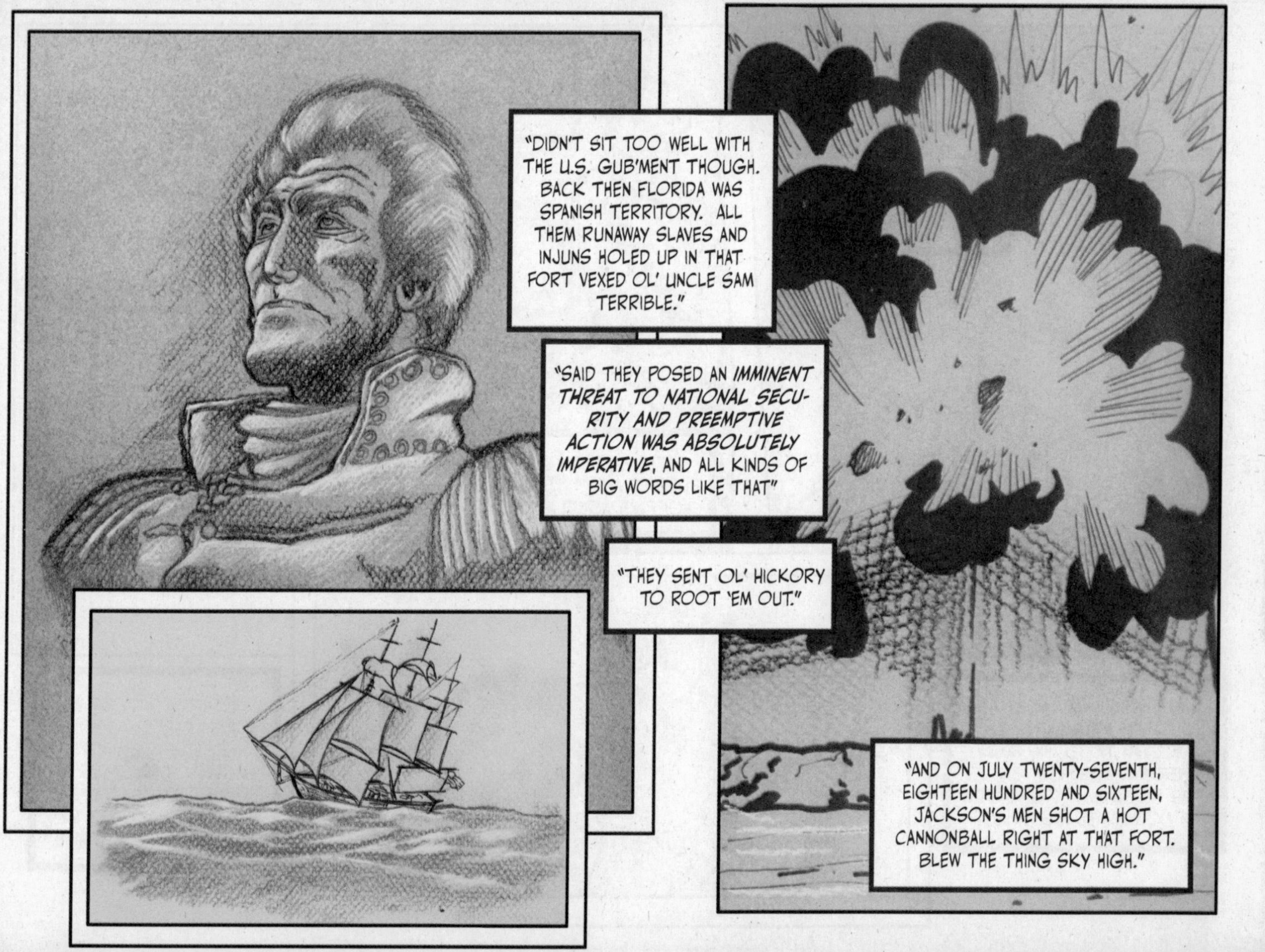
"DIDN'T SIT TOO WELL WITH THE U.S. GUB'MENT THOUGH. BACK THEN FLORIDA WAS SPANISH TERRITORY. ALL THEM RUNAWAY SLAVES AND INJUNS HOLED UP IN THAT FORT VEXED OL' UNCLE SAM TERRIBLE."
"SAID THEY POSED AN *IMMINENT THREAT TO NATIONAL SECURITY AND PREEMPTIVE ACTION WAS ABSOLUTELY IMPERATIVE*, AND ALL KINDS OF BIG WORDS LIKE THAT"
"THEY SENT OL' HICKORY TO ROOT 'EM OUT."
"AND ON JULY TWENTY-SEVENTH, EIGHTEEN HUNDRED AND SIXTEEN, JACKSON'S MEN SHOT A HOT CANNONBALL RIGHT AT THAT FORT. BLEW THE THING SKY HIGH."

"A CHOCTAW WARRIOR GOT A FEW WOMEN AND CHILDREN OUT JUST BEFORE THE THING BLEW. ENOCH WAS WITH THEM BUT HIS MAMA AND DADDY DIED IN THE FORT."

"ENOCH'S BLOOD WAS BOILING. HE WANTED REVENGE."

"THE WARRIOR GAVE HIM THIS BLESSED AXE. TOLD HIM IT WAS FOR CHOPPING WOOD AND KILLING MEN."

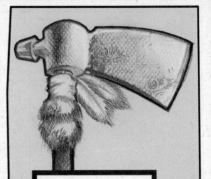

"NOW WAS TIME TO BE FREE. CHOP WOOD. BUILD A NEW HOME. BUT WHEN IT WAS TIME TO FIGHT HE WOULD BE READY."

"AND THAT'S WHAT OL' ENOCH. BUILT HIM A HOME WITH THE CHOCTAW TRIBE. HIS FAMILY NEVER SAW BONDAGE. ENOCH GAVE HIS SON, MY GRAN'DADDY, THE AXE WHEN HE WAS OF AGE."

"HE HAD IT WITH HIM IN SOUTH CAROLINA WHEN HE HELPED STORM FORT WAGNER. THOUSANDS OF SOULS DIED THAT DAY, BUT THAT AXE BROUGHT MY GRAN'DADDY HOME SAFE."

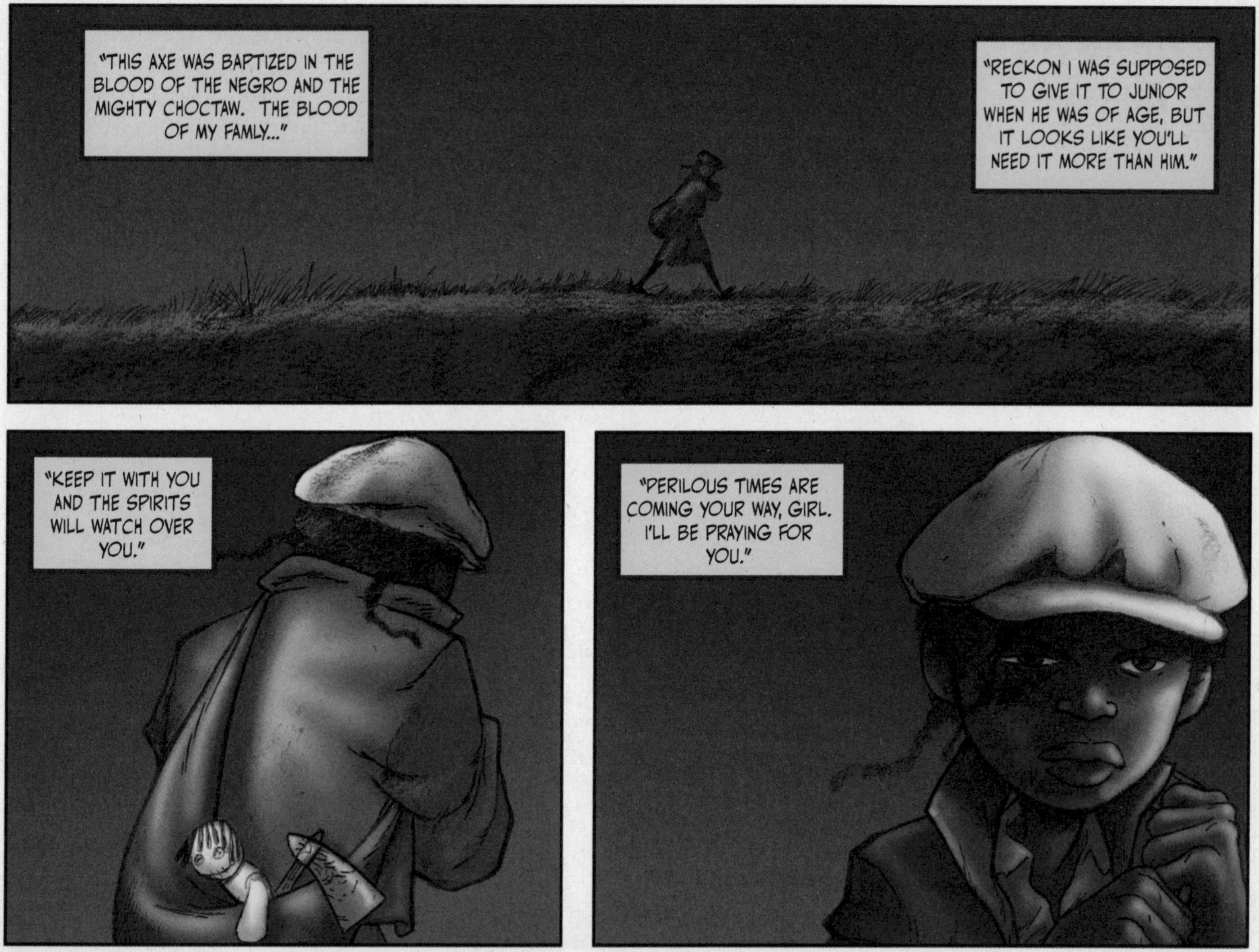
"THIS AXE WAS BAPTIZED IN THE BLOOD OF THE NEGRO AND THE MIGHTY CHOCTAW. THE BLOOD OF MY FAMLY..."
"RECKON I WAS SUPPOSED TO GIVE IT TO JUNIOR WHEN HE WAS OF AGE, BUT IT LOOKS LIKE YOU'LL NEED IT MORE THAN HIM."
"KEEP IT WITH YOU AND THE SPIRITS WILL WATCH OVER YOU."
"PERILOUS TIMES ARE COMING YOUR WAY, GIRL. I'LL BE PRAYING FOR YOU."

# *TRAGEDY ON THE BAYOU*

Special Commentary by Jack Barbour

In the northwest corner of our great state of Mississippi, along the Yazoo river, is the hamlet Charon. Nestled on the great alluvial plain, where cotton is king, Charon is the very definition of "salt of the earth." From the majestic plantations and mansions to the north, the sprawling cotton fields, and the haunting bayous in the south, there is one of the last bastions of Southern grandeur.

The town was renamed from its original moniker, Clarksville, after the War Between the States. It was there, in the waning days of the epic conflict, that General Douglass Matthew Bogg made his last stand against Sherman's Northern marauders. Bogg fought so fiercely that a Yankee writer likened him to Charon, the ancient Greek figure who ferried dead souls into Hades.

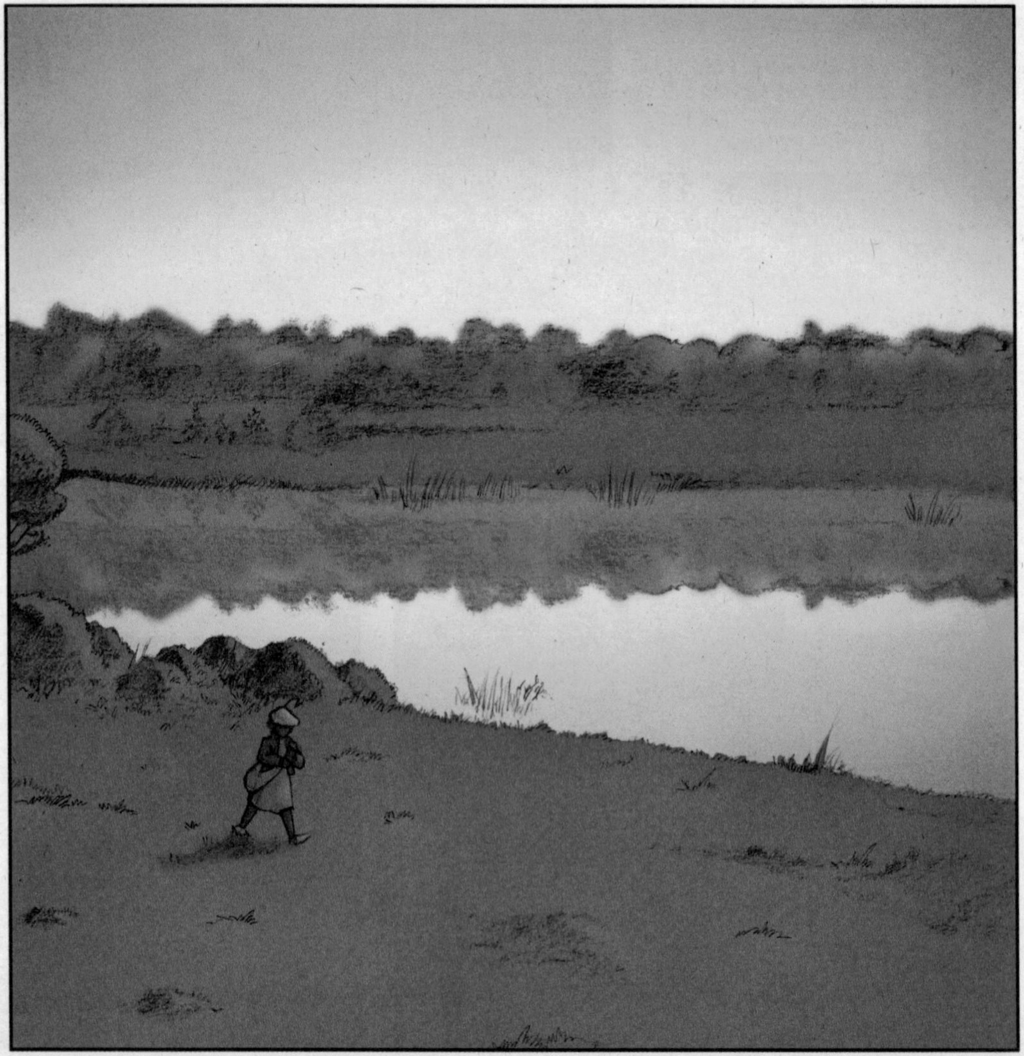

Refusing to surrender, General Bogg fought to the last man and was himself killed. His steadfast gallantry was permanently ingrained upon the minds of Clarksville. They renamed the town Charon, after Bogg's new nom de plume.

It is this writer's sad duty to report that in this great Southern town, a grave tragedy has occurred. A young white girl, Lily Westmoreland, has gone missing. The prime suspect is a negro, Calvin Wagstaff. Wagstaff is a big and burly wretch, with long, sinewy, apelike arms and massive hands. His eyes are devoid of feeling and humanity. One finds it hard to empathize with this criminal.

The Negro is currently in custody, but the white girl's undoubtedly violated body has yet to be found. A shoe found in the Negro suspect's home is the only trace. As I write this article, a massive search for the girl is under way.

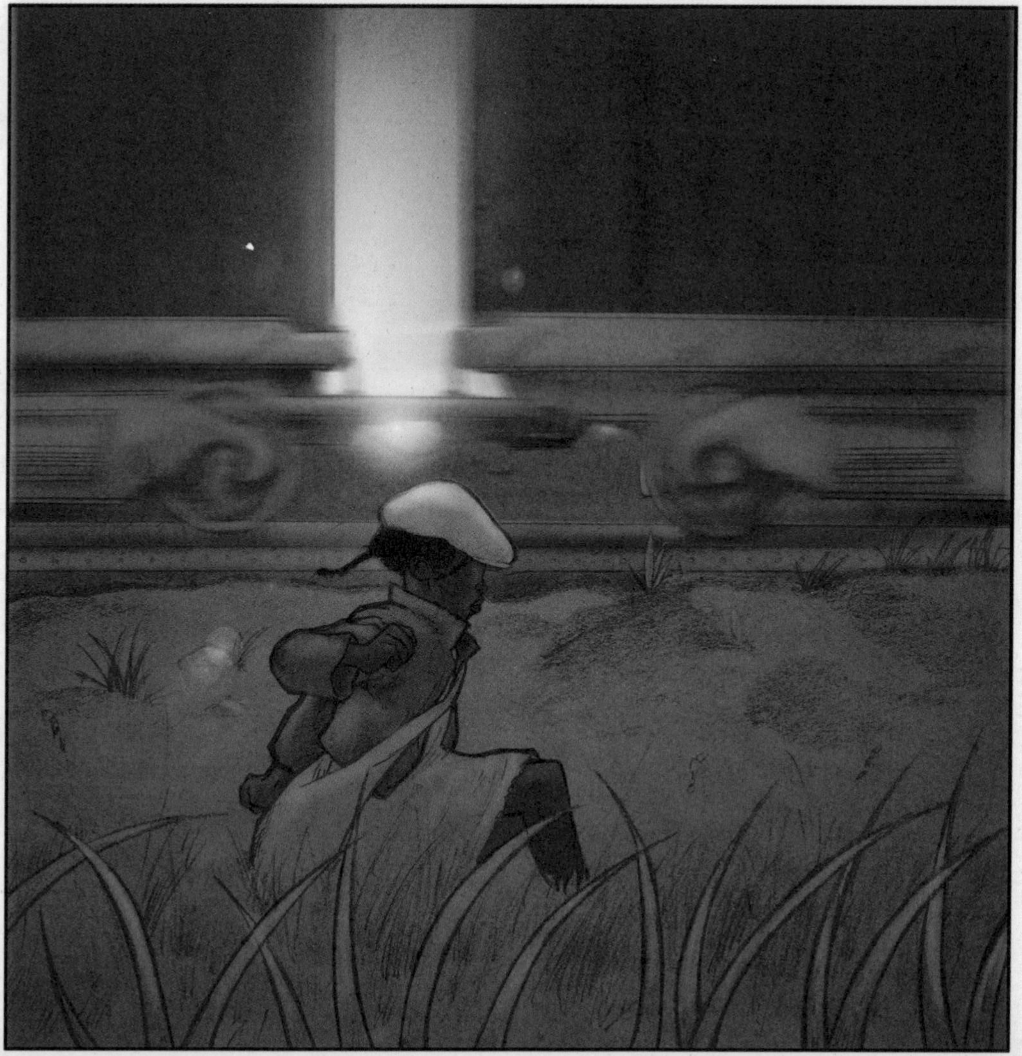

All volunteers in the surrounding counties are encouraged to keep eye and ear pricked for any possible signs of the girl. All Negroes are encouraged to come forward with any information. This writer fears for the safety of the well-behaved Negroes of Charon if this situation is not resolved.

It is indeed ironic that in the place where Douglass Bogg defended a gallant way of life with such ferocity such a tragedy should occur. To this writer it illustrates the wisdom of our forefathers, who foresaw this type of lawlessness in the wake of the fall of Southern culture. We can only pray that the surge of white anger does not boil over and seek to reclaim the glory of our slain ancestors.

*Jack Barbour is an acclaimed historian and author of the novel Red Season.*

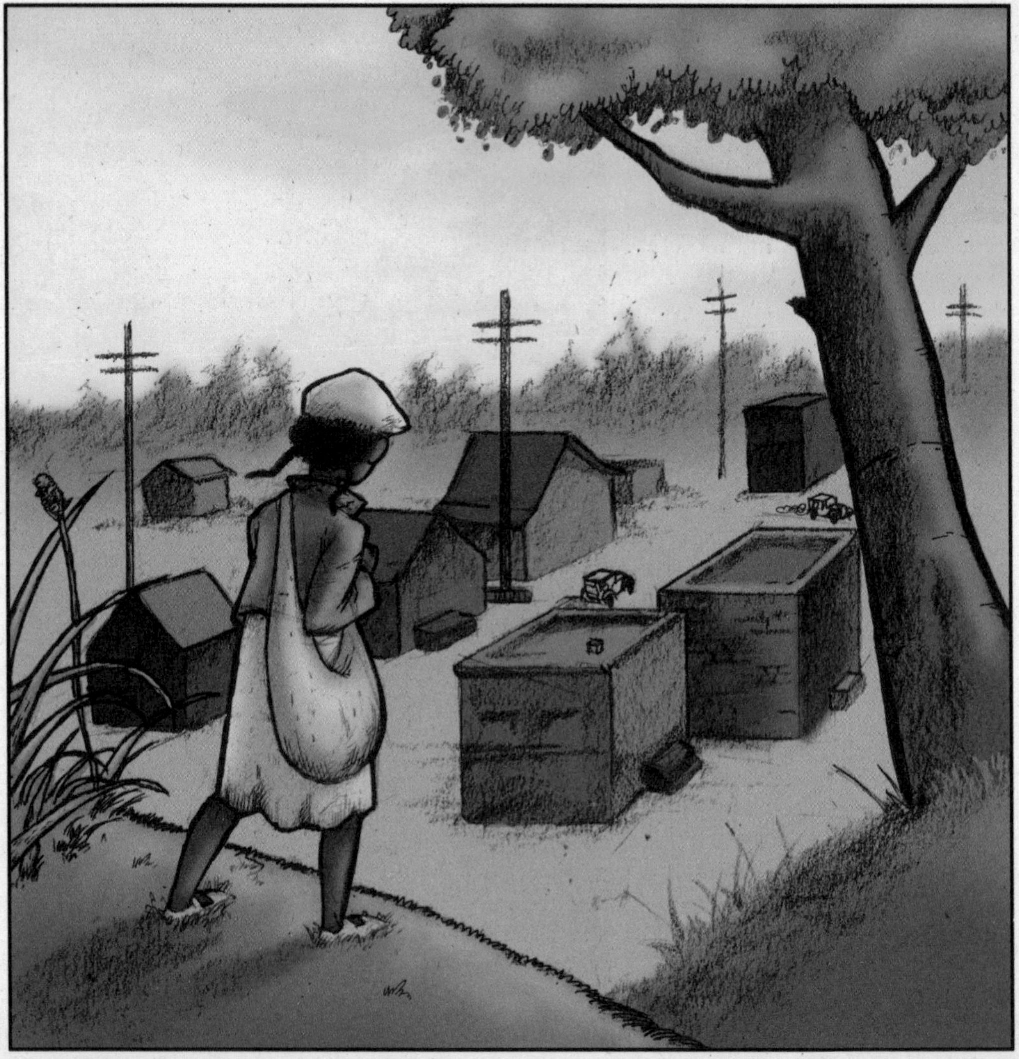

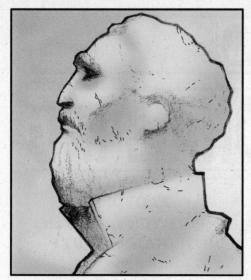

GENERAL
DOUGLASS M.
'HELLHOUND'
BOGG

HERO OF THE WAR OF NORTHERN AGGRESSION

WEATHER
FORECAST

High 83
Low 74
Partly Cloudy

Humid

# THE YAZOO HERALD

LATE
EDITION

June 18, 1933

# NEGRO HELD IN KIDNAPPING

## TRAGEDY ON THE BAYOU

*Special Commentary by Jack Barbour*

In the northwest corner of our great state of Mississippi, along the Yazoo river, is the hamlet Charon. Nestled on the great alluvial plain, where cotton is king, Charon is the very definition of "salt of the earth." From the majestic plantations and mansions to the north, the sprawling cotton fields, and the haunting bayou's in the south, there is one of the last bastions of Southern grandeur.

The town was renamed from its original moniker, Clarksville, after the War Between the States. It was there, in the waning days of the epic conflict, that General Douglass Matthew Bogg made his last stand against Sherman's Northern marauders. Bogg fought so fiercely that a Yankee writer likened him to Charon, the ancient Greek figure who ferried dead souls into Hades.

Refusing to surrender,

## MASSIVE SEARCH UNDERWAY FOR MISSING WHITE GIRL

### VOLUNTEERS POUR IN FROM SURROUNDING COUNTIES

A comprehensive search is under way all around Yazoo County for Lily Ann Westmoreland, age 10. The search is centered around the town of Charon. Volunteers from surrounding delta counties have poured in to assist local sheriff deputies.

Authorities did not comment on the health of the missing girl, but sources indicate sexual molestation. A Negro suspect has yet to provide information on her whereabouts, or condition. Sources inside the Sheriff's department cite "damning eyewitness and physical evidence" as the cause for arresting the Negro man, Calvin Wagstaff, on suspicion of kidnapping and rape.

Miss Eugena Westmoreland, Lily's

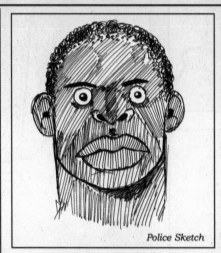

*Police Sketch*

## PRIME SUSPECT: SHARECROPPER CALVIN WAGSTAFF, 33, NEGRO

## YAZOO COUNTY BASEBALL TEAM OPTIMISTIC ON

## 'PRETTY BOY FLOYD' KILLS FOUR G-MEN IN KANSAS CITY

*FBI AGENTS WERE UNARMED*

Four law enforcement officers and a criminal fugitive were shot dead at the Union Station railroad depot in Kansas City, Missouri yesterday morning. According to the official FBI report, the Kansas City Massacre occurred as the result of the attempt by Charles "Pretty Boy" Floyd, Vernon Miller, and Adam Richetti to free their friend, Frank Nash, a federal prisoner. At the time, Nash was in the custody of several law enforcement officers who were returning him to the U.S. Penitentiary at Leavenworth, Kansas, from which he had escaped three years earlier.

However, all of the men alleged to be involved denied involvement. Floyd, in particular, went so far as to write to a newspaper denying involvement in the massacre.

A green Plymouth was parked about six feet away on the right side of Agent Caffrey's car. Looking in the direction of this Plymouth, Agent Lackey saw two men run from behind a car. He noticed that

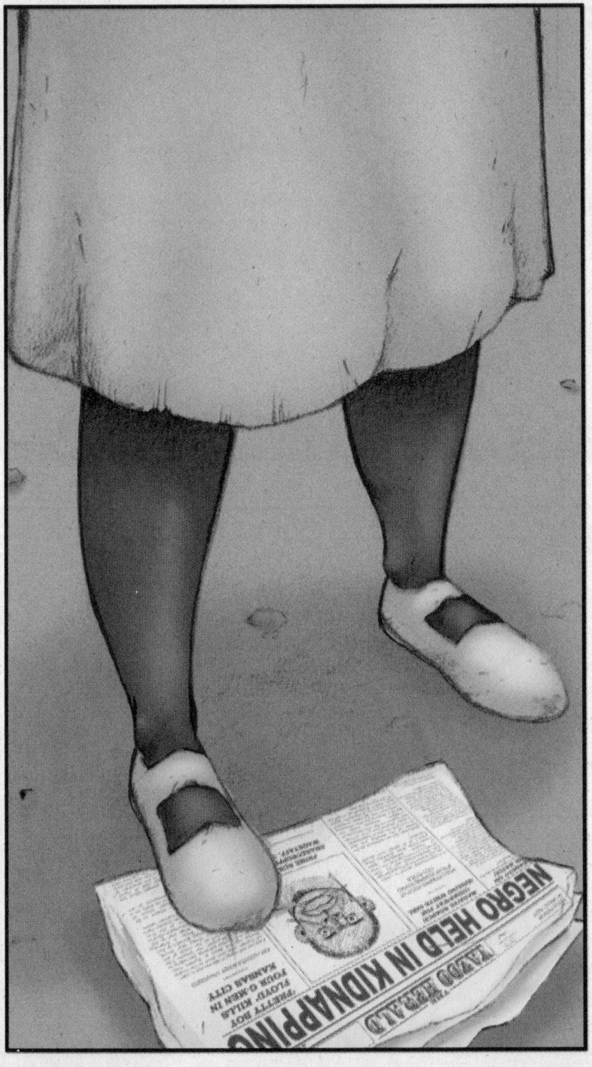
THE HERALD
NEGRO HELD IN KIDNAPPIN
'PRETTY BOY' FLOYD' KILLS FOUR G-MEN IN KANSAS CITY

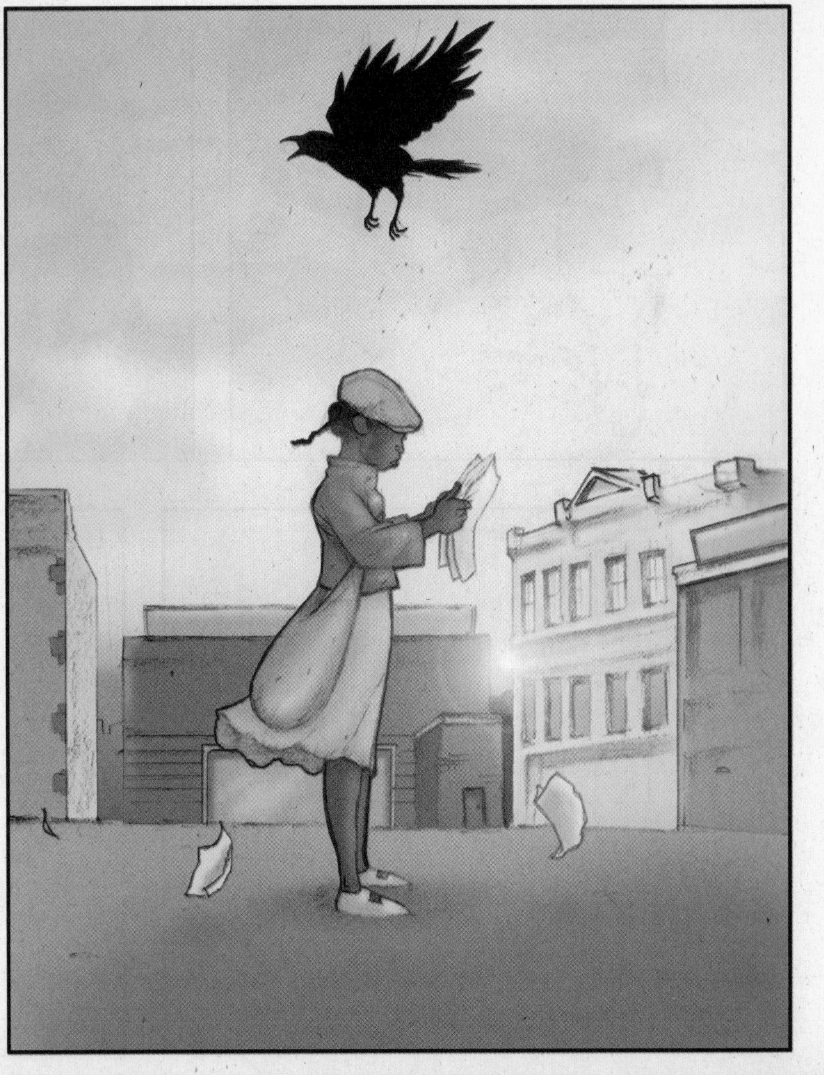

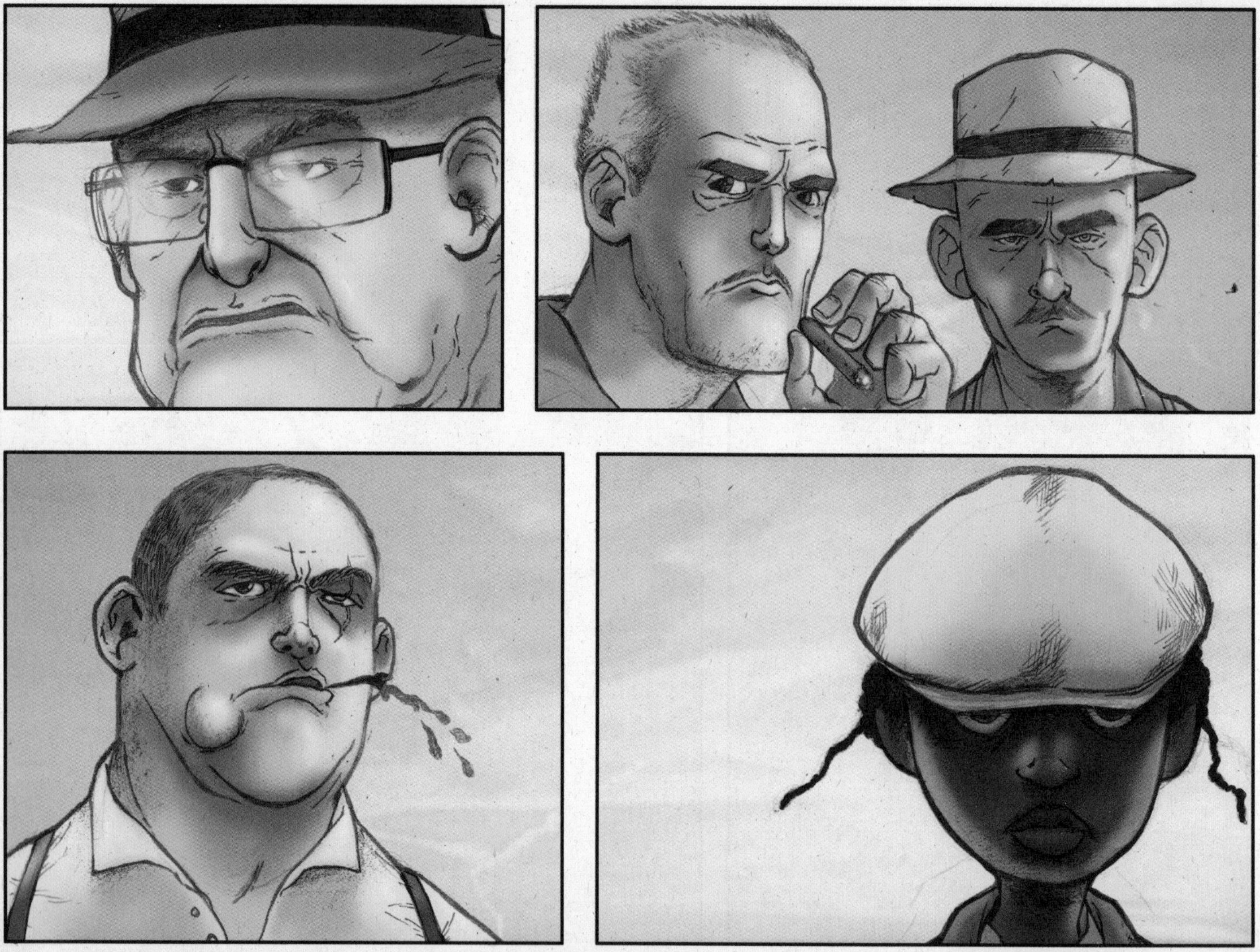

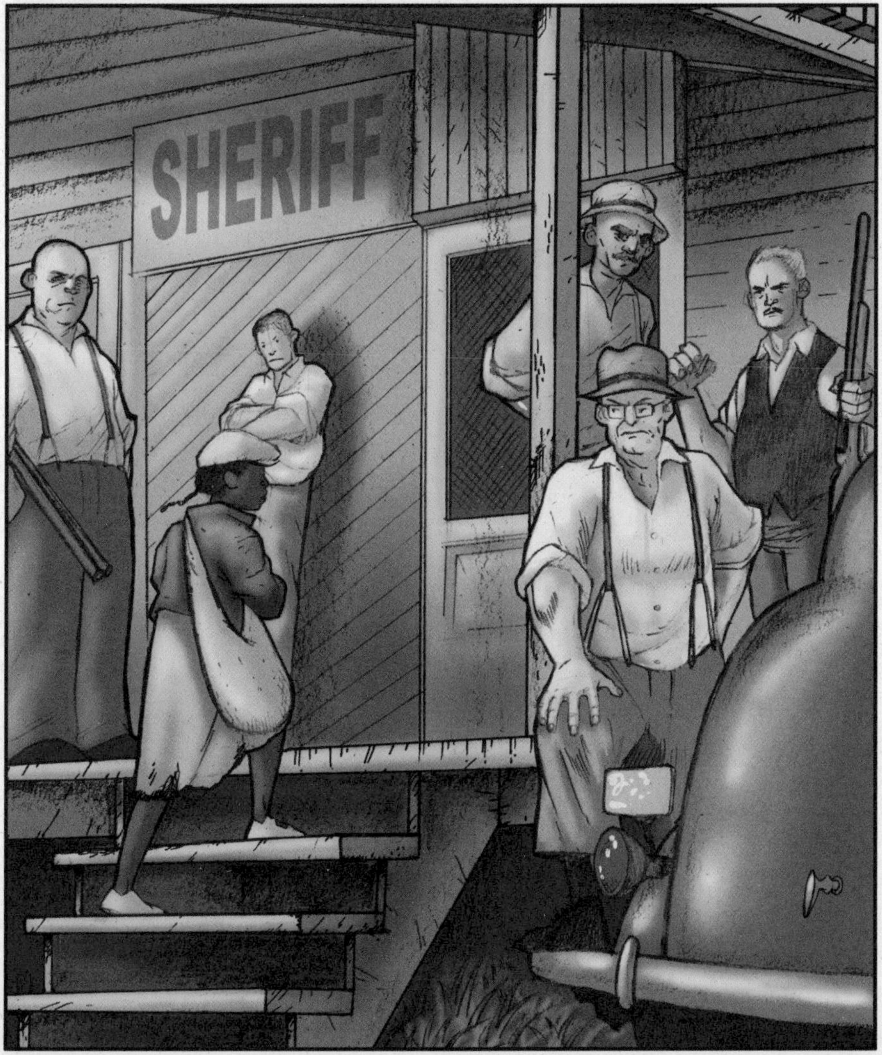
SHERIFF

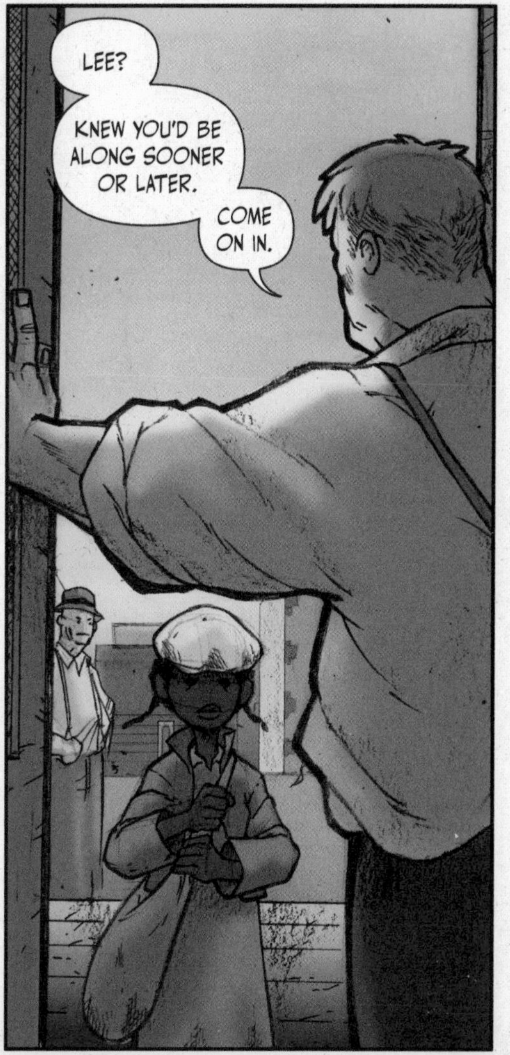
LEE?
KNEW YOU'D BE ALONG SOONER OR LATER.
COME ON IN.

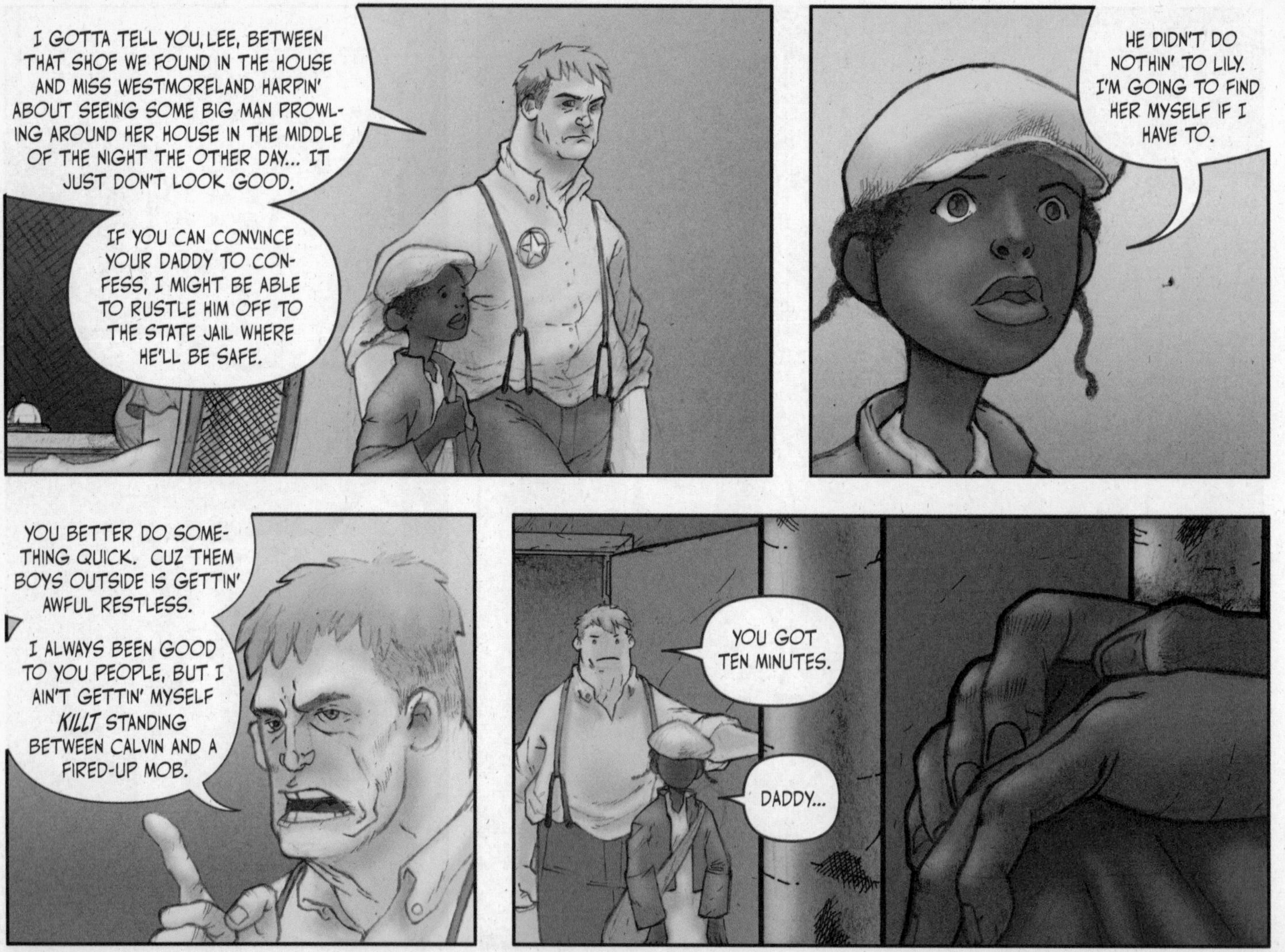
I GOTTA TELL YOU, LEE, BETWEEN THAT SHOE WE FOUND IN THE HOUSE AND MISS WESTMORELAND HARPIN' ABOUT SEEING SOME BIG MAN PROWLING AROUND HER HOUSE IN THE MIDDLE OF THE NIGHT THE OTHER DAY... IT JUST DON'T LOOK GOOD.
IF YOU CAN CONVINCE YOUR DADDY TO CONFESS, I MIGHT BE ABLE TO RUSTLE HIM OFF TO THE STATE JAIL WHERE HE'LL BE SAFE.
HE DIDN'T DO NOTHIN' TO LILY. I'M GOING TO FIND HER MYSELF IF I HAVE TO.
YOU BETTER DO SOMETHING QUICK. CUZ THEM BOYS OUTSIDE IS GETTIN' AWFUL RESTLESS.
I ALWAYS BEEN GOOD TO YOU PEOPLE, BUT I AIN'T GETTIN' MYSELF *KILLT* STANDING BETWEEN CALVIN AND A FIRED-UP MOB.
YOU GOT TEN MINUTES.
DADDY...

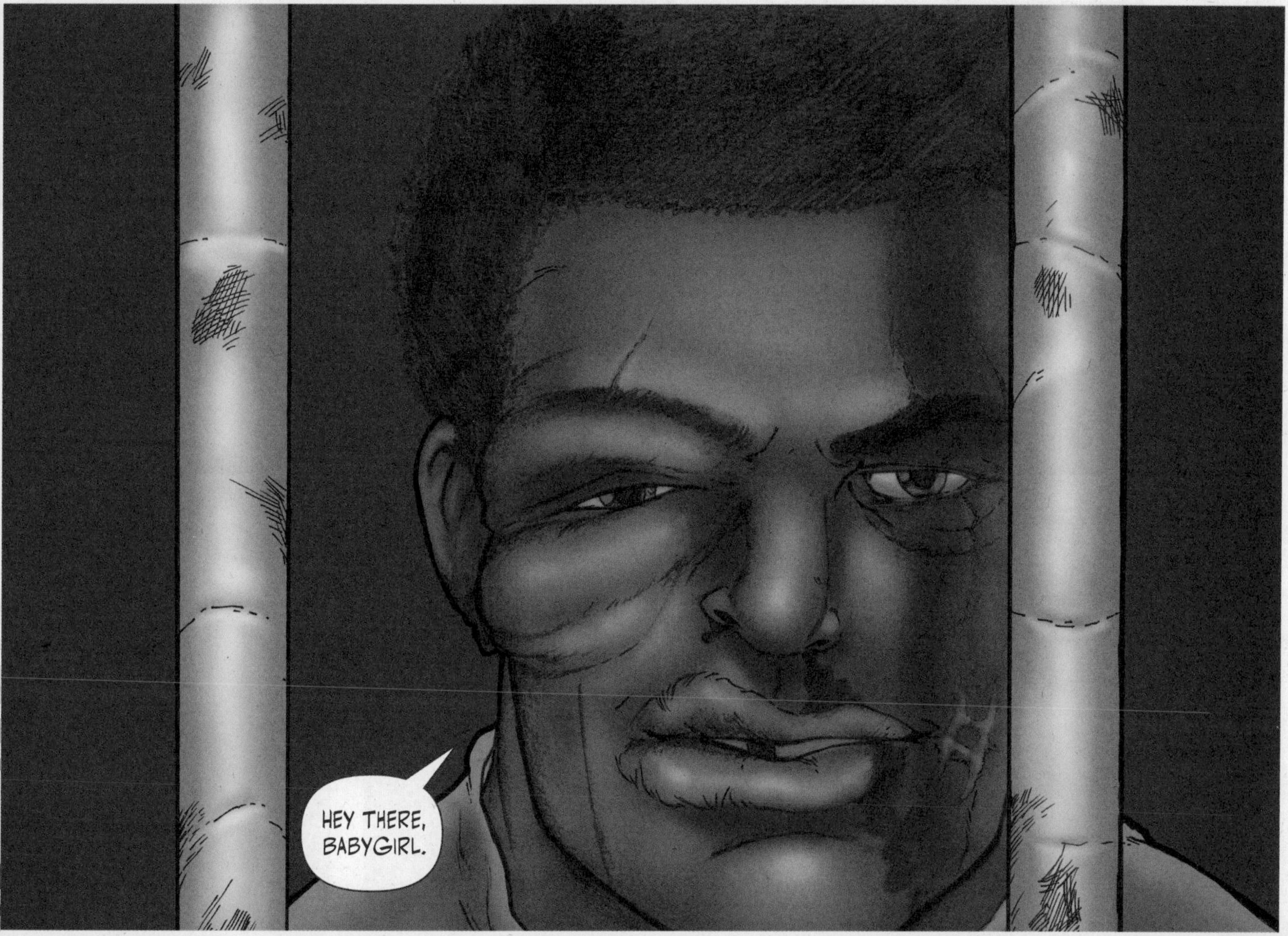
HEY THERE, BABYGIRL.

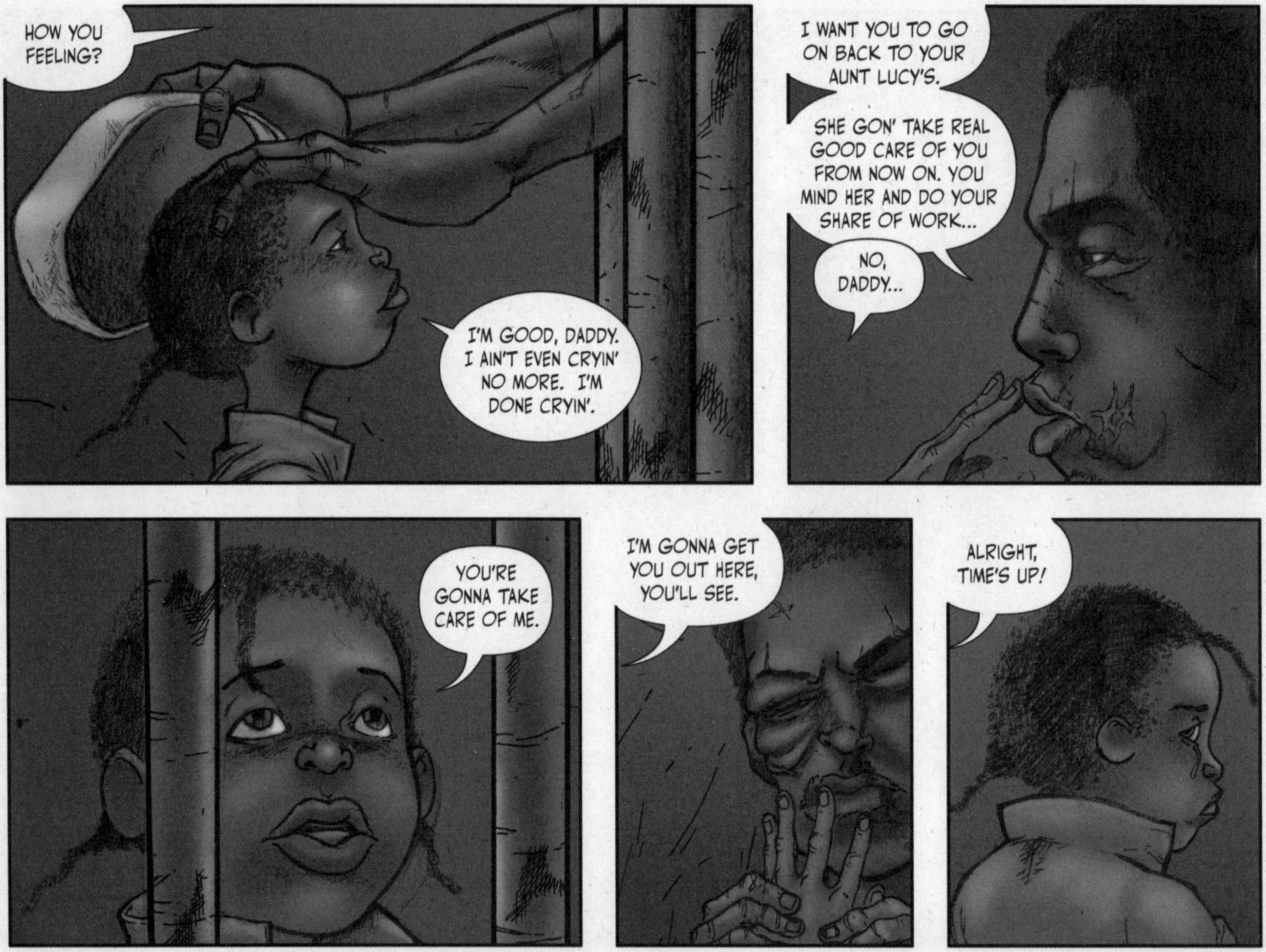
HOW YOU FEELING?
I'M GOOD, DADDY. I AIN'T EVEN CRYIN' NO MORE. I'M DONE CRYIN'.
I WANT YOU TO GO ON BACK TO YOUR AUNT LUCY'S.
SHE GON' TAKE REAL GOOD CARE OF YOU FROM NOW ON. YOU MIND HER AND DO YOUR SHARE OF WORK...
NO, DADDY...
YOU'RE GONNA TAKE CARE OF ME.
I'M GONNA GET YOU OUT HERE, YOU'LL SEE.
ALRIGHT, TIME'S UP!

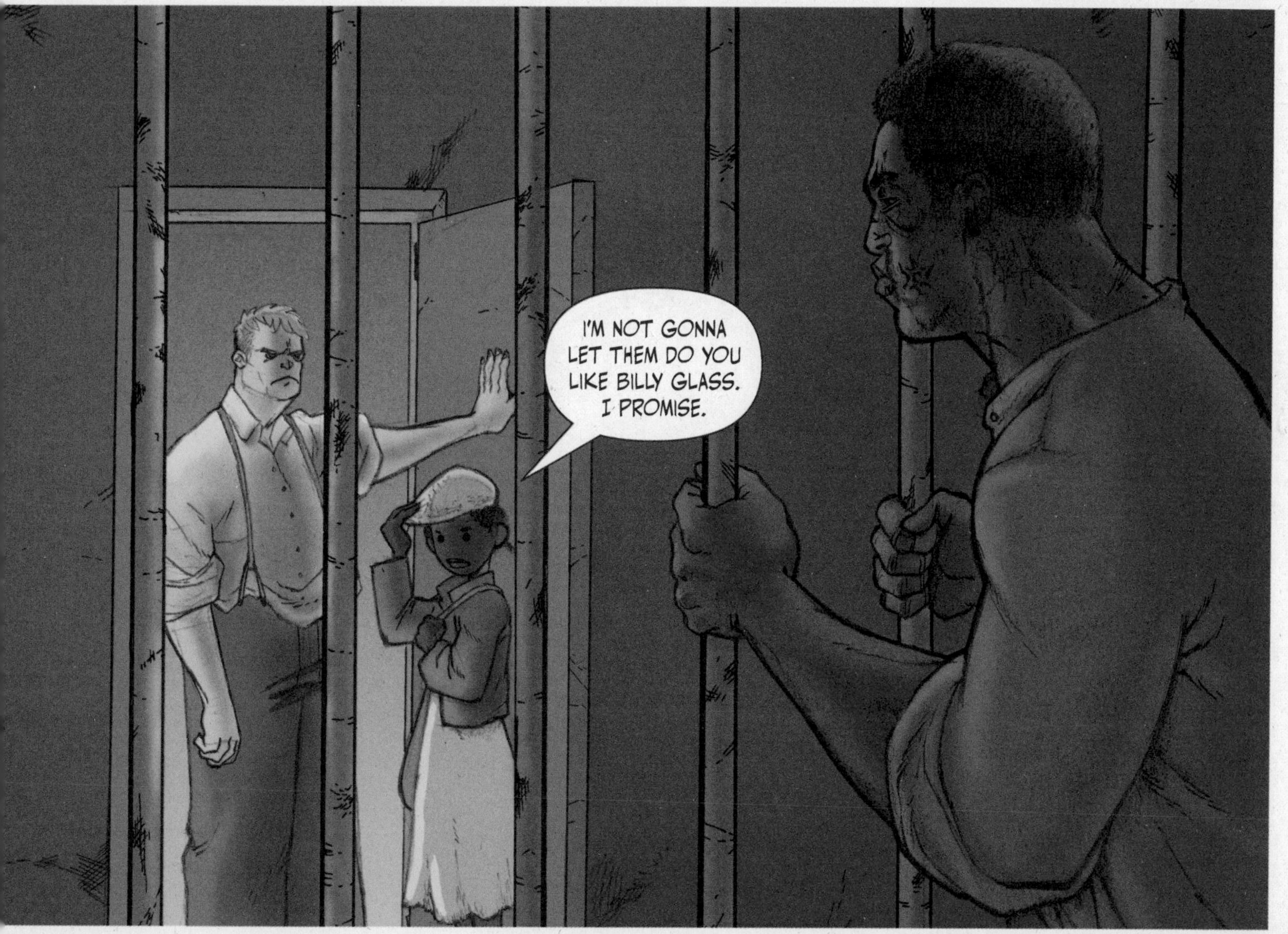
I'M NOT GONNA LET THEM DO YOU LIKE BILLY GLASS. I PROMISE.

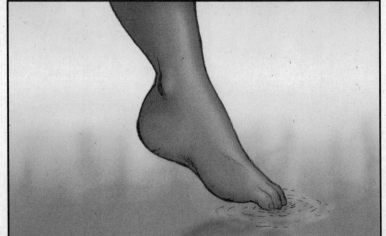

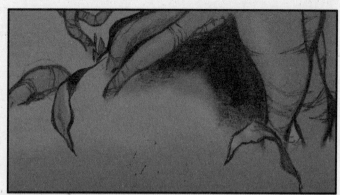

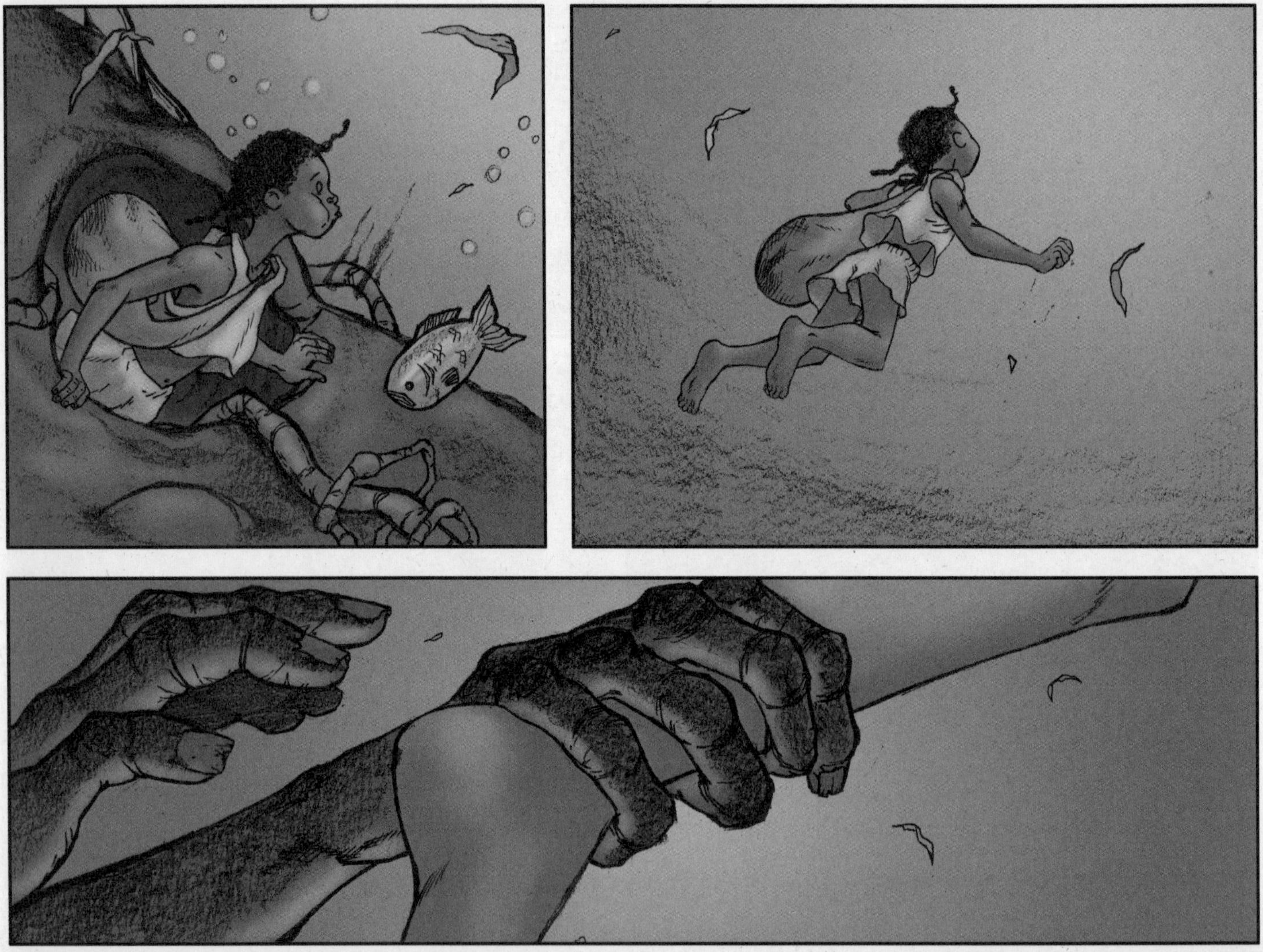

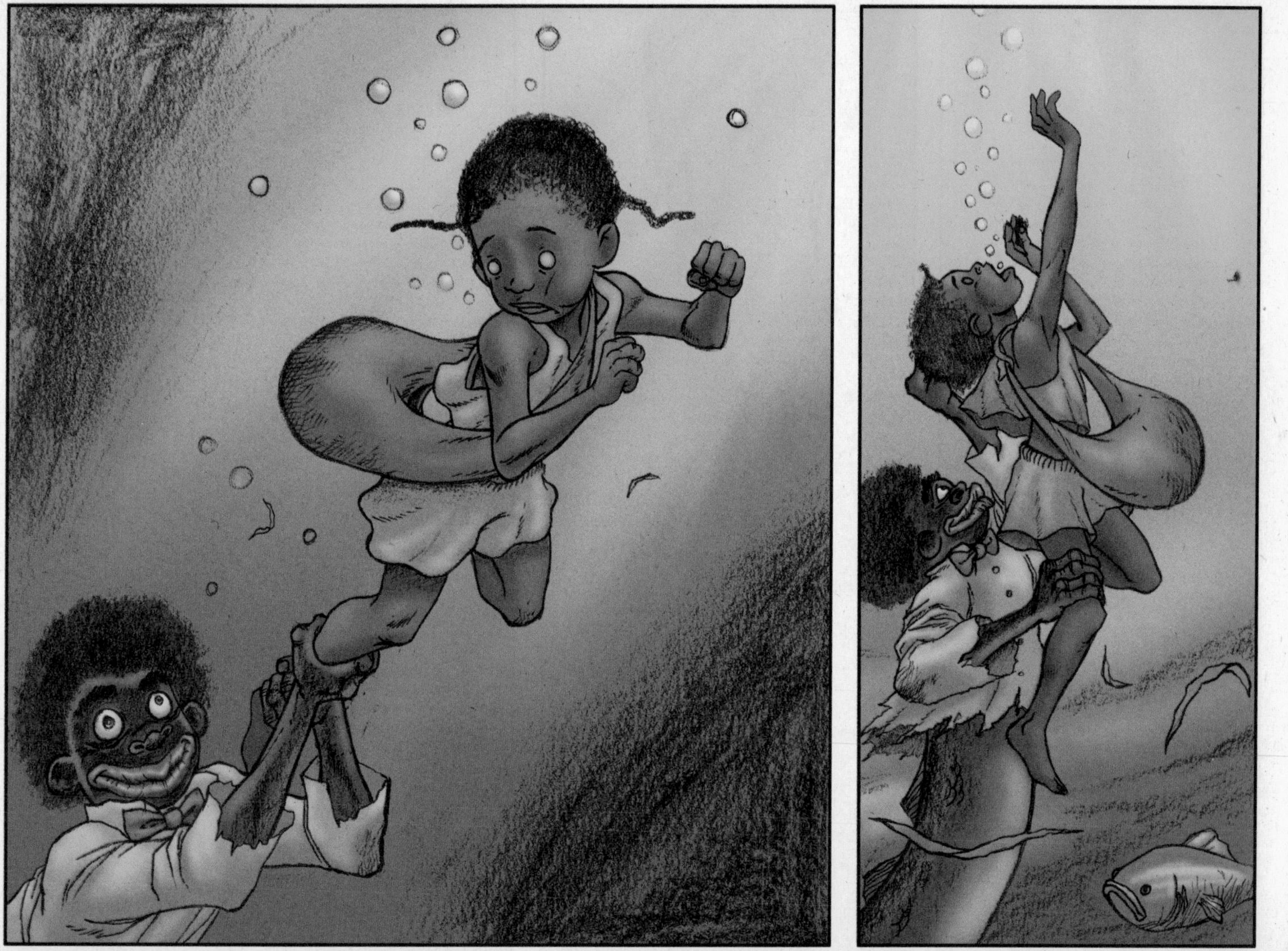

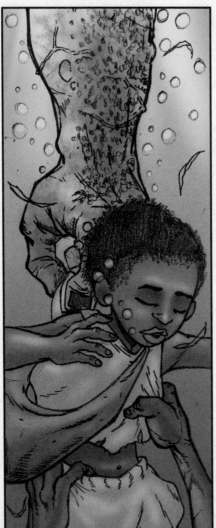

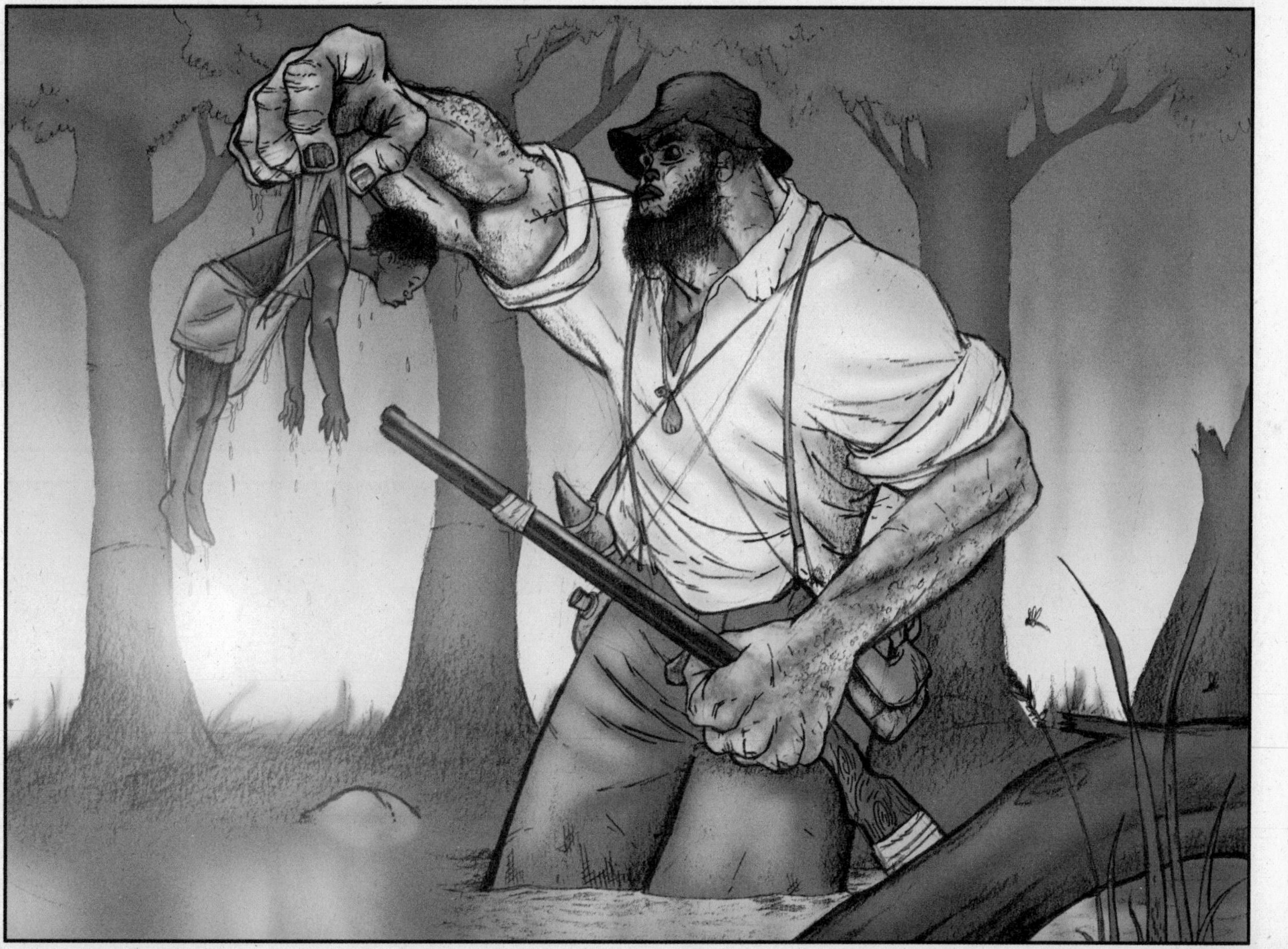

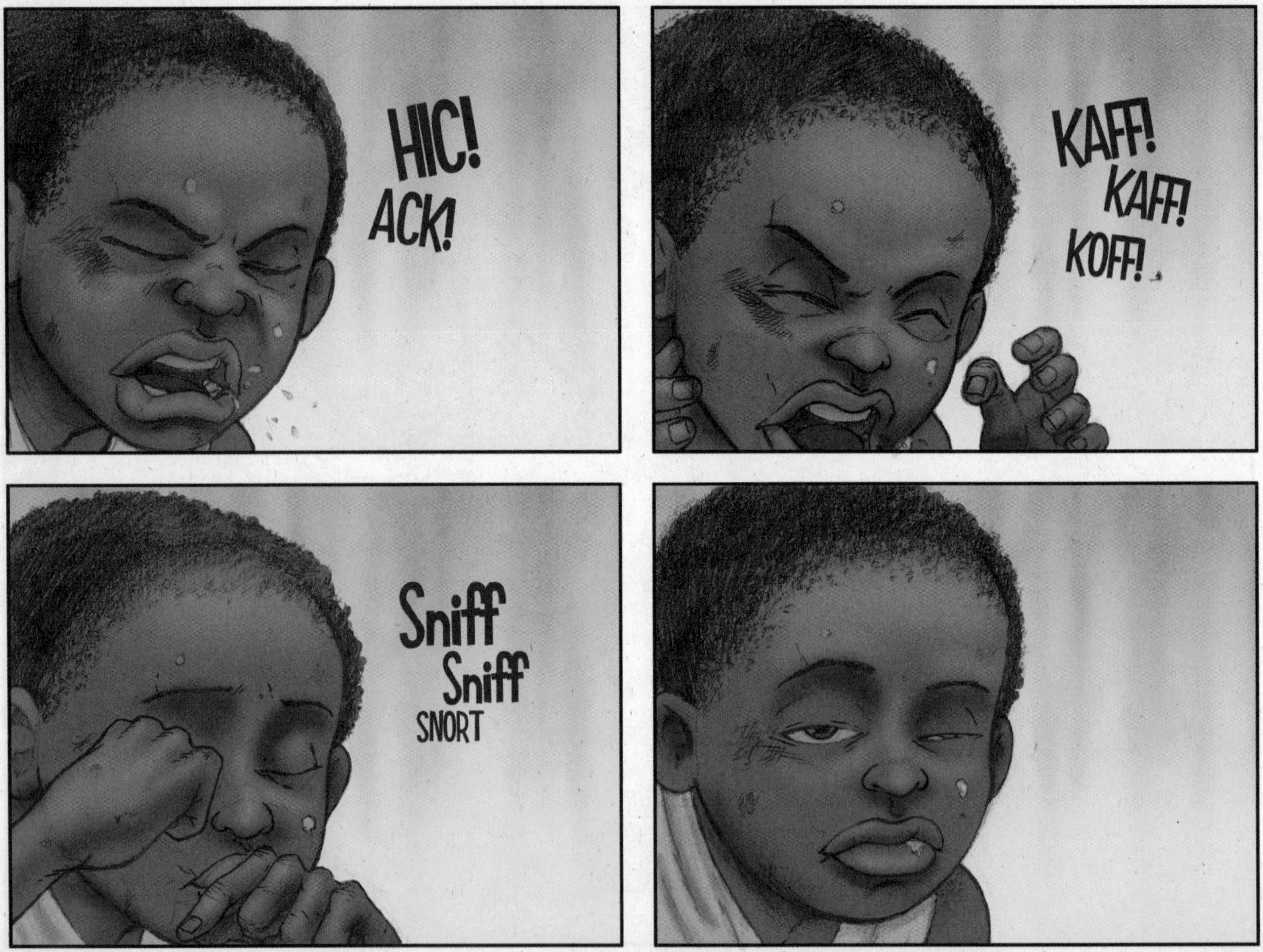
HIC!
ACK!
KAFF!
KAFF!
KOFF!
Sniff
Sniff
SNORT

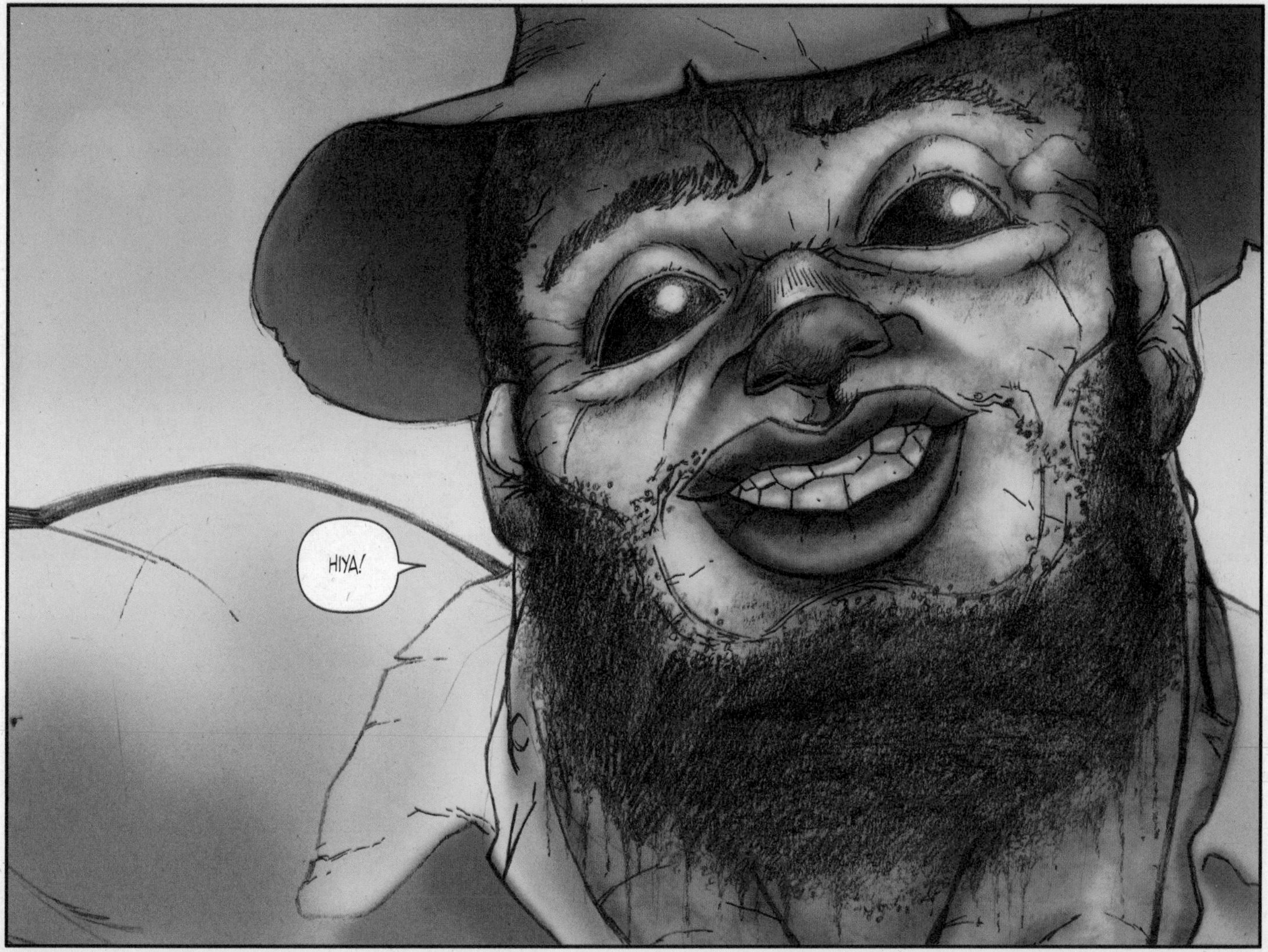
HIYA!

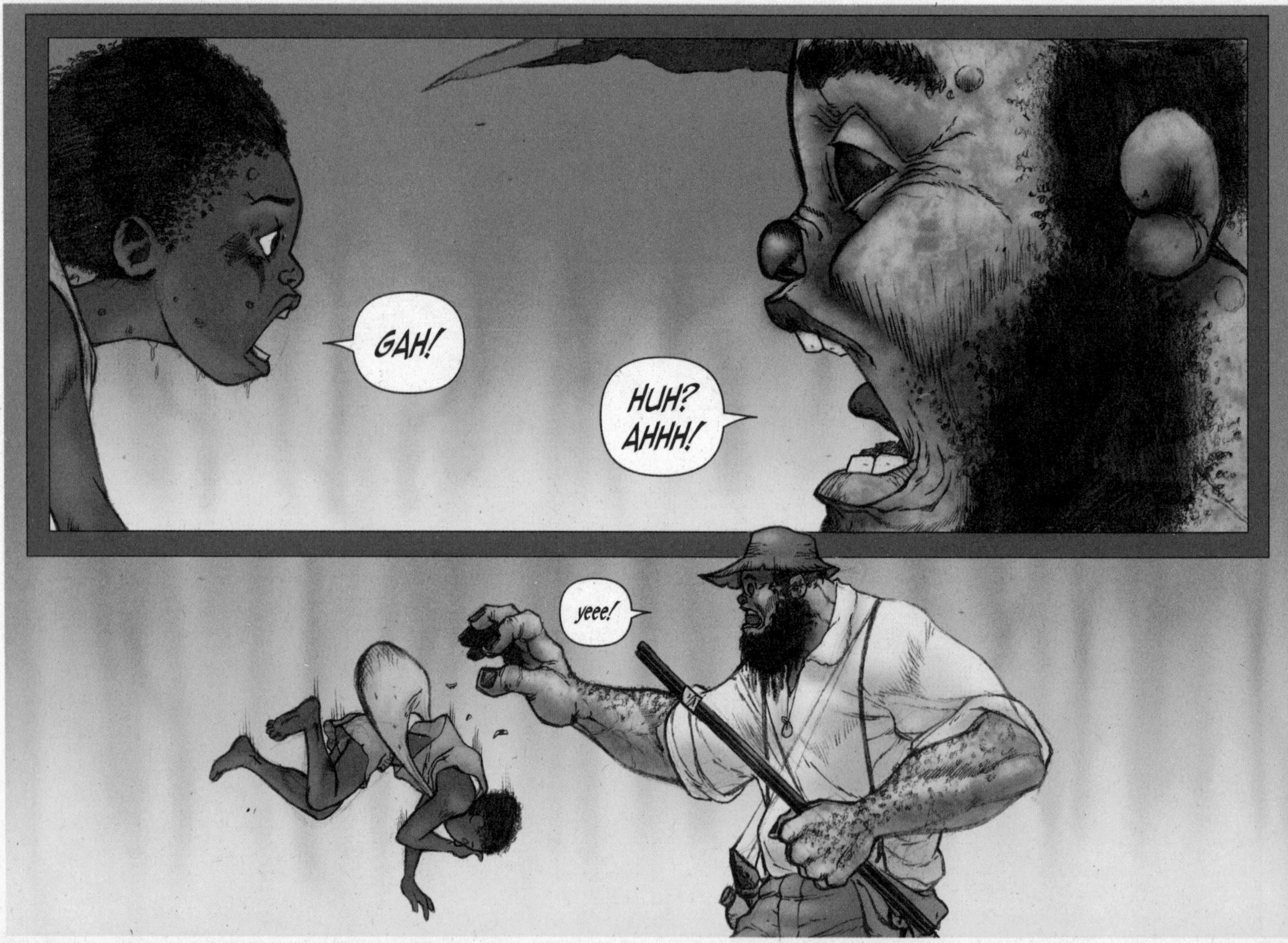
GAH!
HUH? AHHH!
yeee!

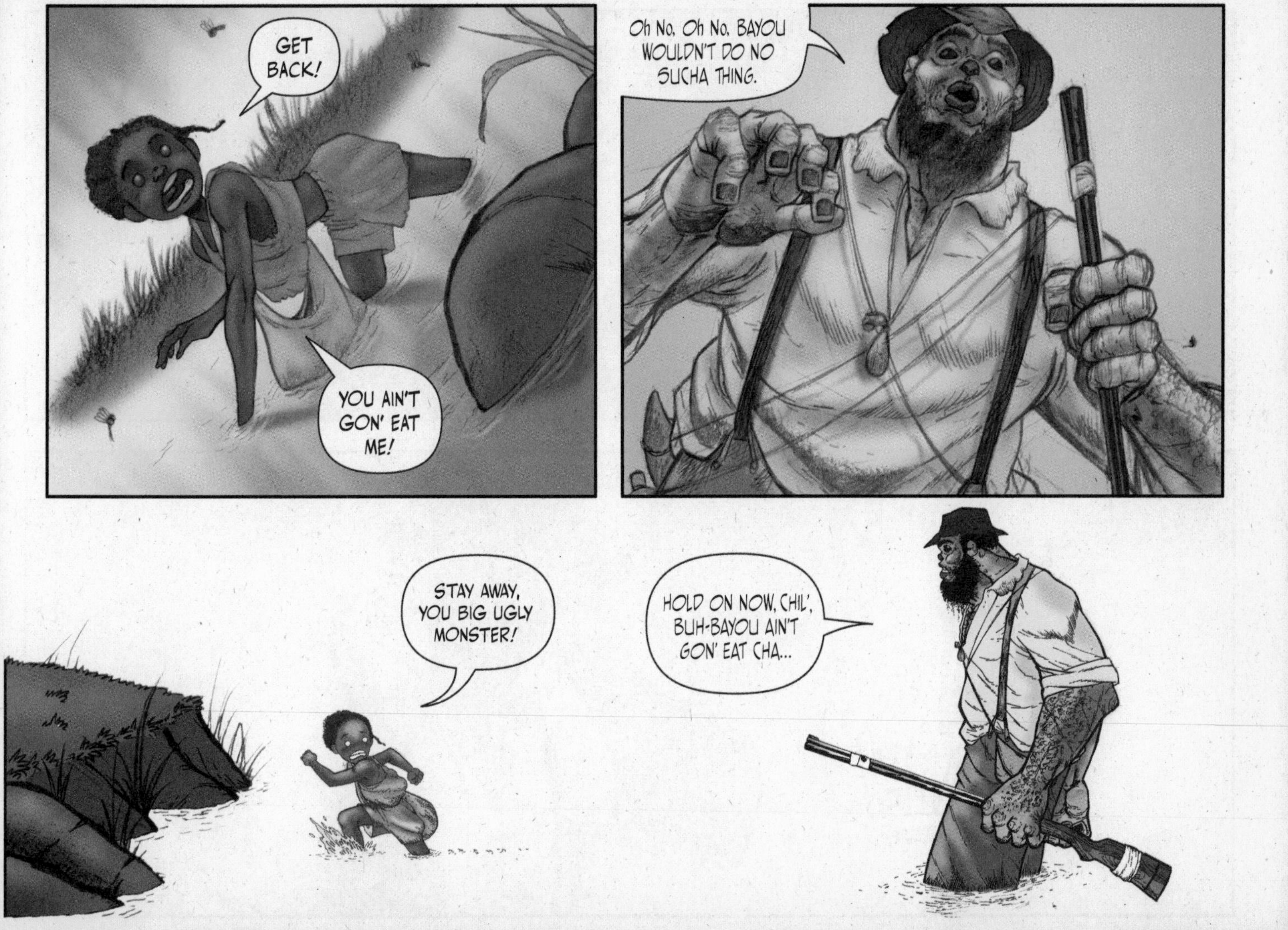
GET BACK!
YOU AIN'T GON' EAT ME!
Oh No, Oh No, BAYOU WOULDN'T DO NO SUCHA THING.
STAY AWAY, YOU BIG UGLY MONSTER!
HOLD ON NOW, CHIL', BUH-BAYOU AIN'T GON' EAT CHA...

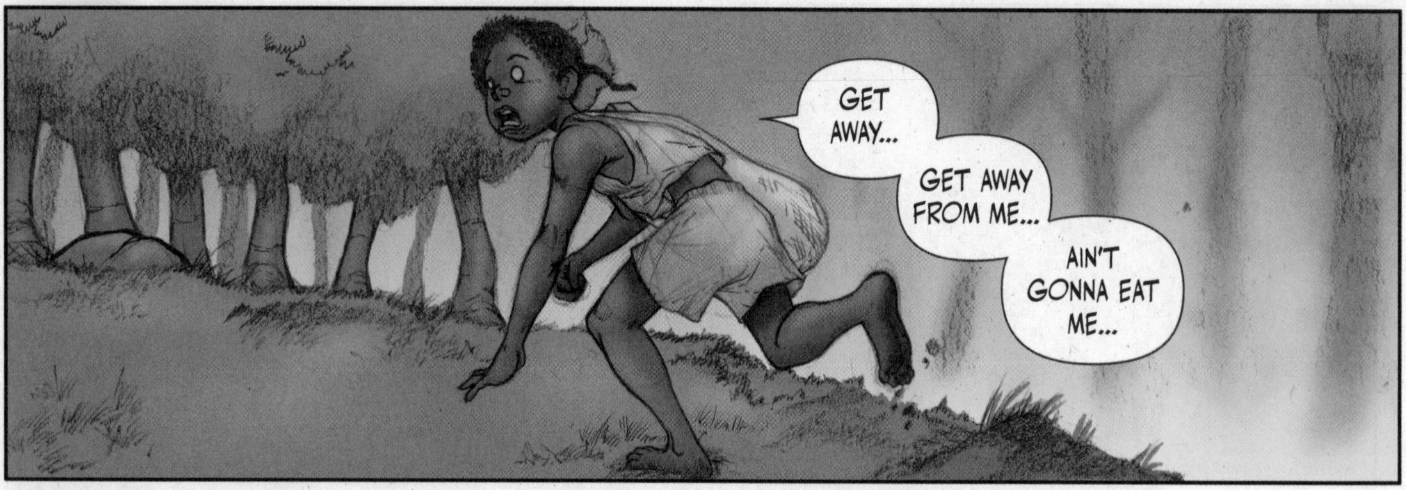
GET AWAY...
GET AWAY FROM ME...
AIN'T GONNA EAT ME...
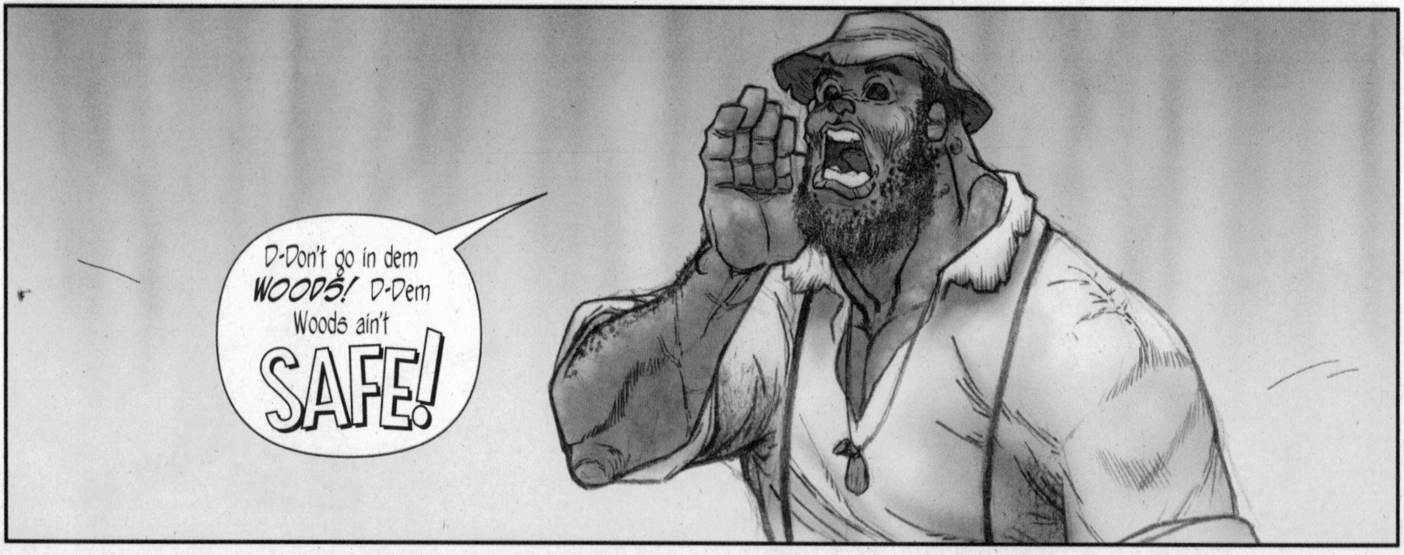
D-Don't go in dem WOODS! D-Dem Woods ain't SAFE!

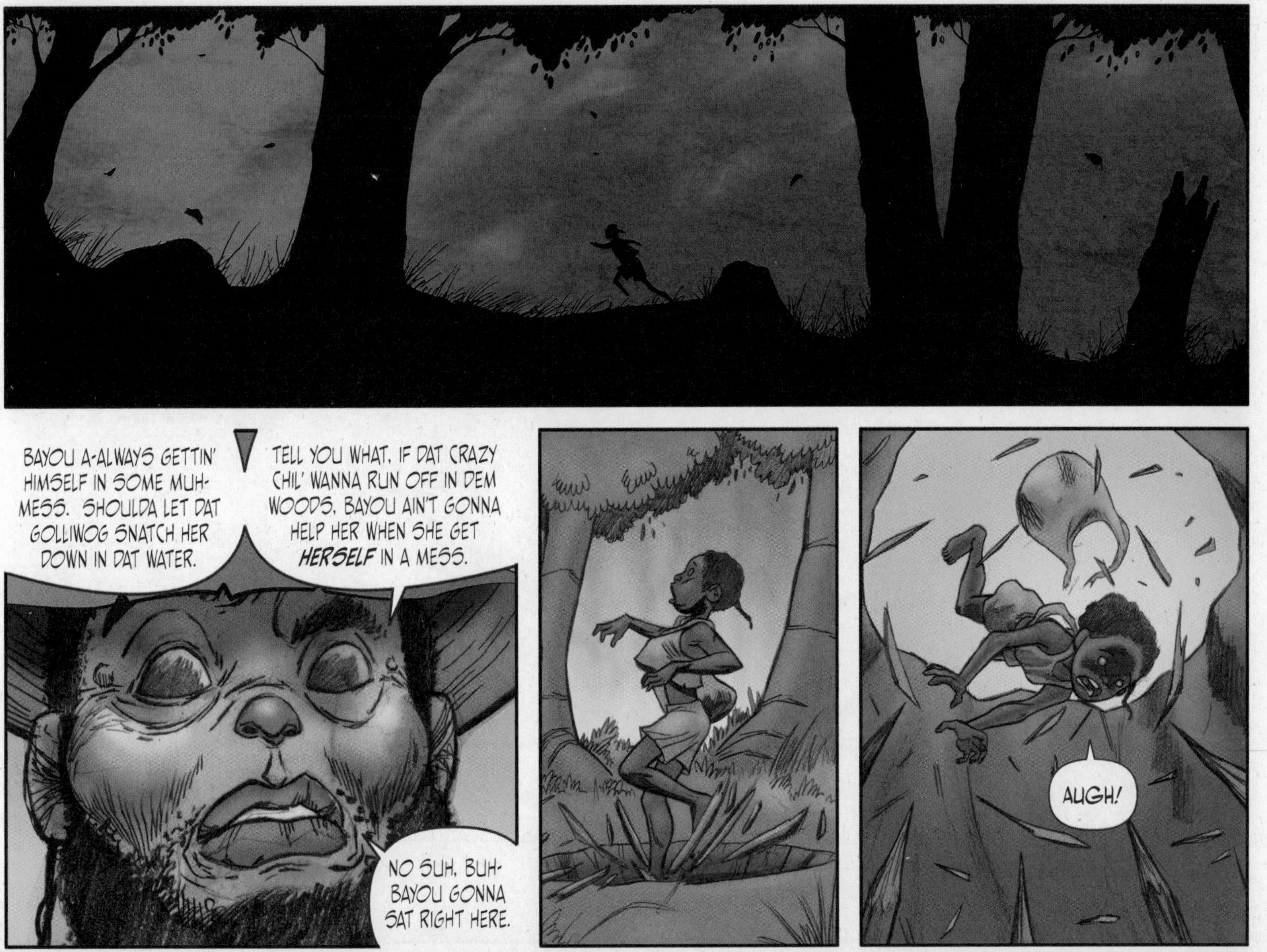
BAYOU A-ALWAYS GETTIN' HIMSELF IN SOME MUH-MESS. SHOULDA LET DAT GOLLIWOG SNATCH HER DOWN IN DAT WATER.
TELL YOU WHAT. IF DAT CRAZY CHIL' WANNA RUN OFF IN DEM WOODS, BAYOU AIN'T GONNA HELP HER WHEN SHE GET ***HERSELF*** IN A MESS.
NO SUH, BUH-BAYOU GONNA SAT RIGHT HERE.
AUGH!

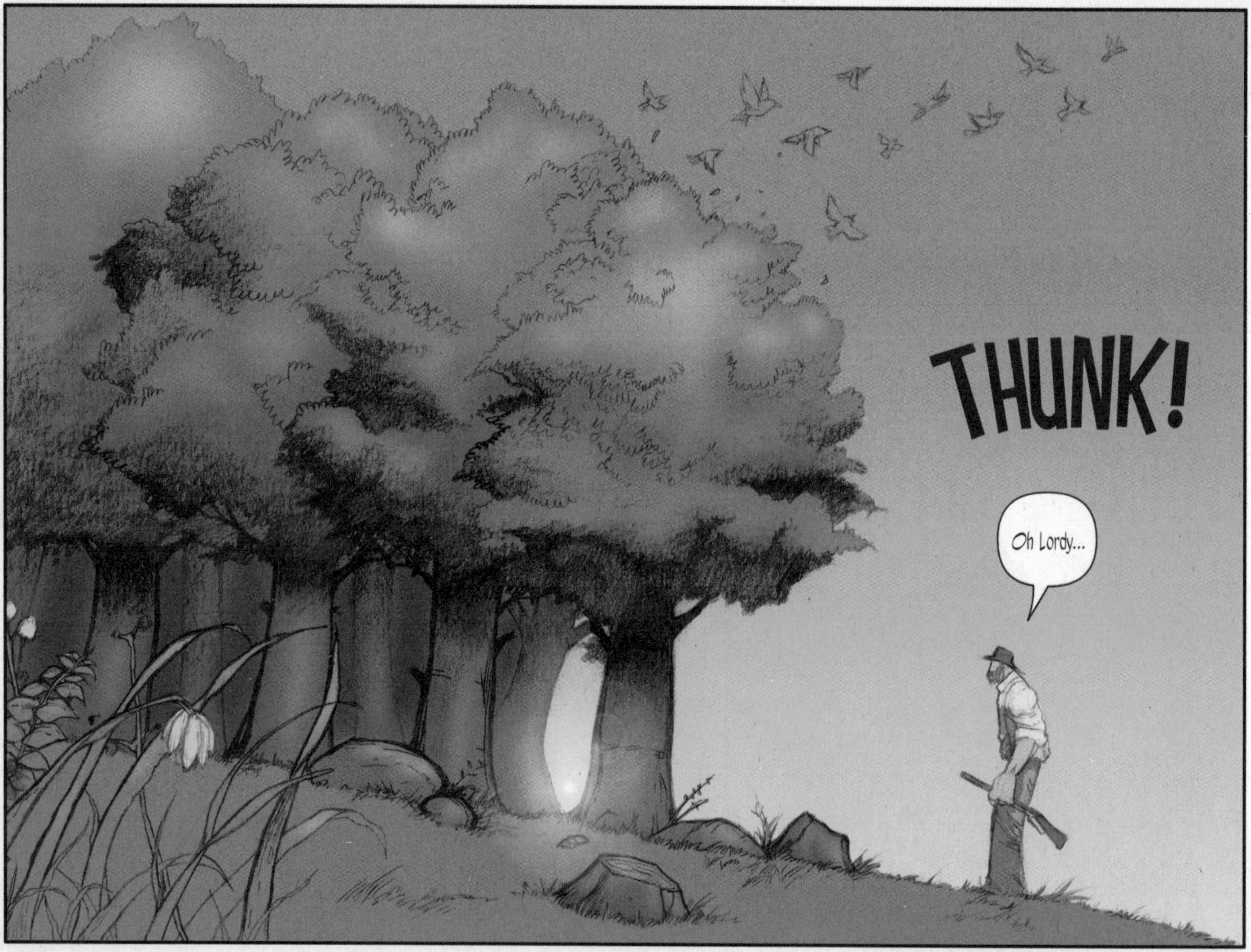
THUNK!
Oh Lordy...

BZZZAYOOOOO!
MISTUH BZZZAYOU. TSK. TSK TSK. WHATCHOO THINK YOU A-DOIN'?
DE BZZZZOSS IS GONNA THROW A BIG OL' FIT!
YOU FORGET WHAT HAPPENED TO YOU LAST TIME WHEN YOU HELPED THAT WICKED OL' RABBIT?
GO' ON AND GIT YOU TRIFLIN' GNAT, YOU!
PIP!
EEP!

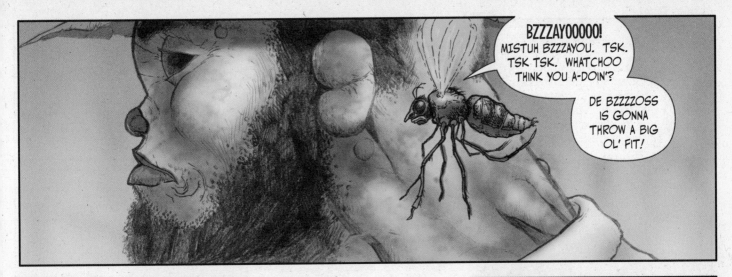

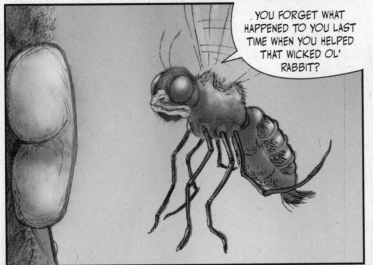

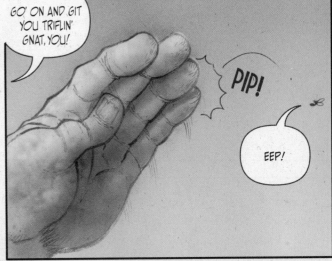

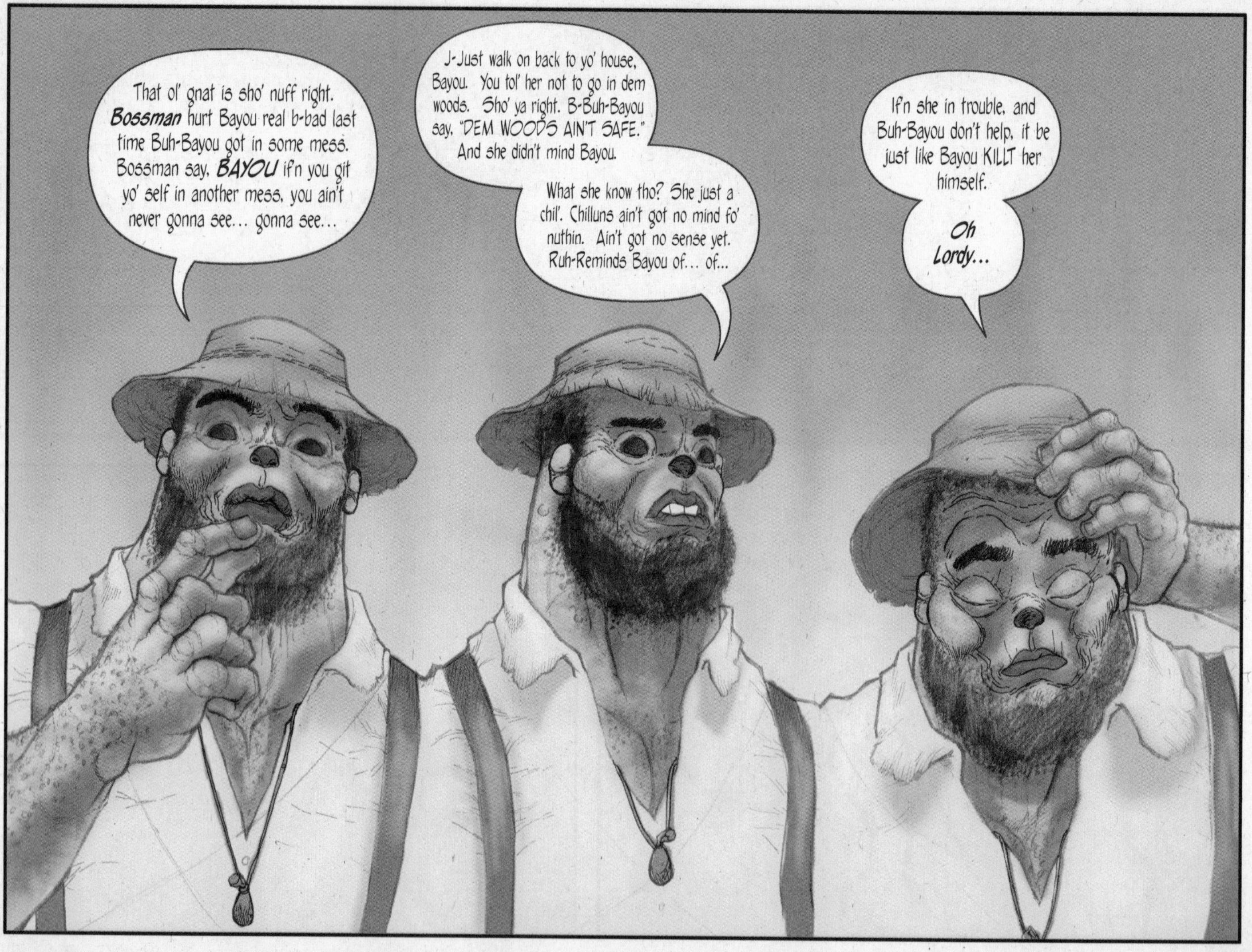
That ol' gnat is sho' nuff right. **Bossman** hurt Bayou real b-bad last time Buh-Bayou got in some mess. Bossman say, **BAYOU** if'n you git yo' self in another mess, you ain't never gonna see... gonna see...
J-Just walk on back to yo' house, Bayou. You tol' her not to go in dem woods. Sho' ya right. B-Buh-Bayou say, "DEM WOODS AIN'T SAFE." And she didn't mind Bayou.
What she know tho? She just a chil'. Chilluns ain't got no mind fo' nuthin. Ain't got no sense yet. Ruh-Reminds Bayou of... of...
If'n she in trouble, and Buh-Bayou don't help, it be just like Bayou KILLT her himself.
*Oh Lordy...*

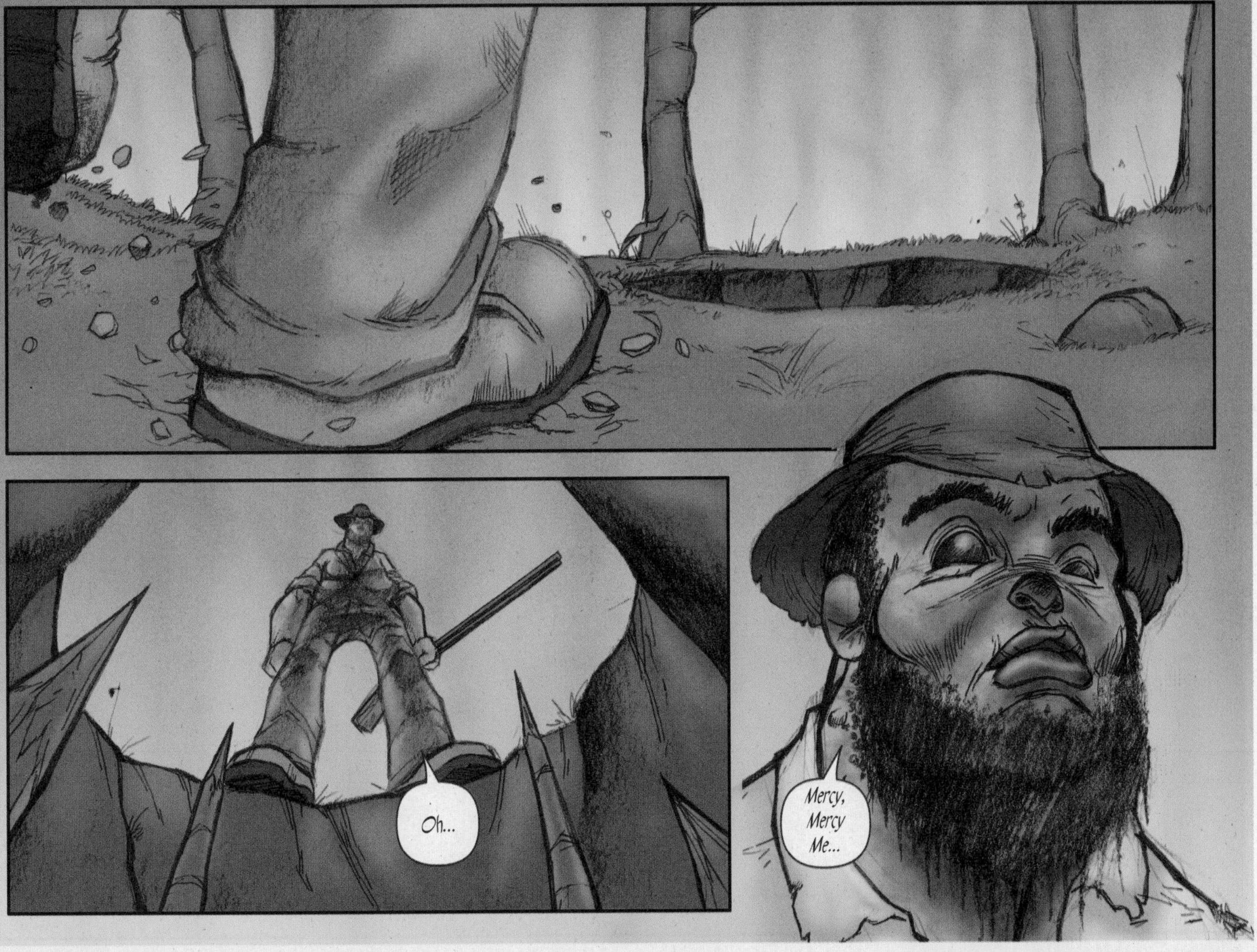
Oh...
Mercy, Mercy Me...

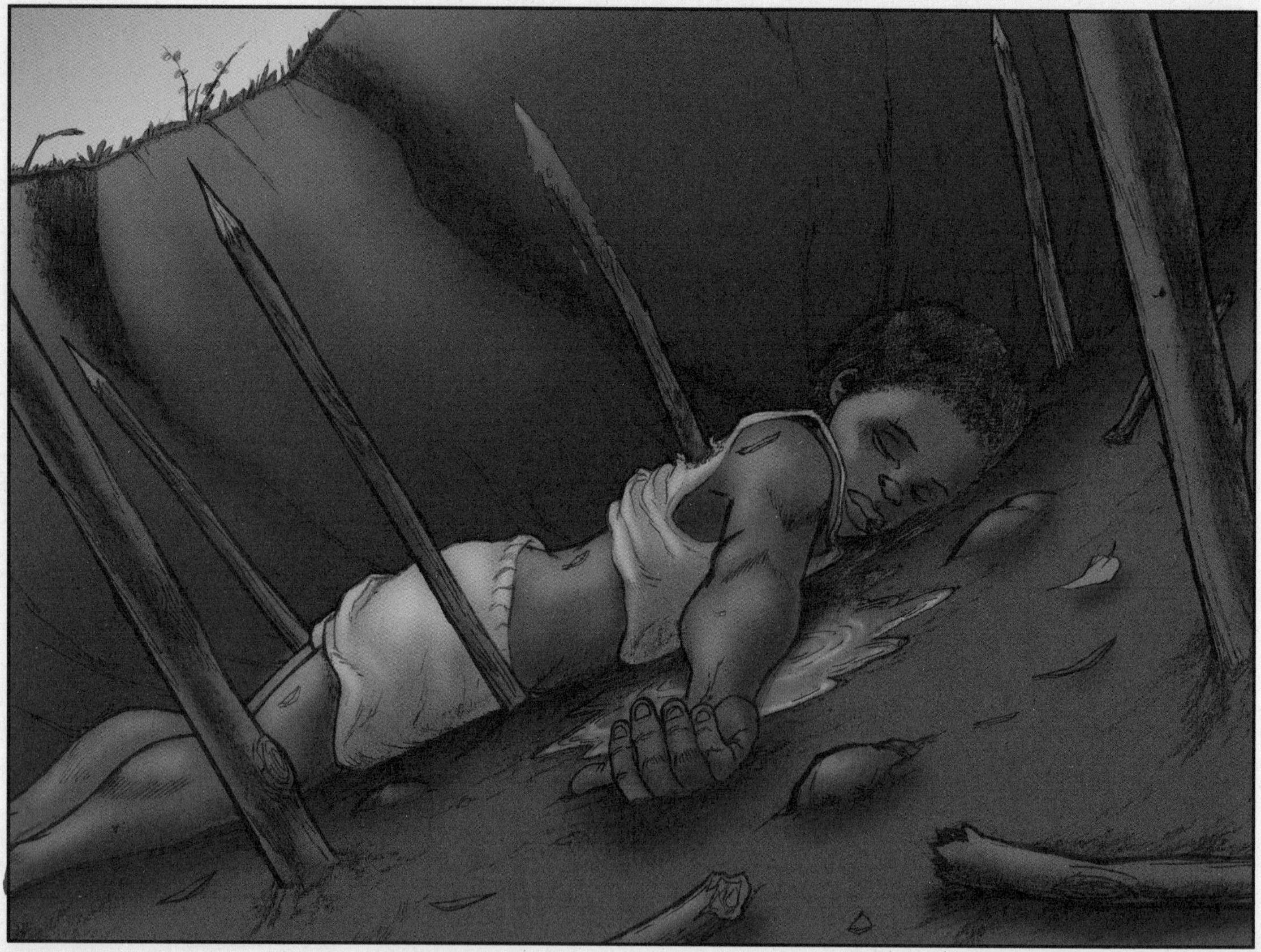

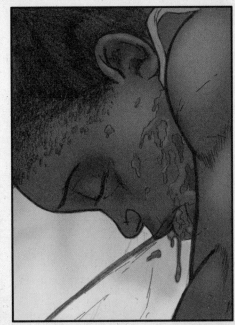

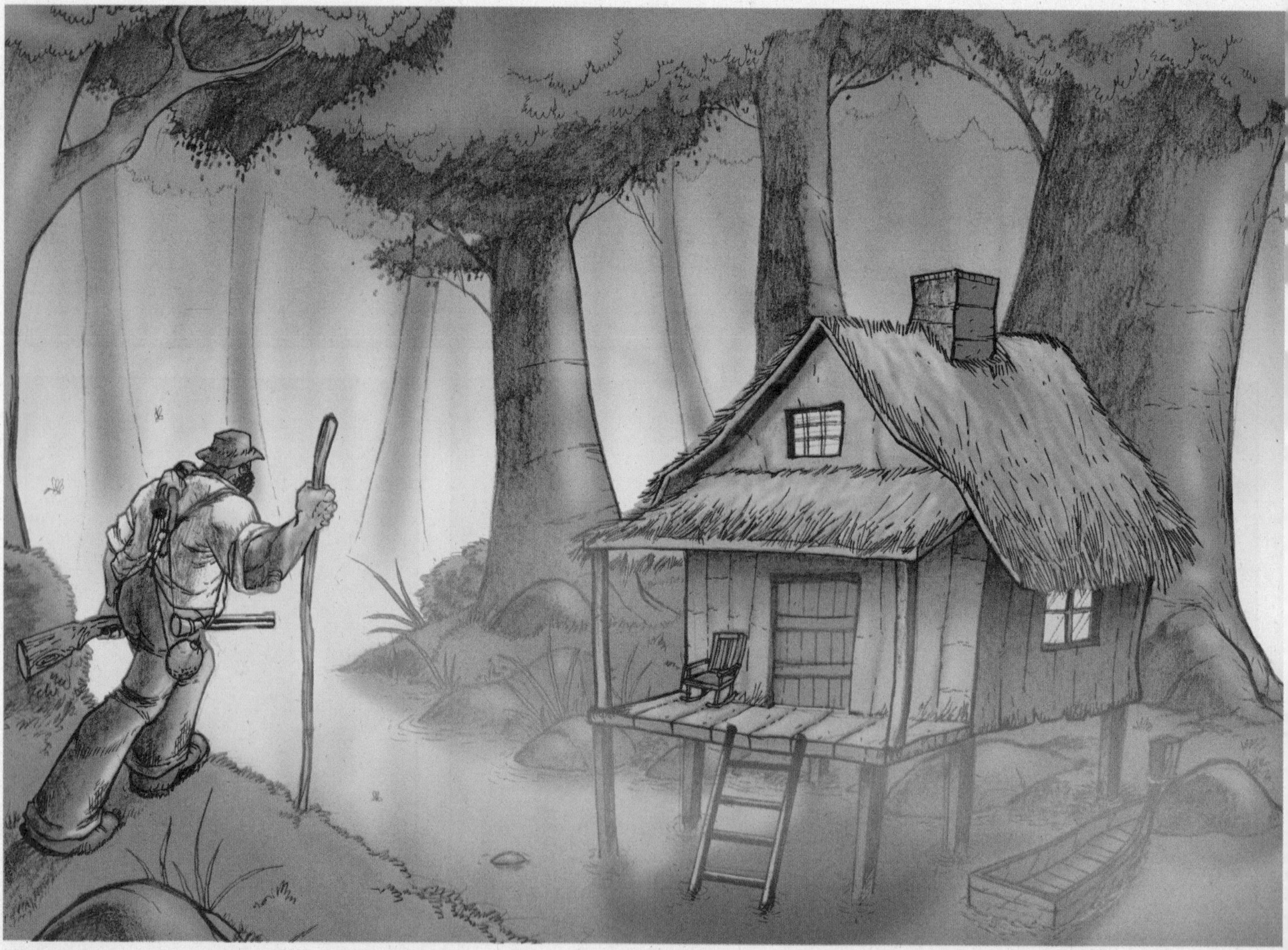

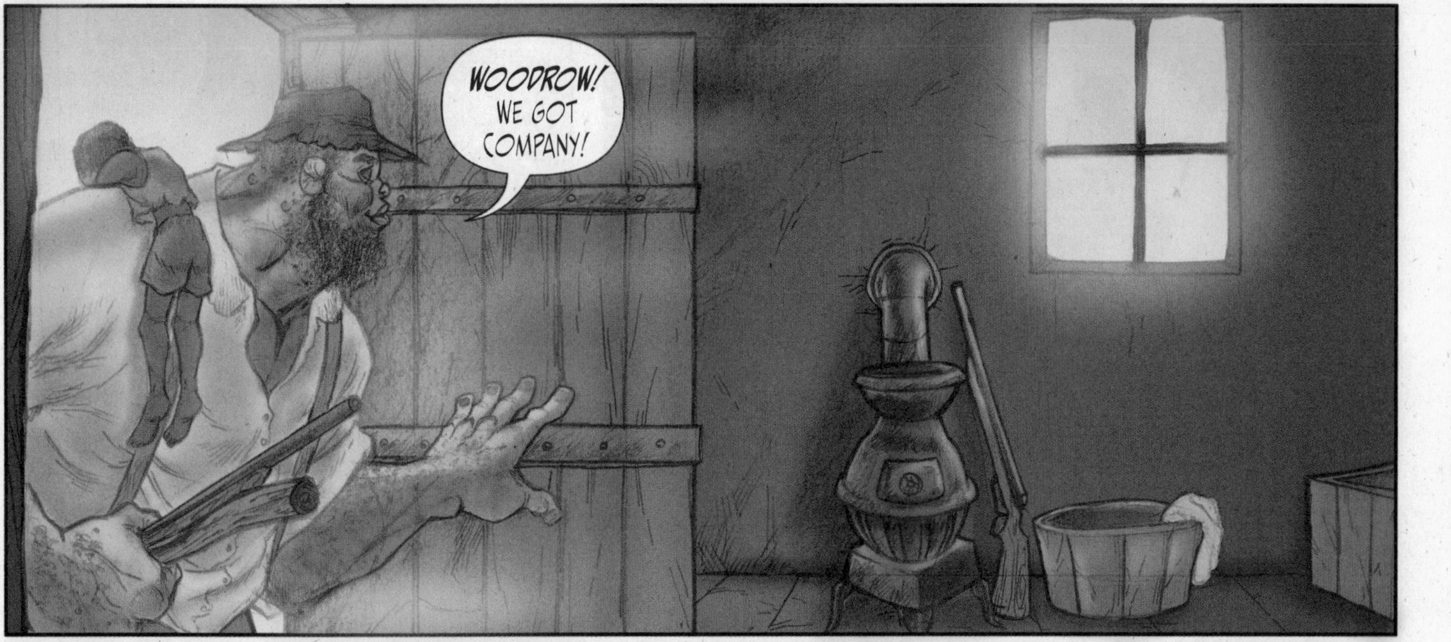
WOODROW! WE GOT COMPANY!

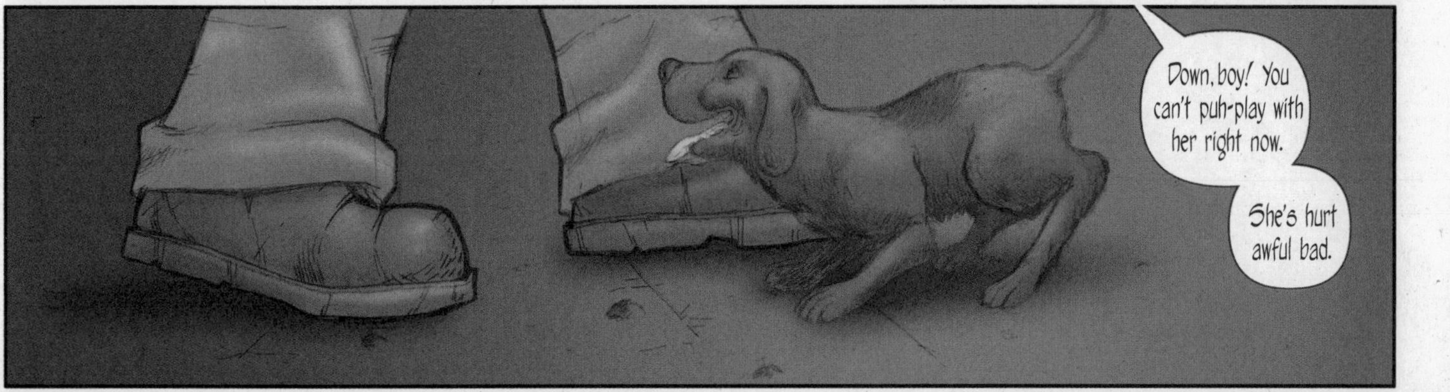
Down, boy! You can't puh-play with her right now.
She's hurt awful bad.

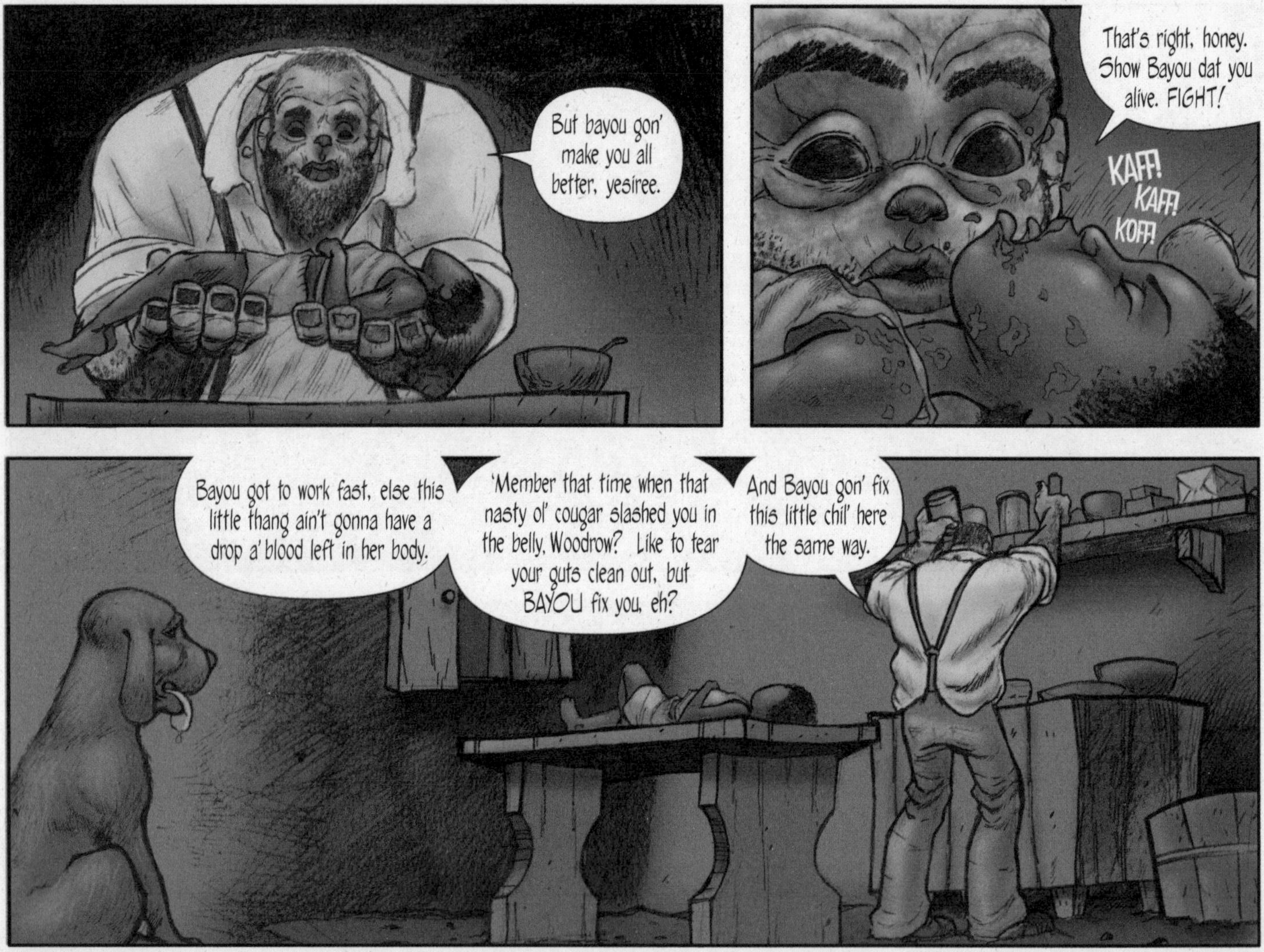

But bayou gon' make you all better, yesiree.
That's right, honey. Show Bayou dat you alive. FIGHT!
KAFF! KAFF! KOFF!
Bayou got to work fast, else this little thang ain't gonna have a drop a' blood left in her body.
'Member that time when that nasty ol' cougar slashed you in the belly, Woodrow? Like to tear your guts clean out, but BAYOU fix you, eh?
And Bayou gon' fix this little chil' here the same way.

Little o' dis.

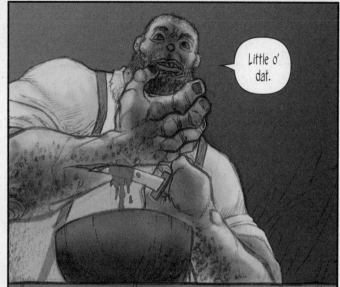

Little o' dat.

NNGG!

Now, jus' gotta sew it up...

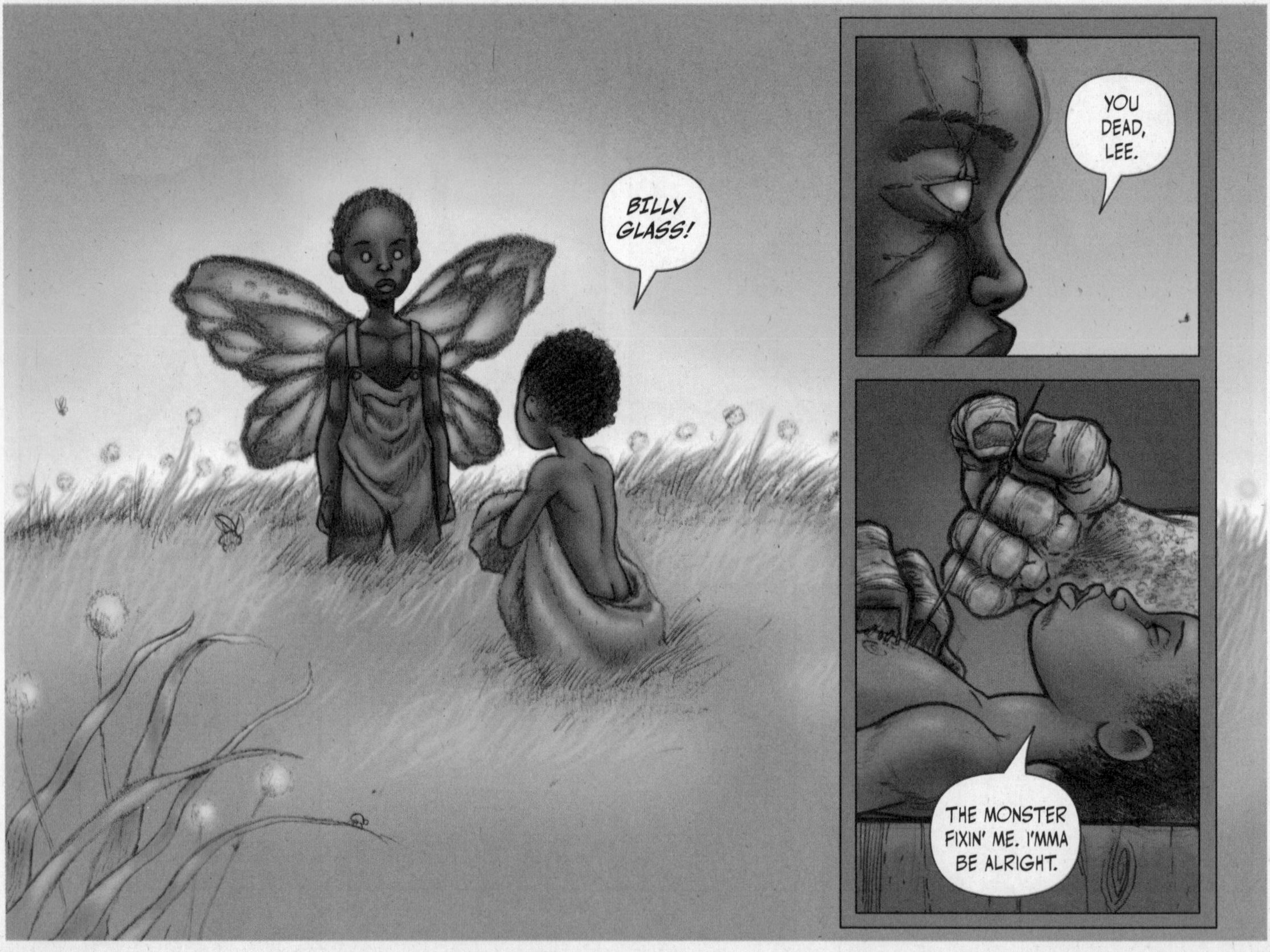
BILLY GLASS!
YOU DEAD, LEE.
THE MONSTER FIXIN' ME. I'MMA BE ALRIGHT.

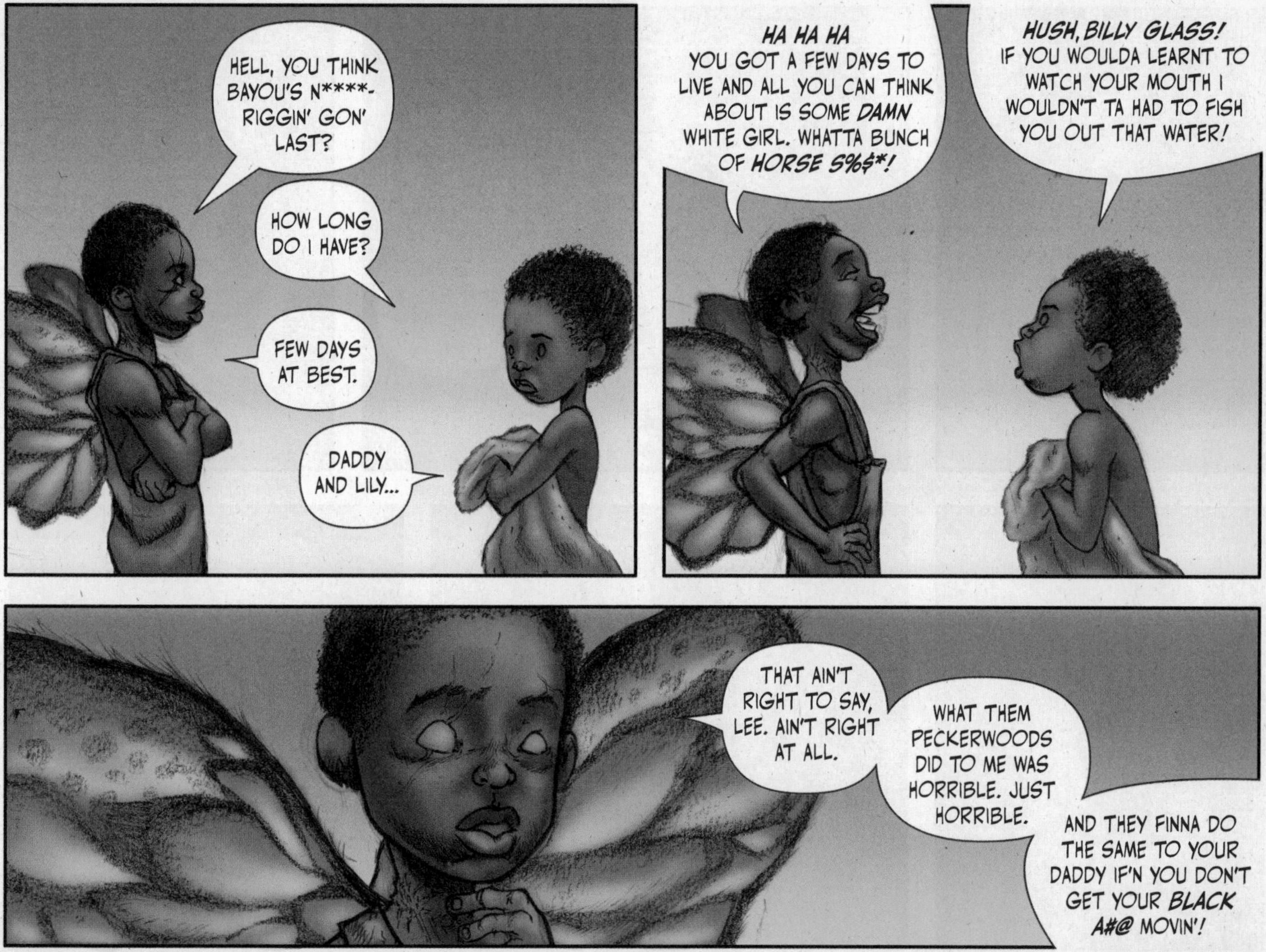

HELL, YOU THINK BAYOU'S N****-RIGGIN' GON' LAST?
HOW LONG DO I HAVE?
FEW DAYS AT BEST.
DADDY AND LILY...
HA HA HA YOU GOT A FEW DAYS TO LIVE AND ALL YOU CAN THINK ABOUT IS SOME DAMN WHITE GIRL. WHATTA BUNCH OF HORSE S%$*!
HUSH, BILLY GLASS! IF YOU WOULDA LEARNT TO WATCH YOUR MOUTH I WOULDN'T TA HAD TO FISH YOU OUT THAT WATER!
THAT AIN'T RIGHT TO SAY, LEE. AIN'T RIGHT AT ALL.
WHAT THEM PECKERWOODS DID TO ME WAS HORRIBLE. JUST HORRIBLE.
AND THEY FINNA DO THE SAME TO YOUR DADDY IF'N YOU DON'T GET YOUR BLACK A#@ MOVIN'!

time...

UGH... EVERY TIME I BLACK OUT, I WAKE UP IN SOME STRANGE PLACE.

LAST THING I REMEMBER WAS...

EW. GUESS I WASN'T DREAMIN'.

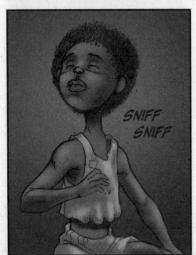

SNIFF SNIFF

!

BURP!

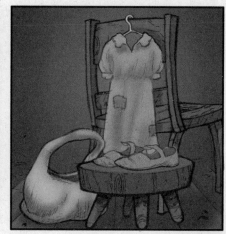

COME TO MY HOUSE...

FIND NO... 'BODY 'ROUND!

ME AND MY BABY, WE GON'

SHAKE EM ON DOOOWN

MUST I HOLLER...

YEEAAH...

must i... SHAKE EM' OOOOON DOWN...

ONE and ONE is two...

TWO and TWO is fo'

GOT YOU, woman, I SURE AIN'T GON' LET YOU GO!

MUST I HOLLER...

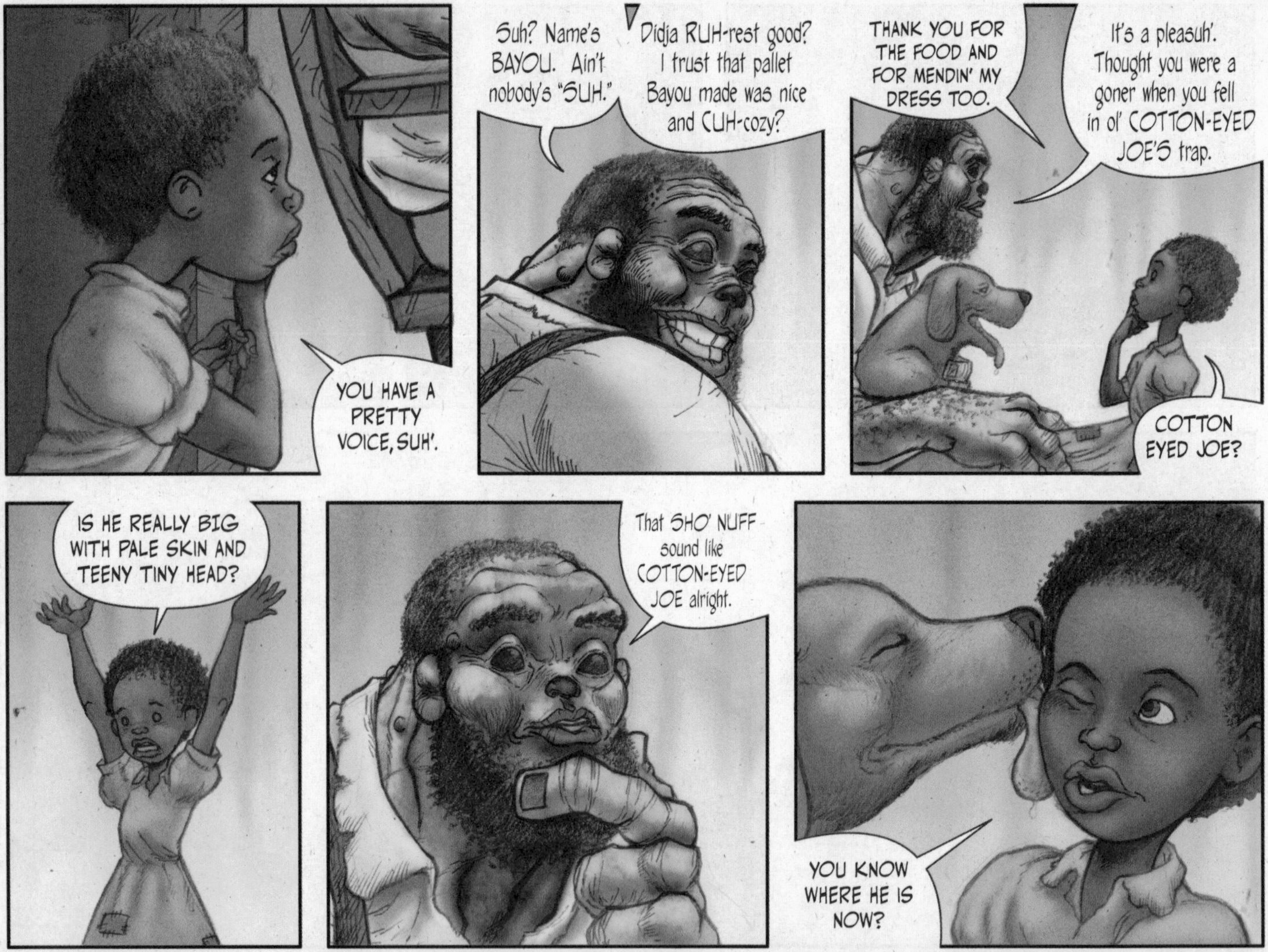
YOU HAVE A PRETTY VOICE, SUH'.
Suh? Name's BAYOU. Ain't nobody's "SUH."
Didja RUH-rest good? I trust that pallet Bayou made was nice and CUH-cozy?
THANK YOU FOR THE FOOD AND FOR MENDIN' MY DRESS TOO.
It's a pleasuh'. Thought you were a goner when you fell in ol' COTTON-EYED JOE'S trap.
COTTON EYED JOE?
IS HE REALLY BIG WITH PALE SKIN AND TEENY TINY HEAD?
That SHO' NUFF sound like COTTON-EYED JOE alright.
YOU KNOW WHERE HE IS NOW?

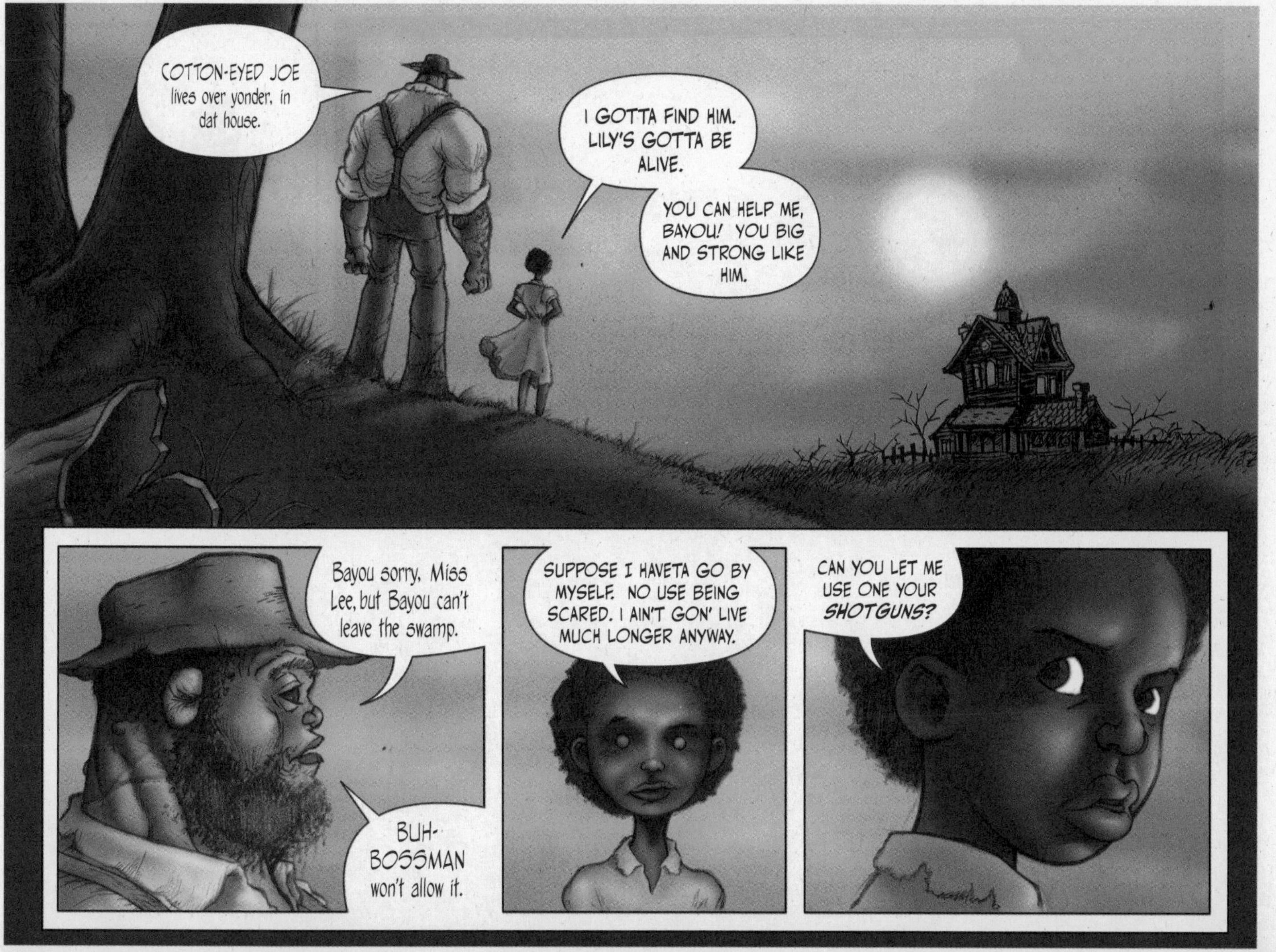
COTTON-EYED JOE lives over yonder, in dat house.
I GOTTA FIND HIM. LILY'S GOTTA BE ALIVE.
YOU CAN HELP ME, BAYOU! YOU BIG AND STRONG LIKE HIM.
Bayou sorry, Miss Lee, but Bayou can't leave the swamp.
BUH-BOSSMAN won't allow it.
SUPPOSE I HAVETA GO BY MYSELF. NO USE BEING SCARED. I AIN'T GON' LIVE MUCH LONGER ANYWAY.
CAN YOU LET ME USE ONE YOUR *SHOTGUNS?*

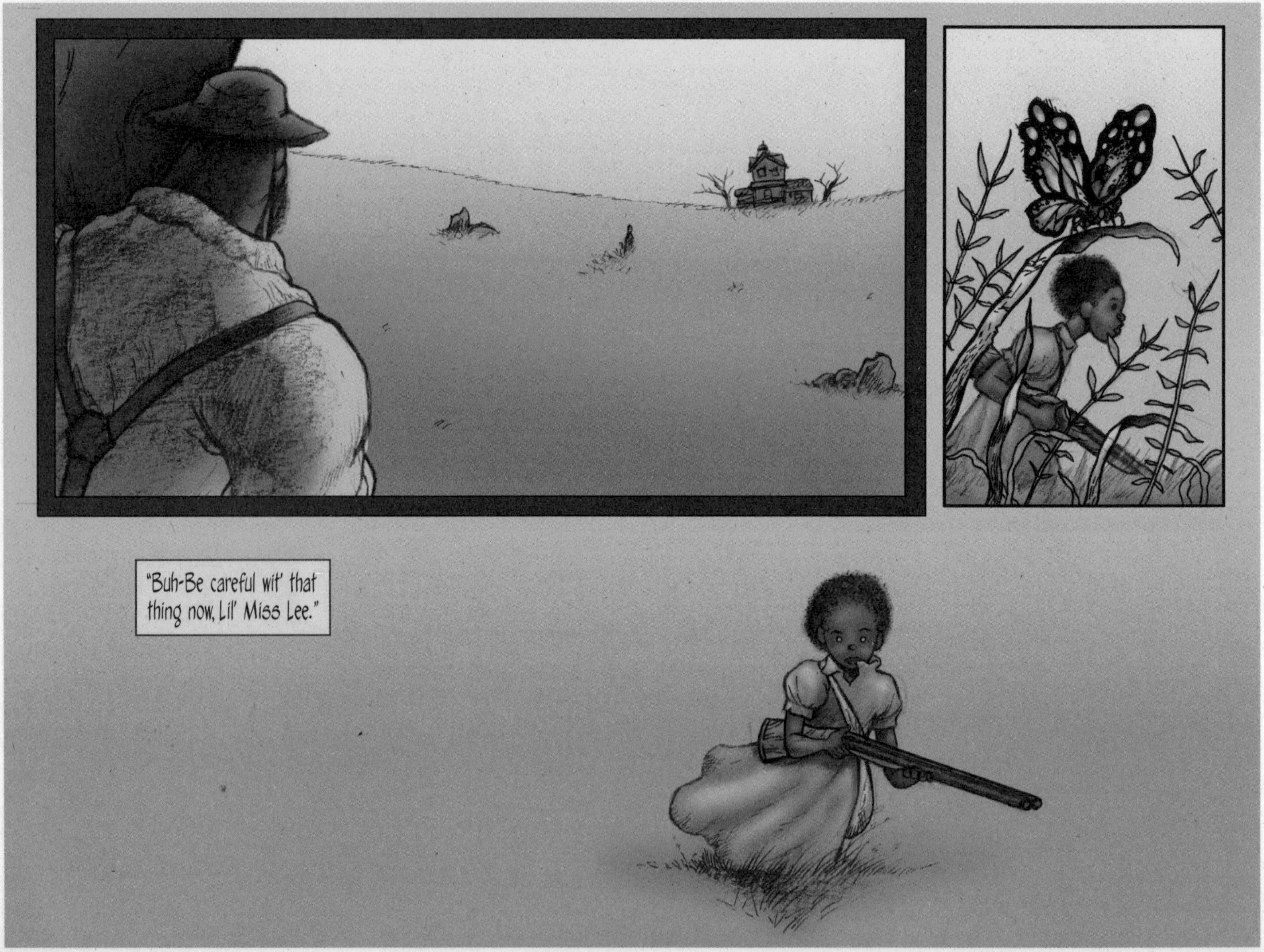
"Buh-Be careful wit' that thing now, Lil' Miss Lee."

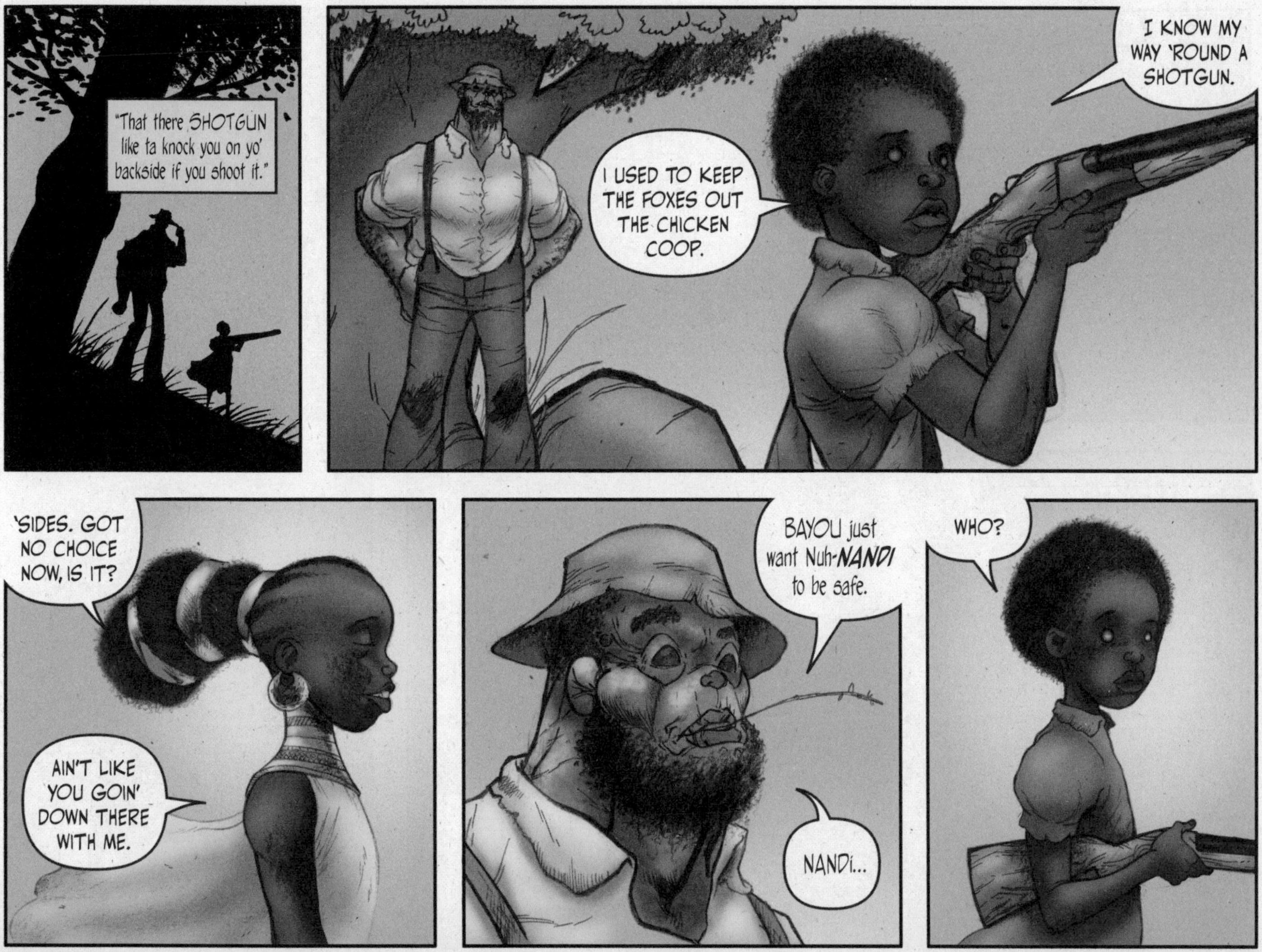
"That there SHOTGUN like ta knock you on yo' backside if you shoot it."
I KNOW MY WAY 'ROUND A SHOTGUN.
I USED TO KEEP THE FOXES OUT THE CHICKEN COOP.
'SIDES. GOT NO CHOICE NOW, IS IT?
AIN'T LIKE YOU GOIN' DOWN THERE WITH ME.
BAYOU just want Nuh-NANDI to be safe.
NANDI...
WHO?

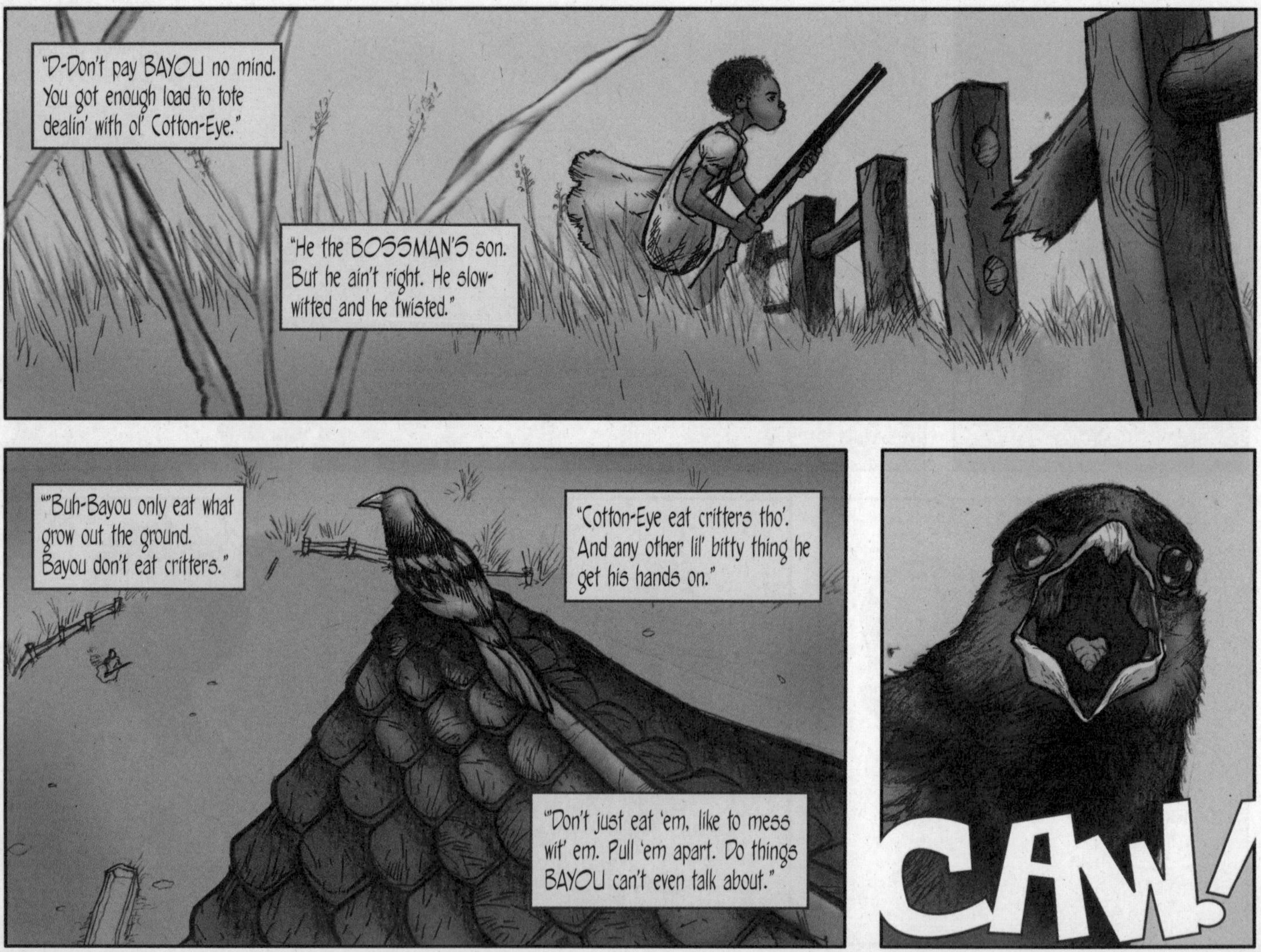
"D-Don't pay BAYOU no mind. You got enough load to tote dealin' with ol' Cotton-Eye."
"He the BOSSMAN'S son. But he ain't right. He slow-witted and he twisted."
""Buh-Bayou only eat what grow out the ground. Bayou don't eat critters."
"Cotton-Eye eat critters tho'. And any other lil' bitty thing he get his hands on."
""Don't just eat 'em, like to mess wit' em. Pull 'em apart. Do things BAYOU can't even talk about."
CAW!

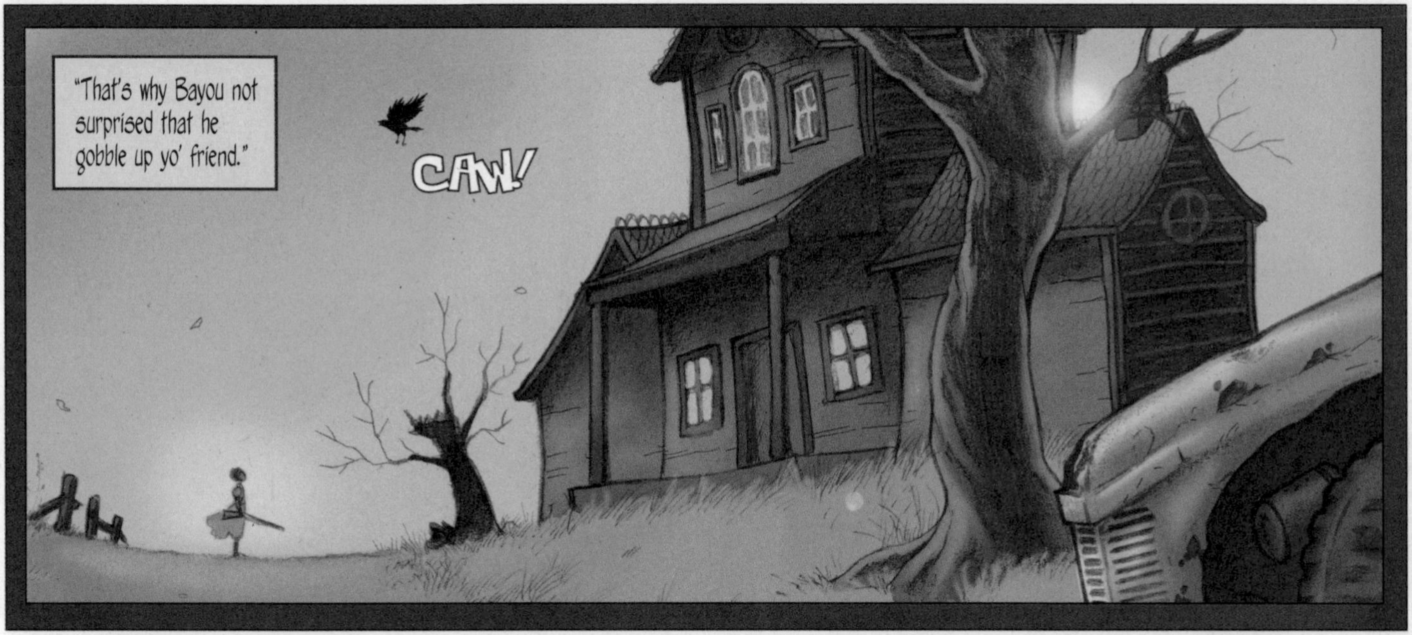
"That's why Bayou not surprised that he gobble up yo' friend."
CAW!

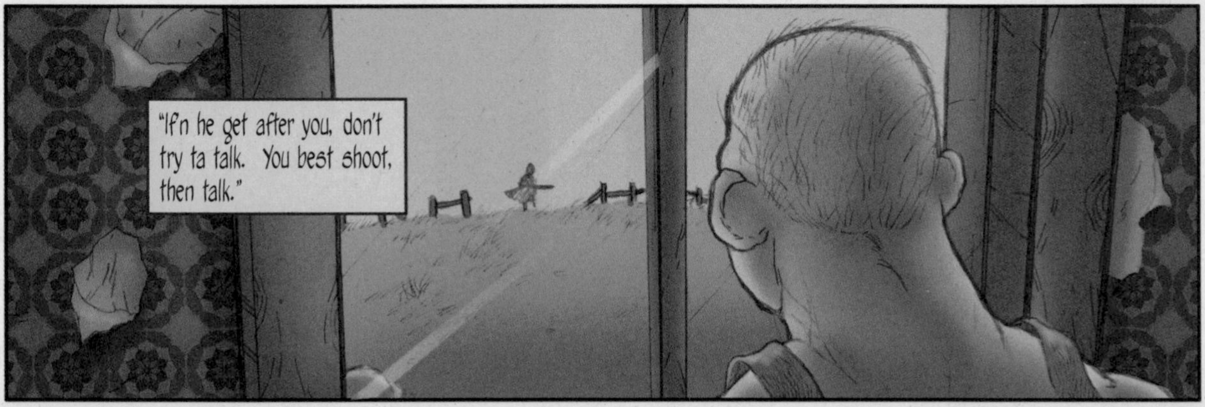
"If'n he get after you, don't try ta talk. You best shoot, then talk."

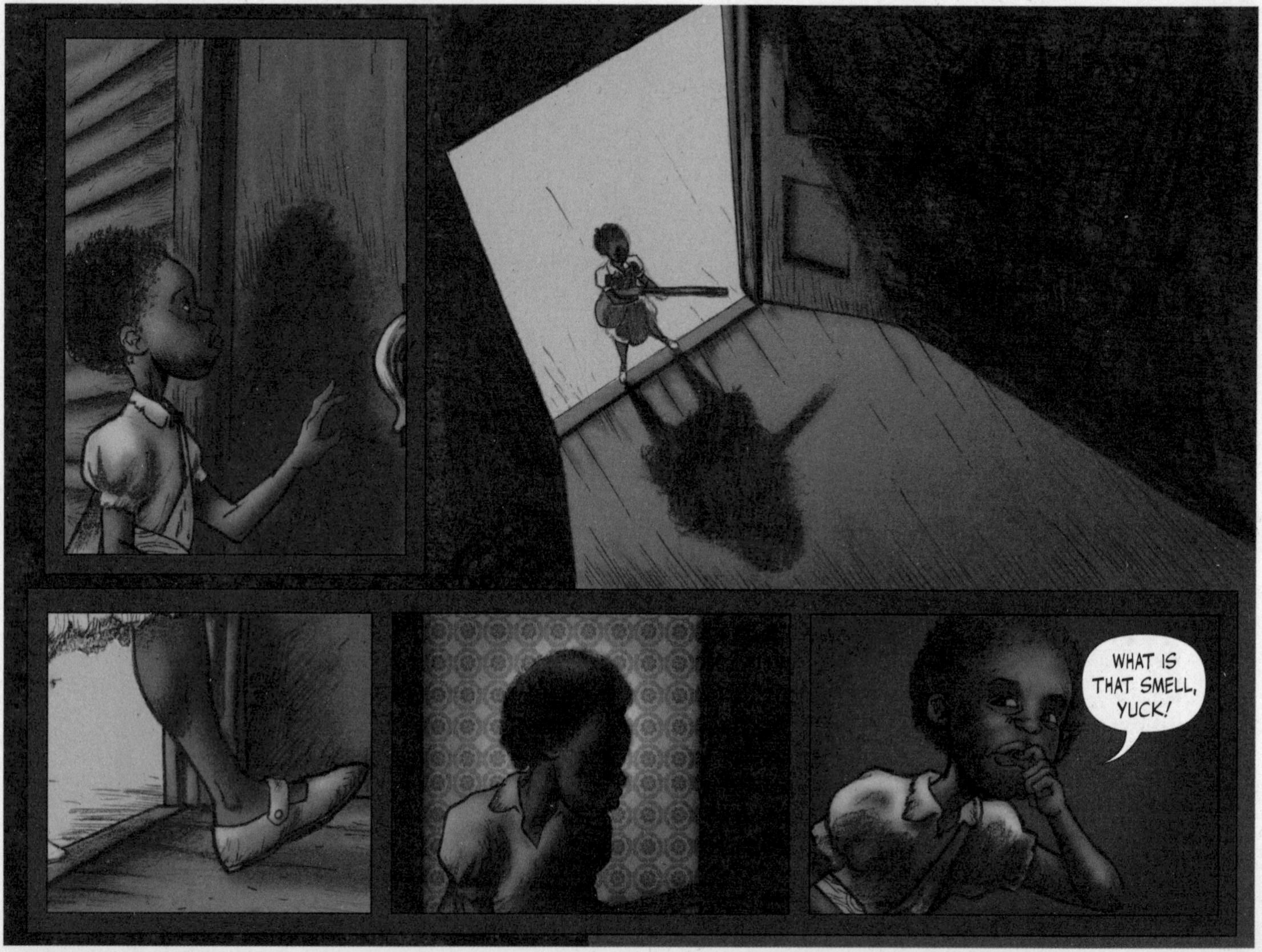
WHAT IS THAT SMELL, YUCK!

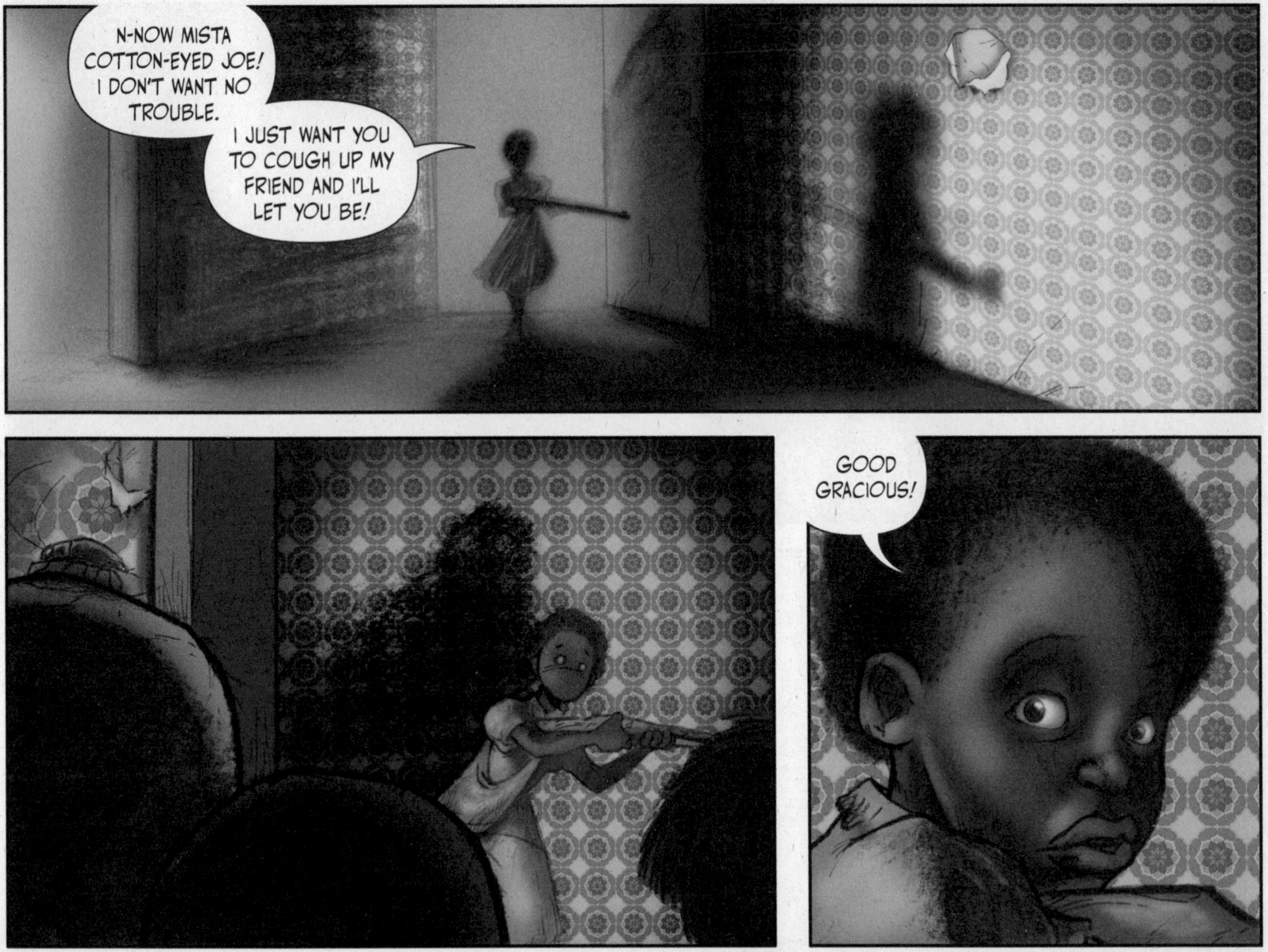
N-NOW MISTA COTTON-EYED JOE! I DON'T WANT NO TROUBLE.
I JUST WANT YOU TO COUGH UP MY FRIEND AND I'LL LET YOU BE!
GOOD GRACIOUS!

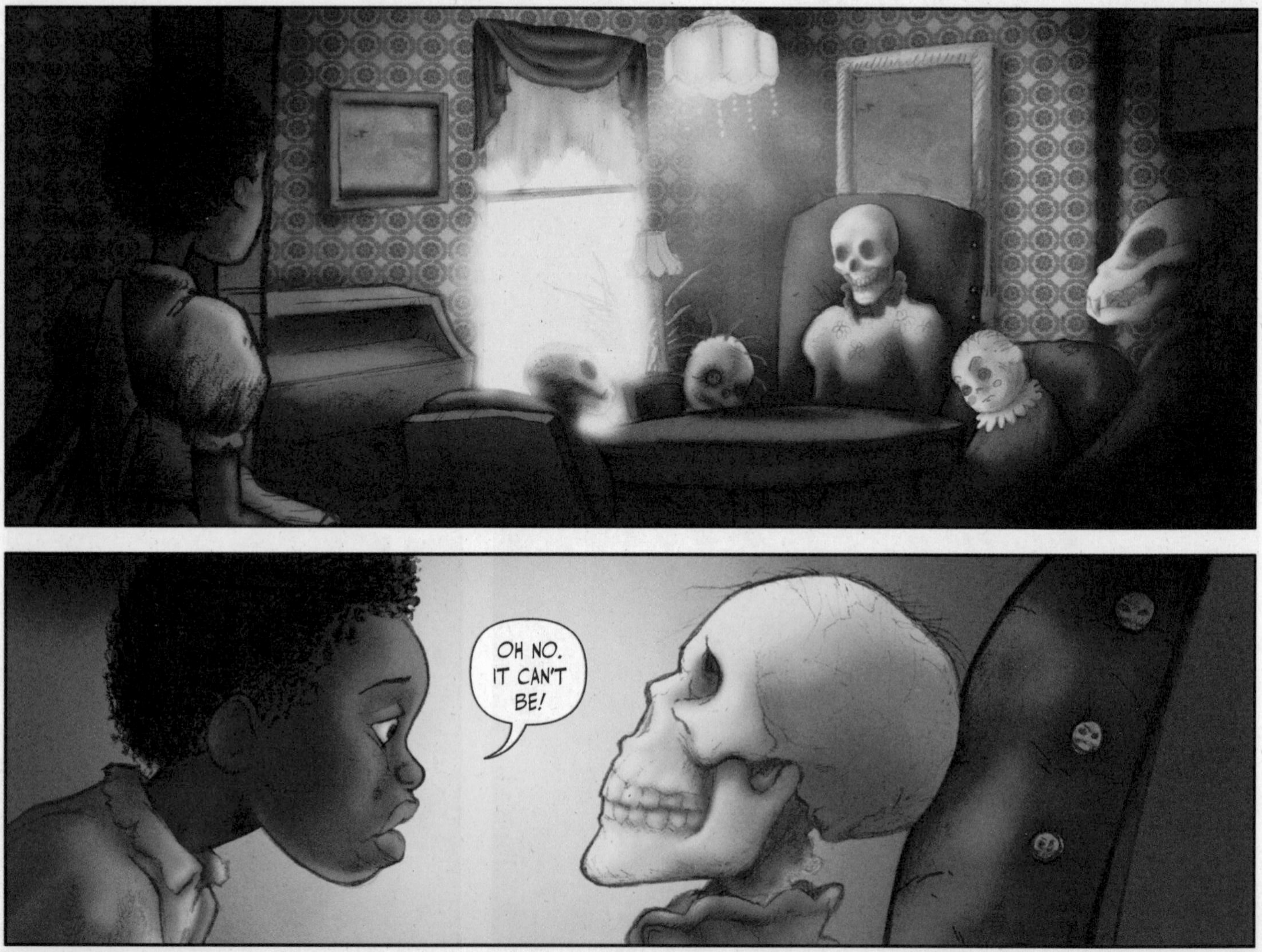
OH NO. IT CAN'T BE!

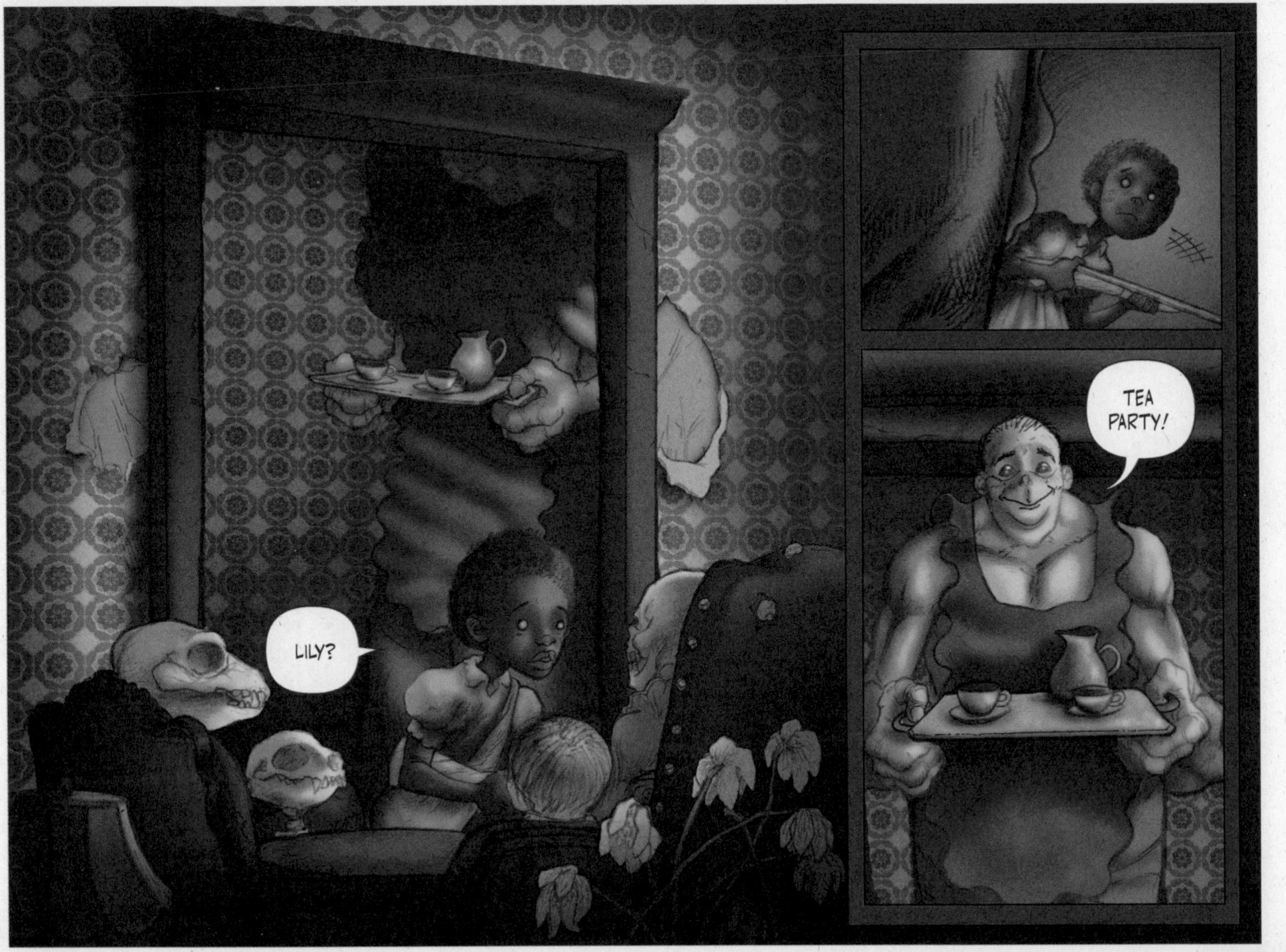
LILY?
TEA PARTY!

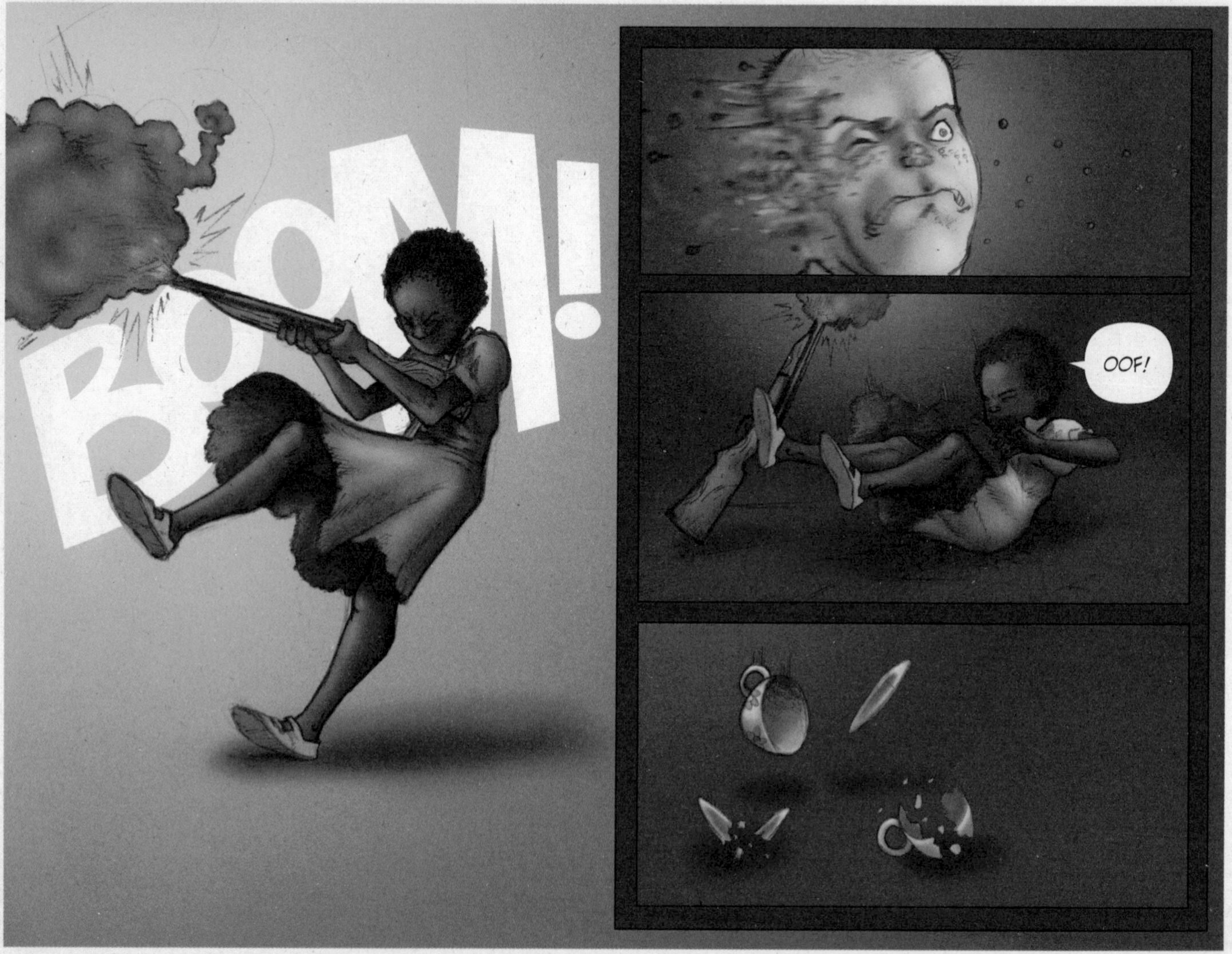
BOOM!
OOF!

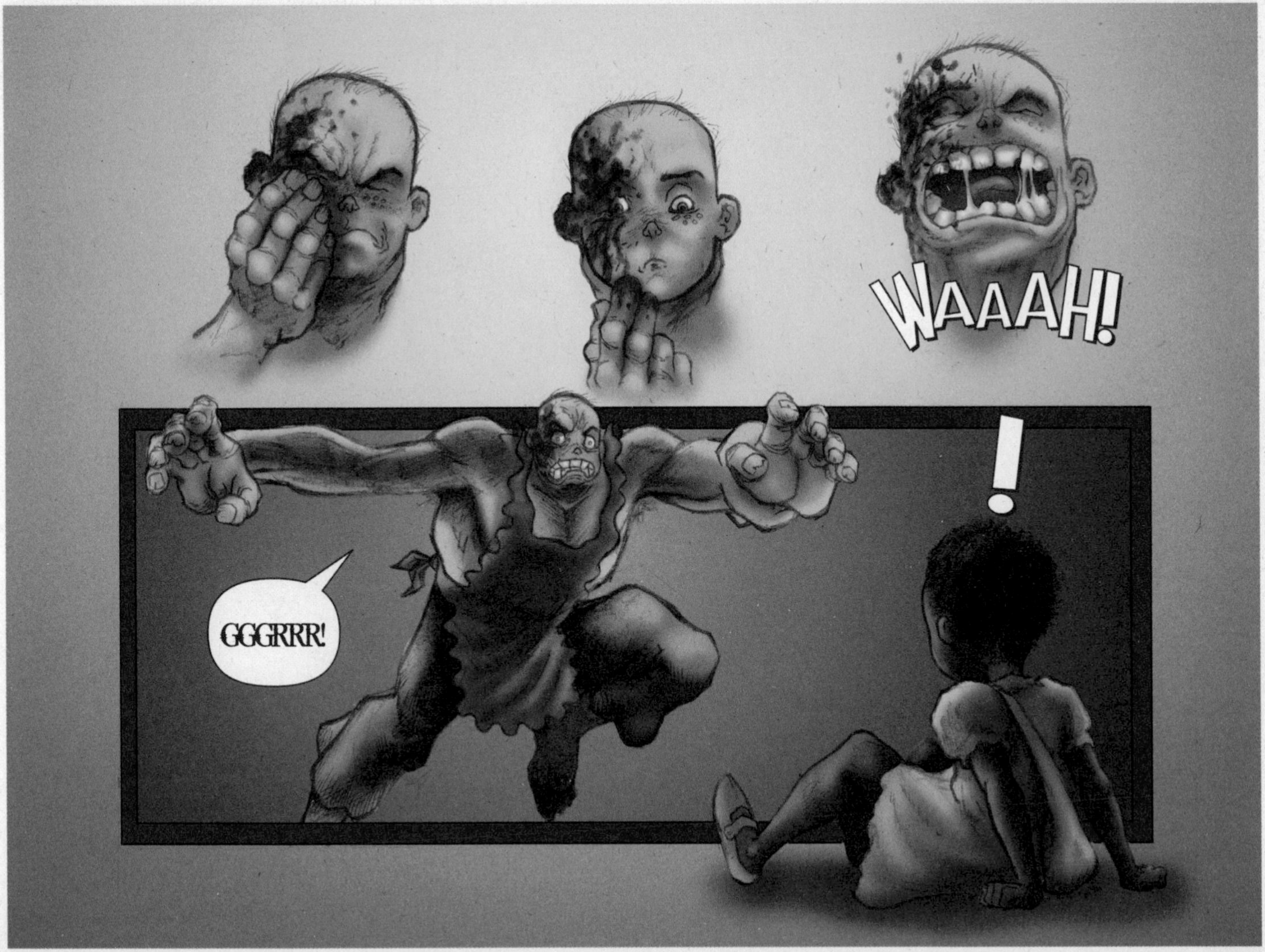
WAAAH!
!
GGGRRR!

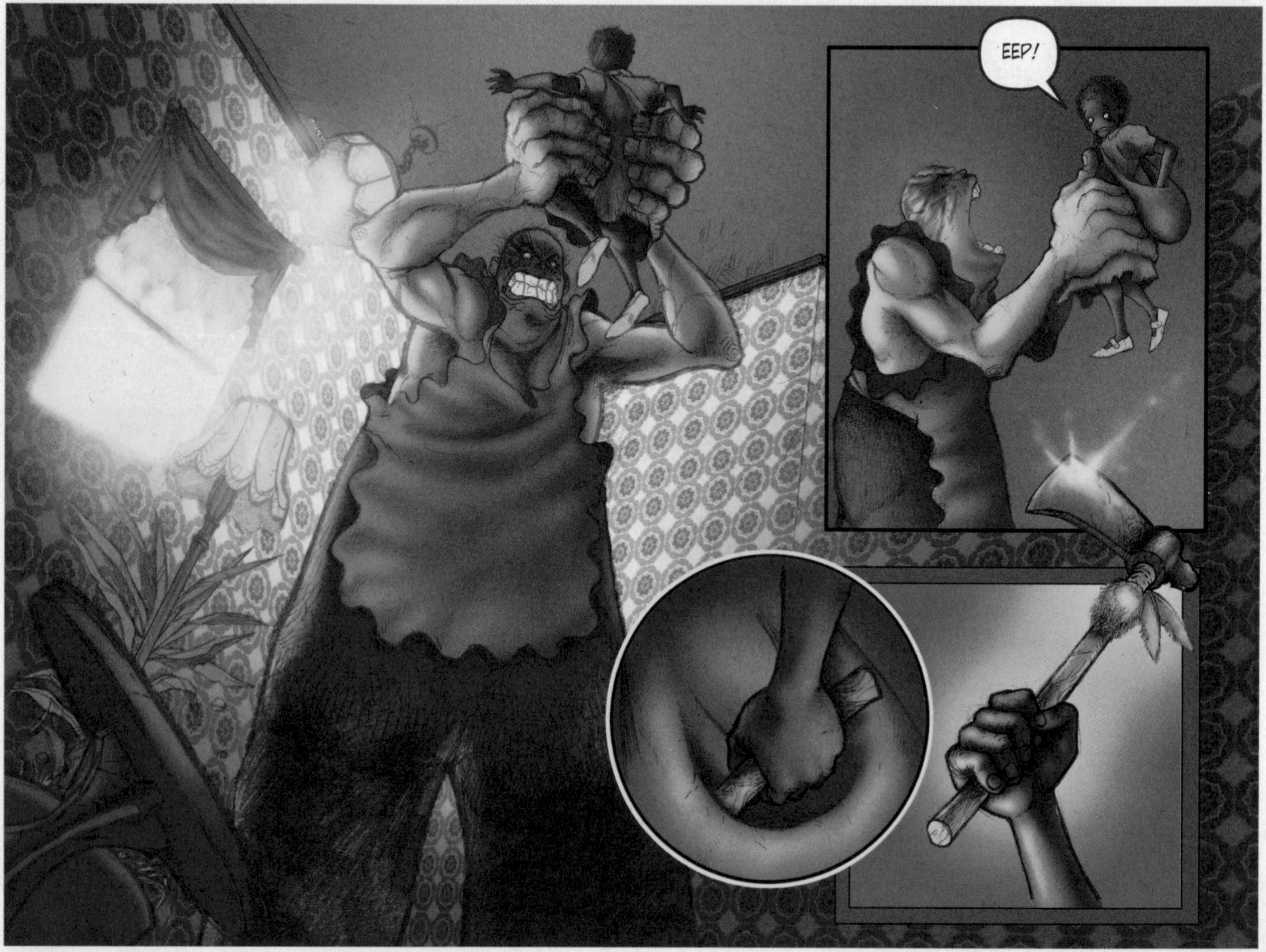
EEP!

AAAAIIIEEEEEEEEEEE!!

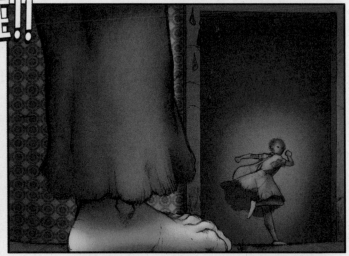

THUNK!

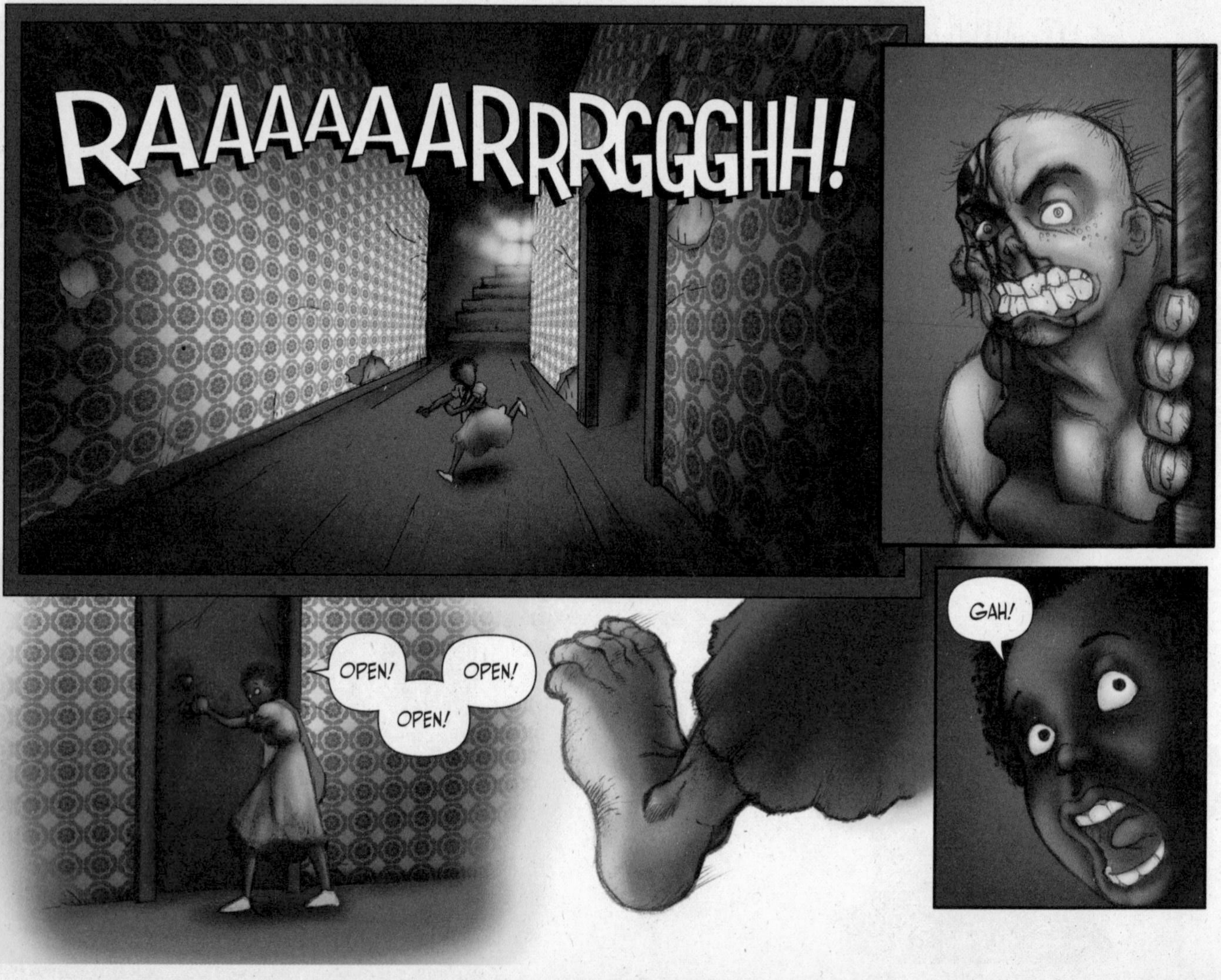
RAAAAAARRRGGGHH!
OPEN!
OPEN!
OPEN!
GAH!

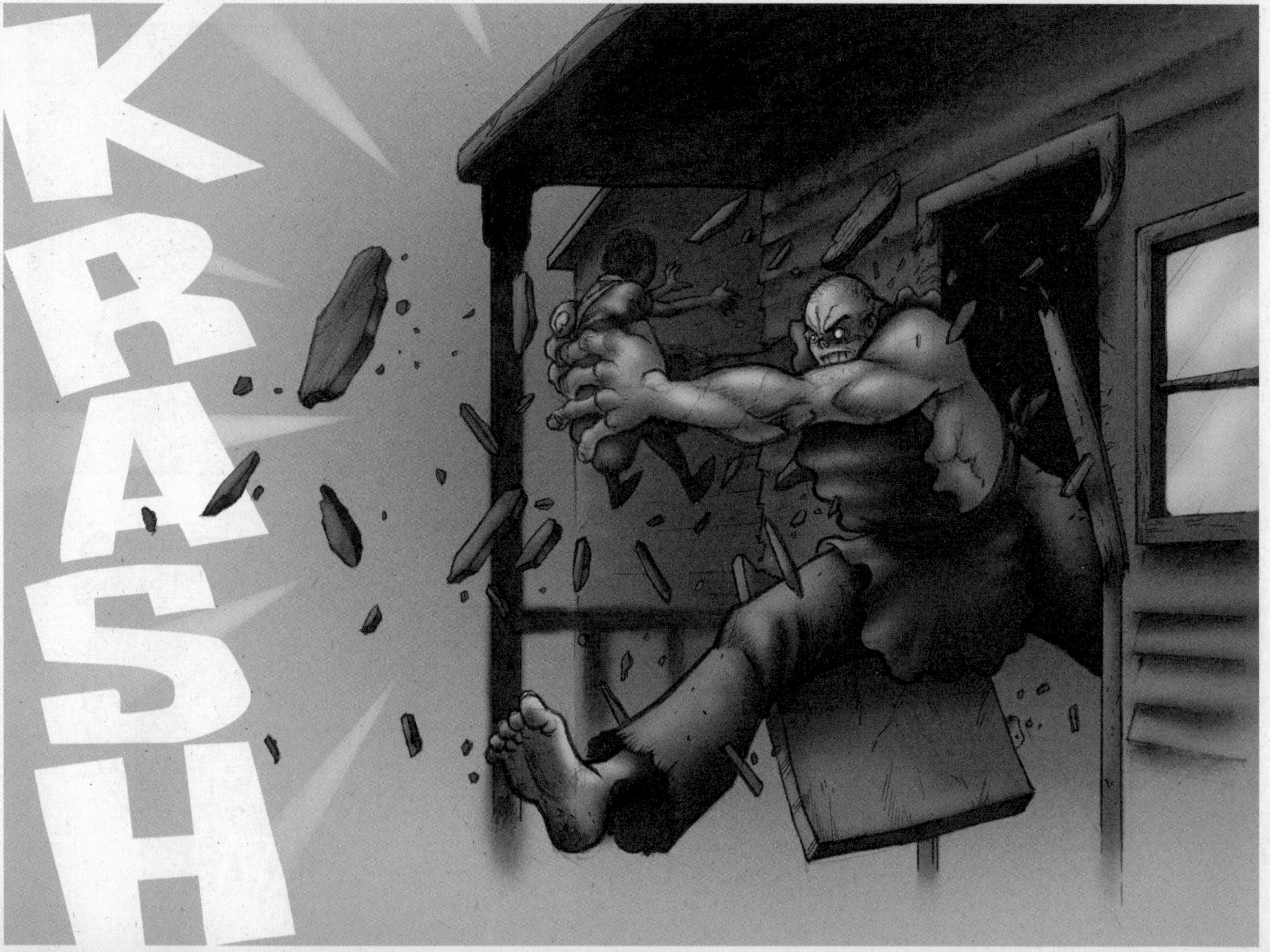
KRASH!

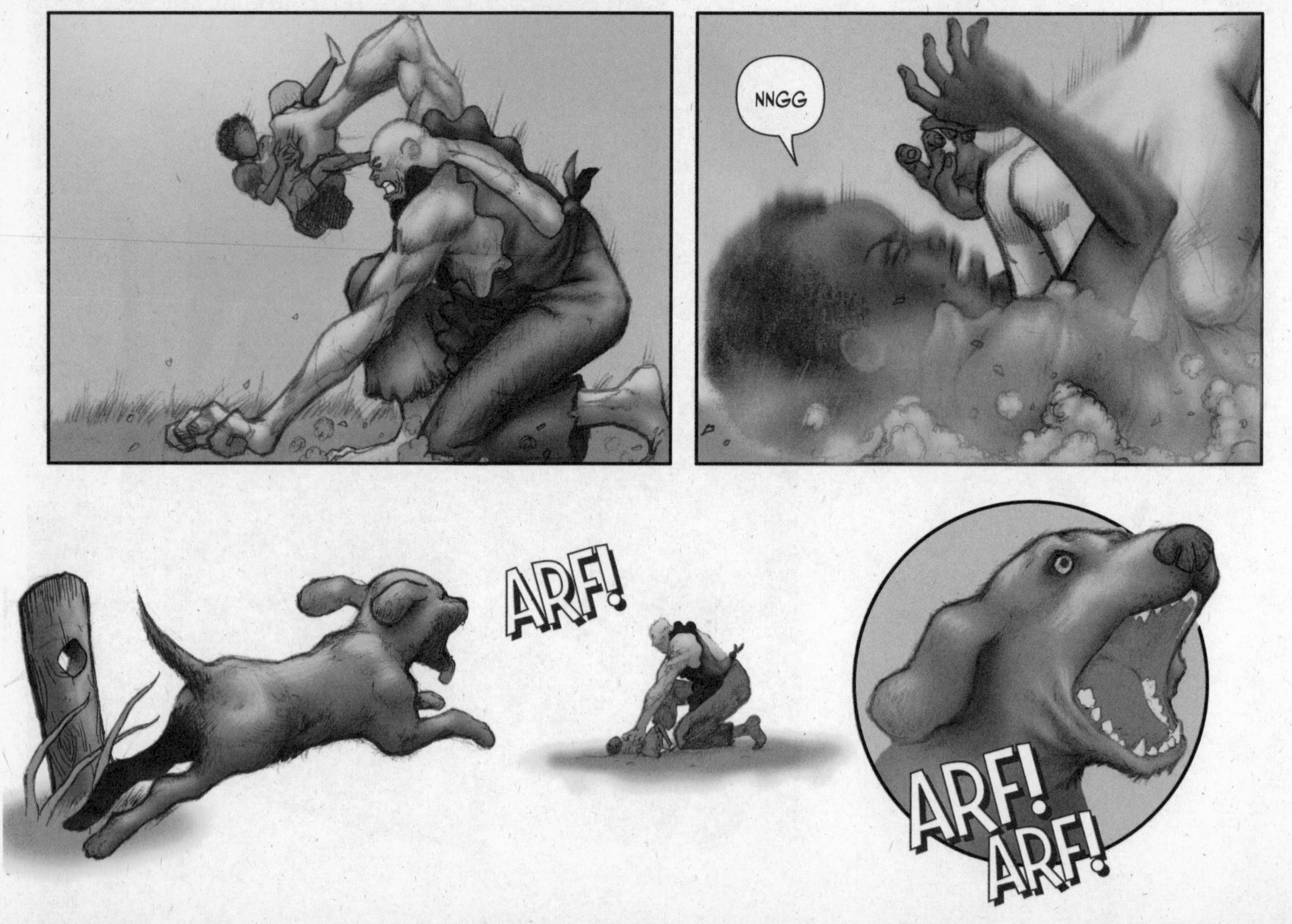
NNGG
ARF!
ARF!
ARF!

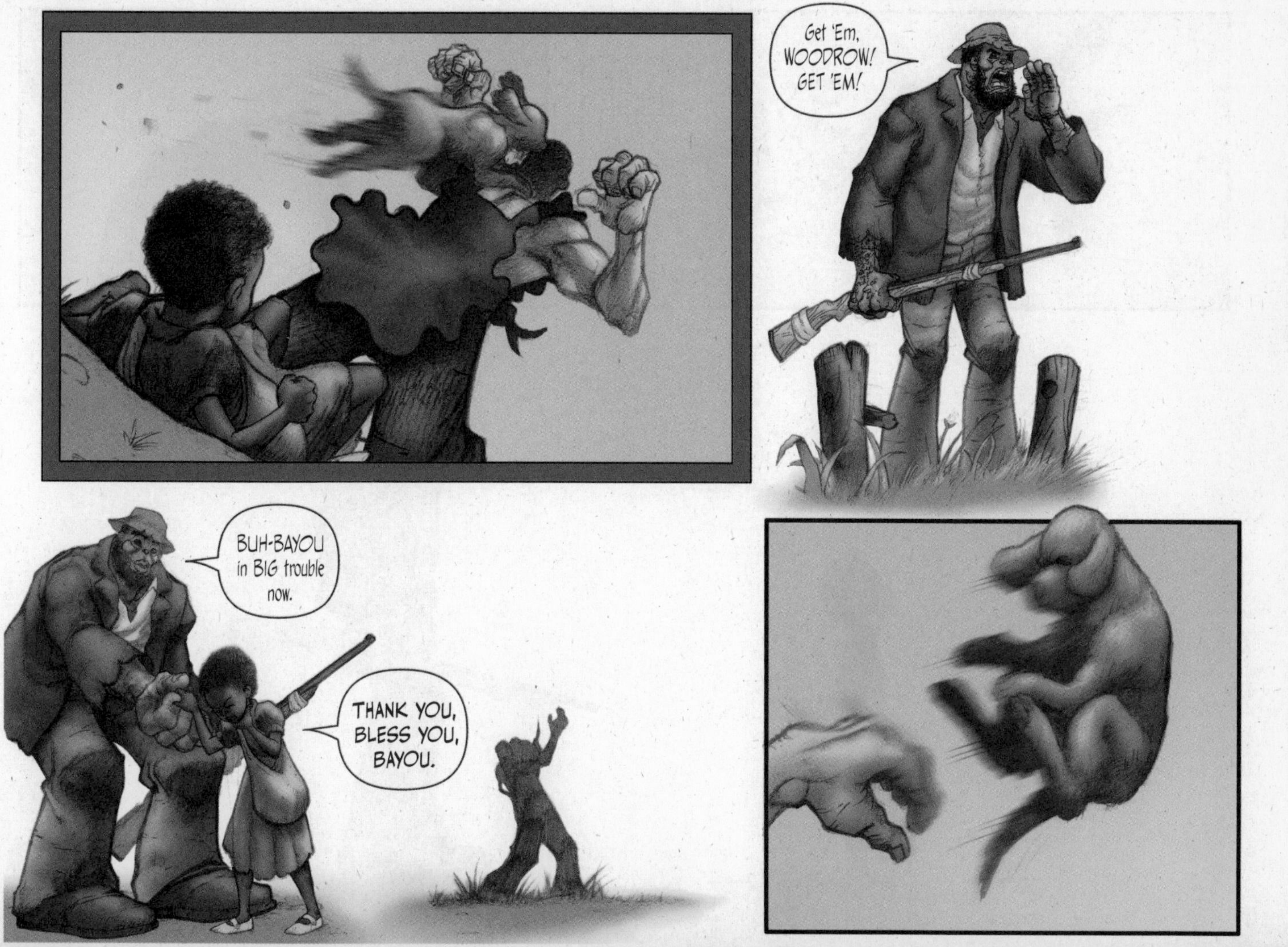
Get 'Em, WOODROW! GET 'EM!
BUH-BAYOU in BIG trouble now.
THANK YOU, BLESS YOU, BAYOU.

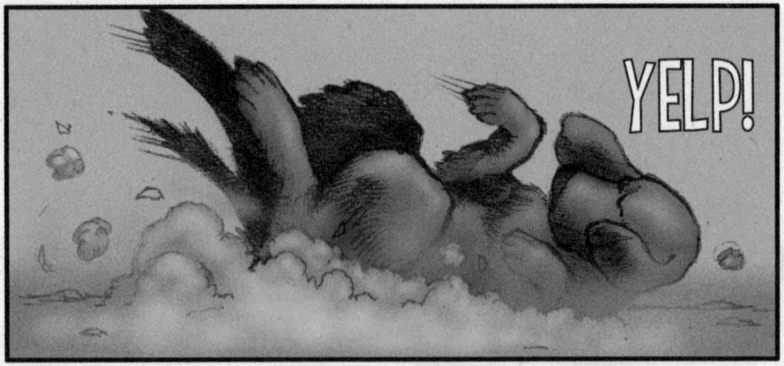
YELP!

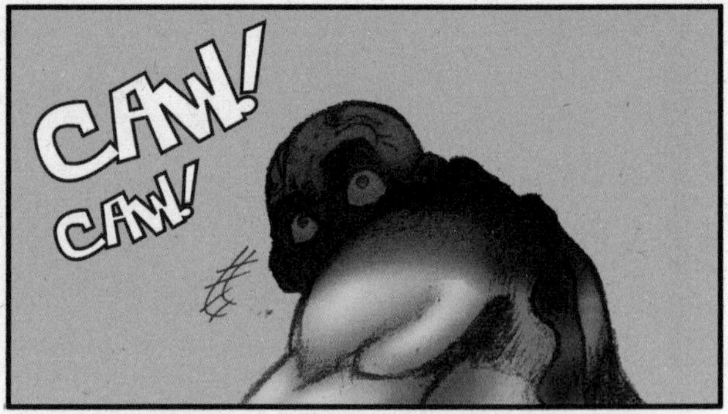
CAW!
CAW!

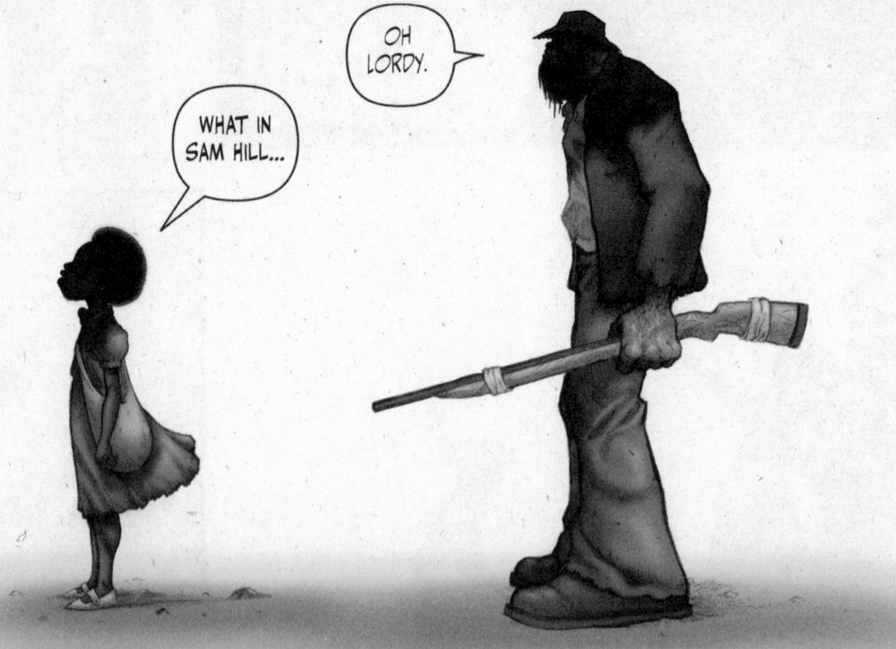
OH LORDY.
WHAT IN SAM HILL...

JIM CROWS!!

EEP!

CAW! CAW! CAW! CAW! CAW! CAW!

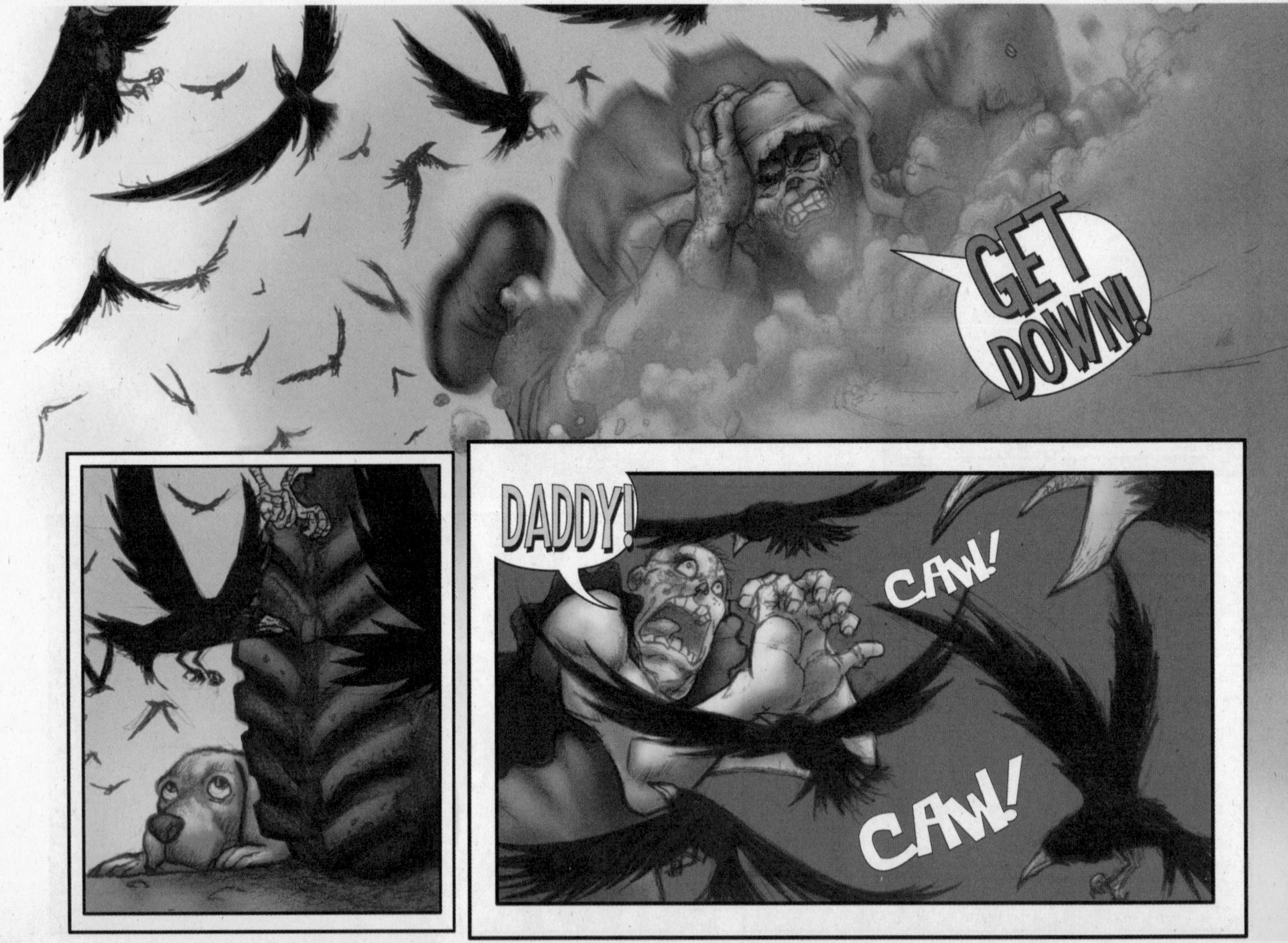
GET DOWN!
DADDY!
CAW!
CAW!

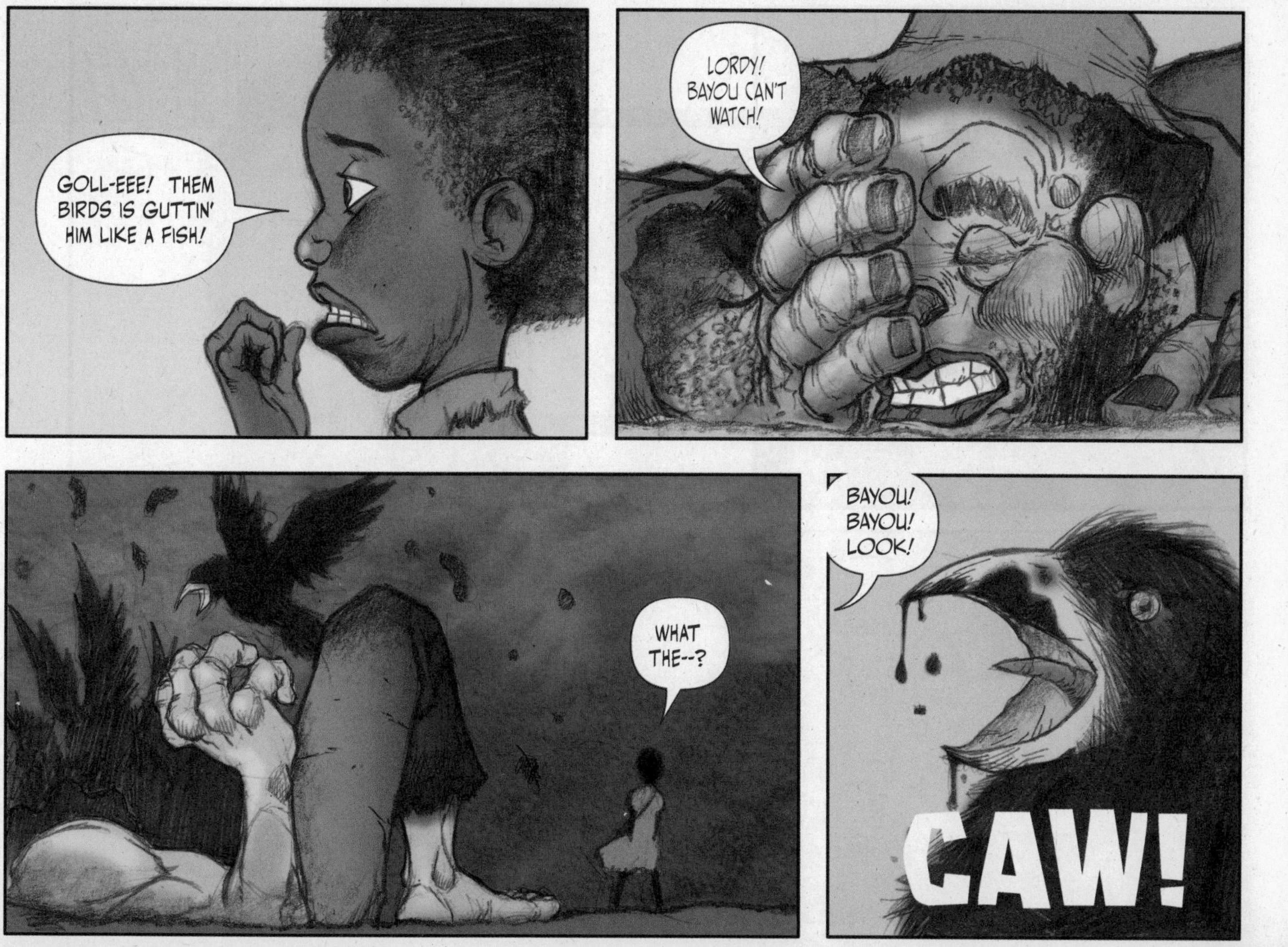
GOLL-EEE! THEM BIRDS IS GUTTIN' HIM LIKE A FISH!
LORDY! BAYOU CAN'T WATCH!
WHAT THE--?
BAYOU! BAYOU! LOOK!
CAW!

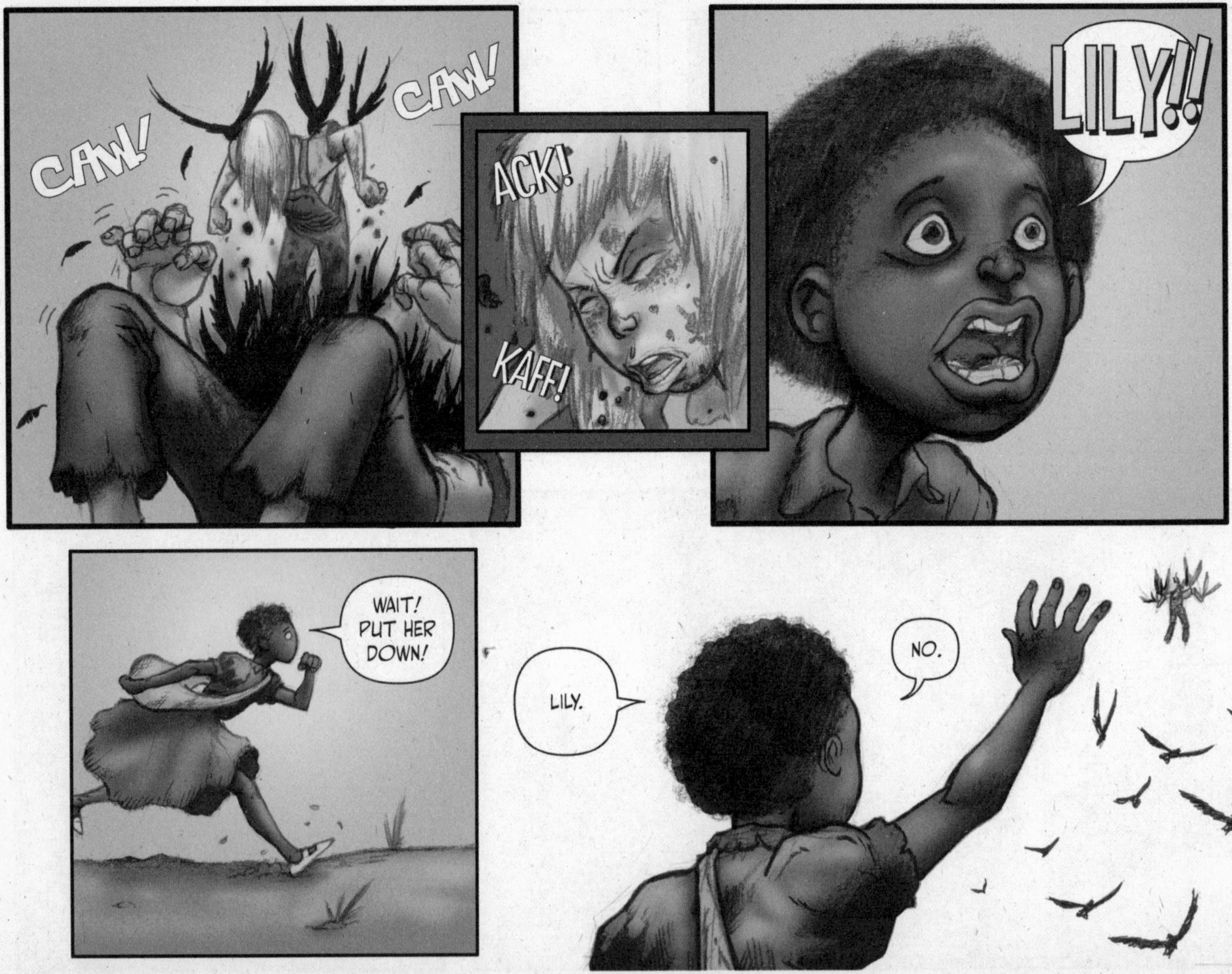
CAW!
CAW!
ACK!
KAFF!
LILY!!!
WAIT! PUT HER DOWN!
LILY.
NO.

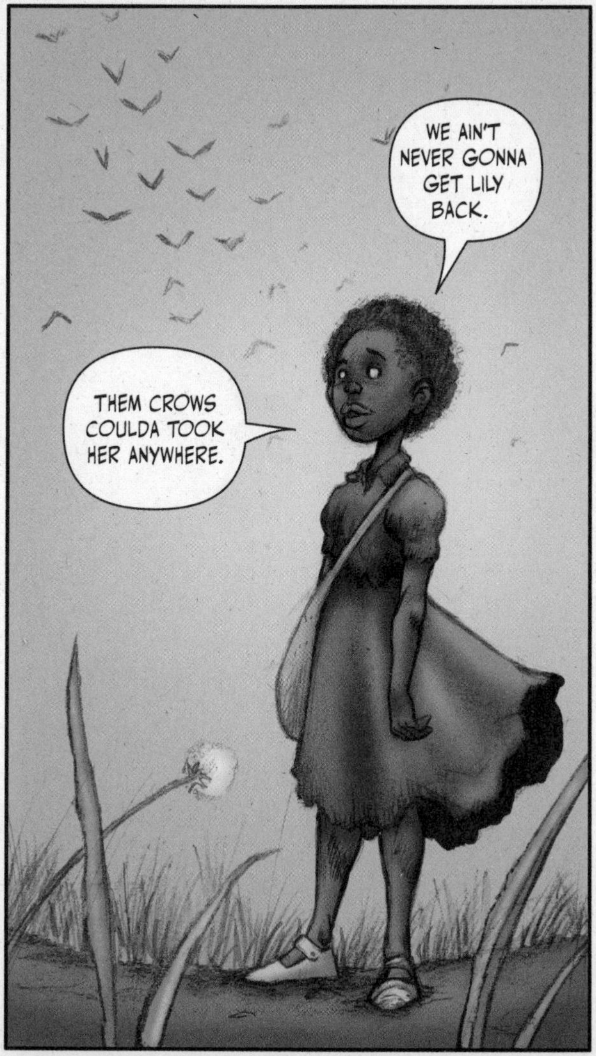
WE AIN'T NEVER GONNA GET LILY BACK.
THEM CROWS COULDA TOOK HER ANYWHERE.

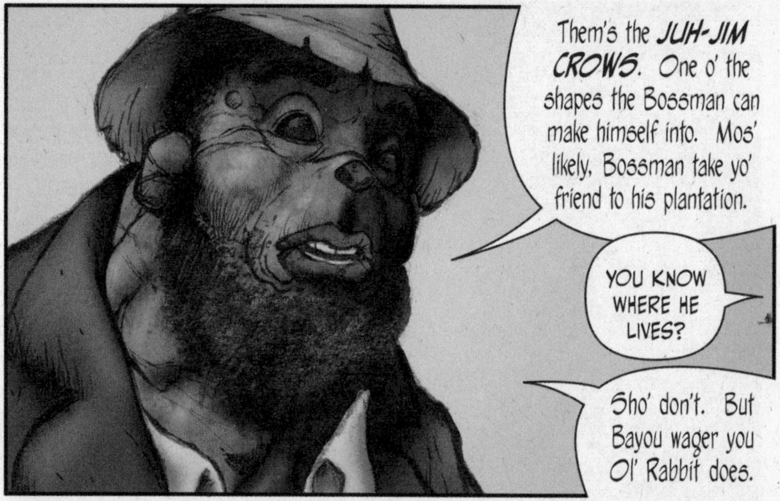
Them's the JUH-JIM CROWS. One o' the shapes the Bossman can make himself into. Mos' likely, Bossman take yo' friend to his plantation.
YOU KNOW WHERE HE LIVES?
Sho' don't. But Bayou wager you Ol' Rabbit does.

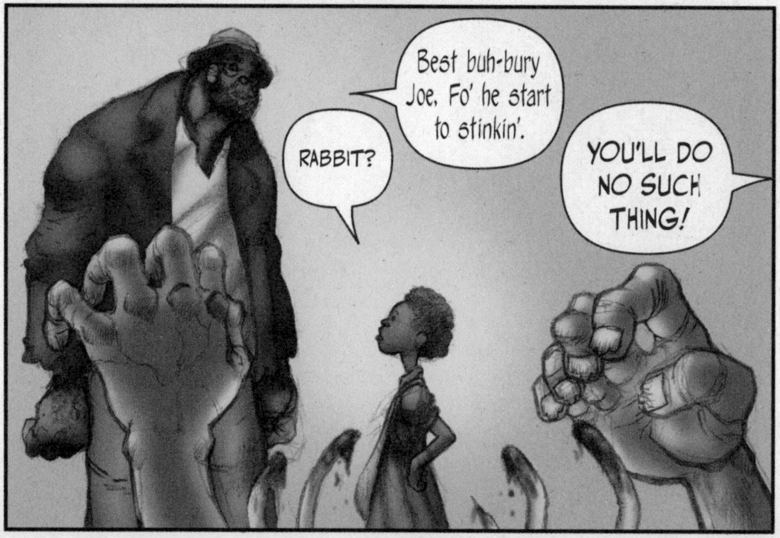
Best buh-bury Joe, Fo' he start to stinkin'.
RABBIT?
YOU'LL DO NO SUCH THING!

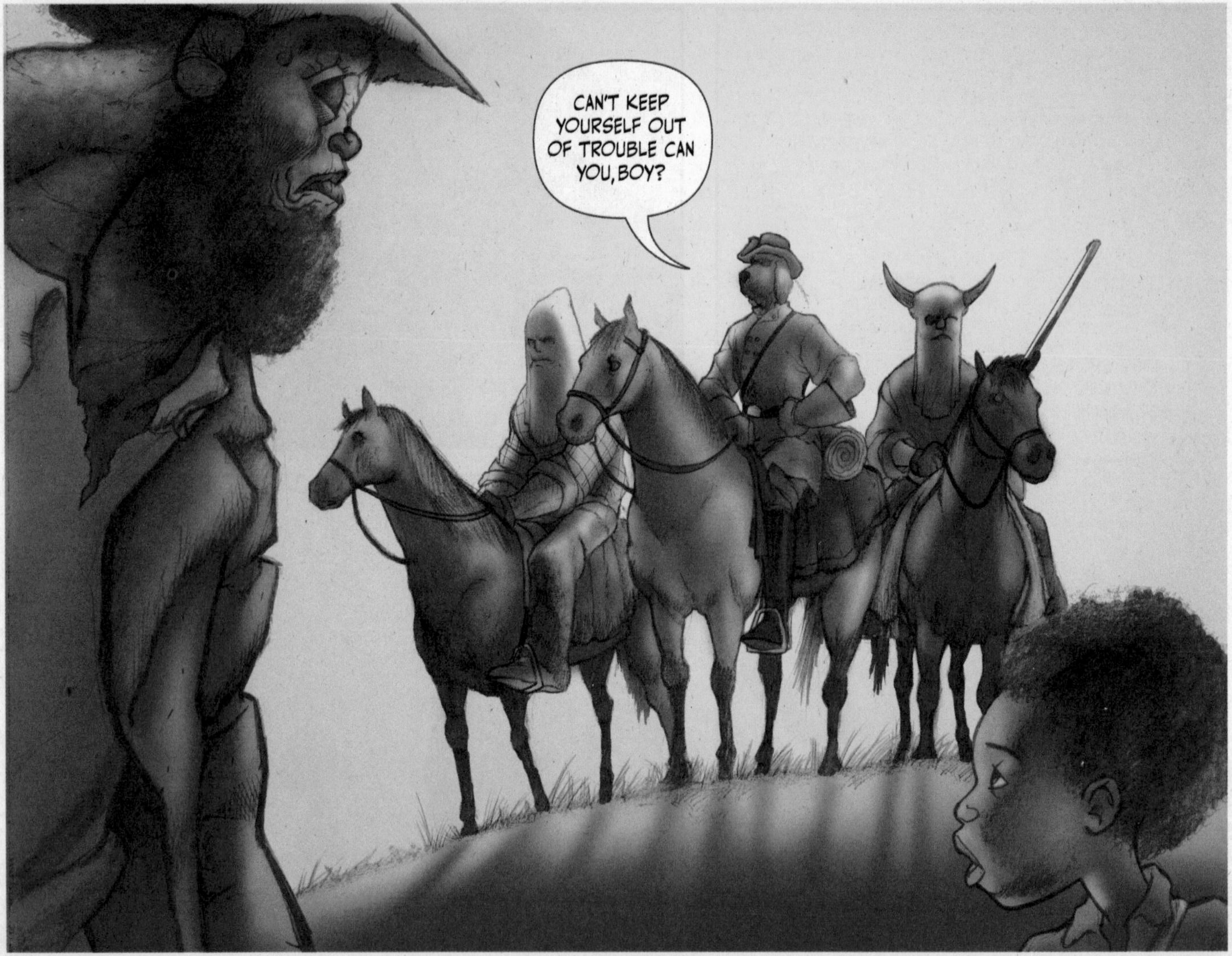
CAN'T KEEP YOURSELF OUT OF TROUBLE CAN YOU, BOY?

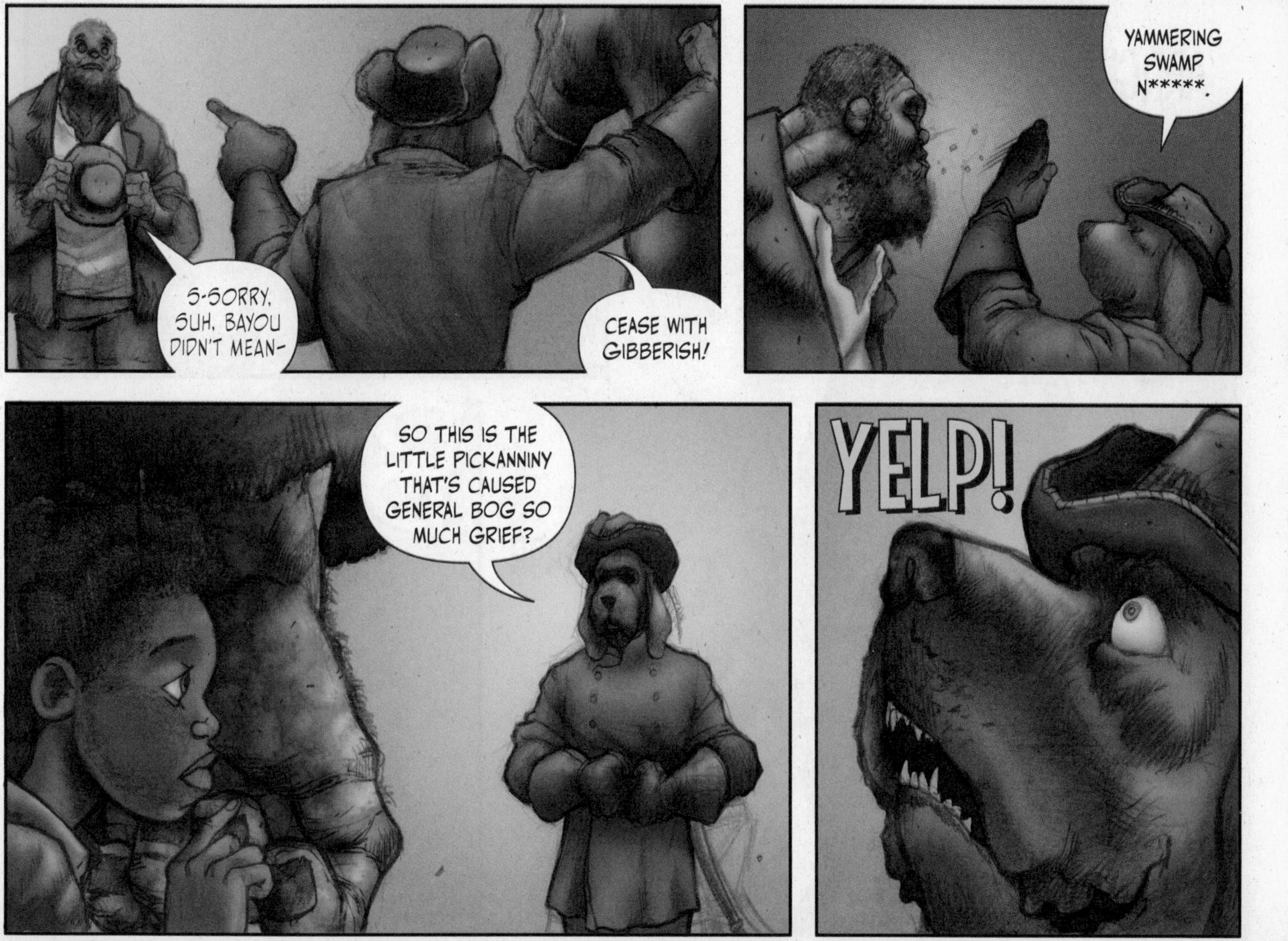
S-SORRY, SUH, BAYOU DIDN'T MEAN-
CEASE WITH GIBBERISH!
YAMMERING SWAMP N*****.
SO THIS IS THE LITTLE PICKANNINY THAT'S CAUSED GENERAL BOG SO MUCH GRIEF?
YELP!

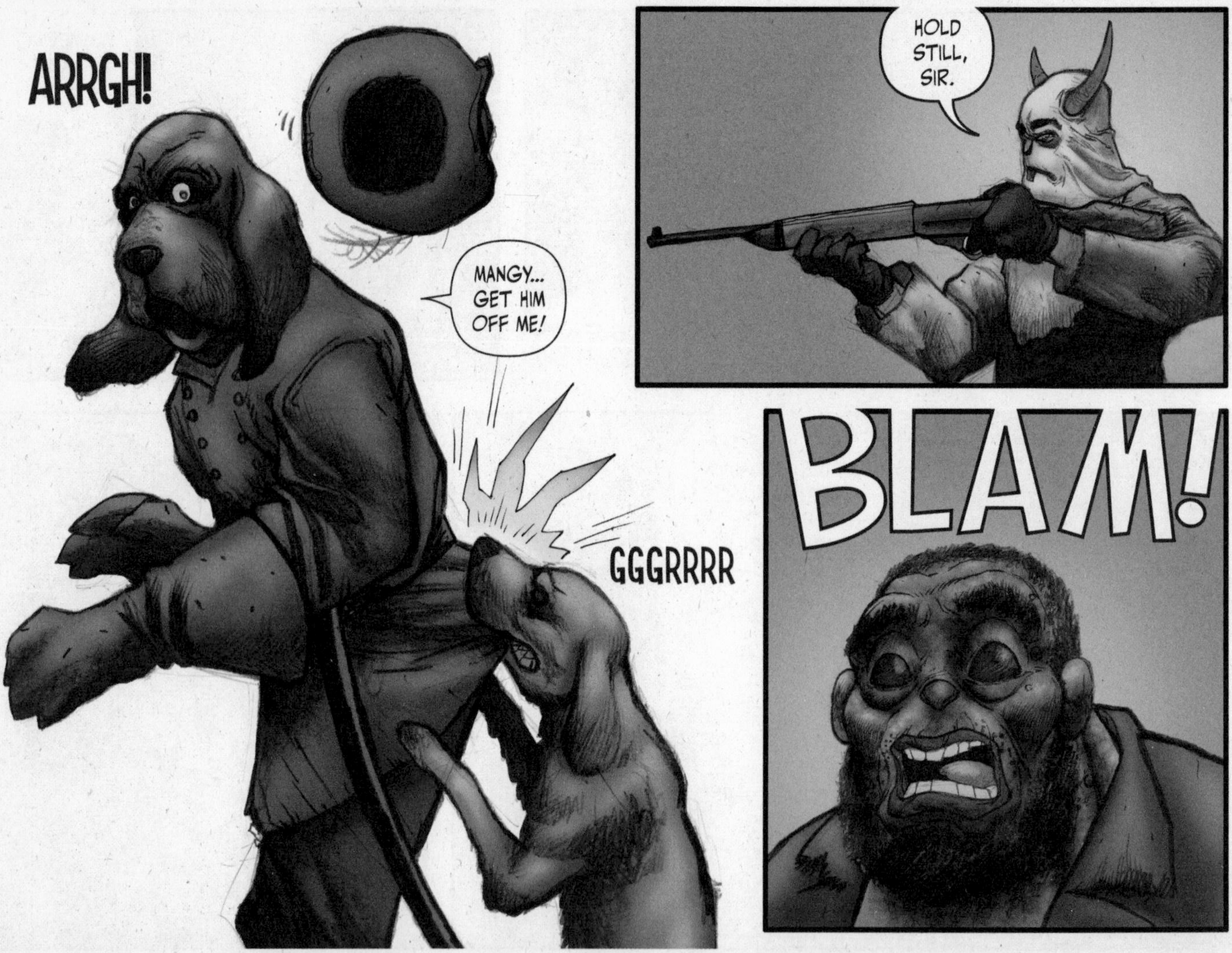
ARRGH!
MANGY... GET HIM OFF ME!
GGGRRRR
HOLD STILL, SIR.
BLAM!

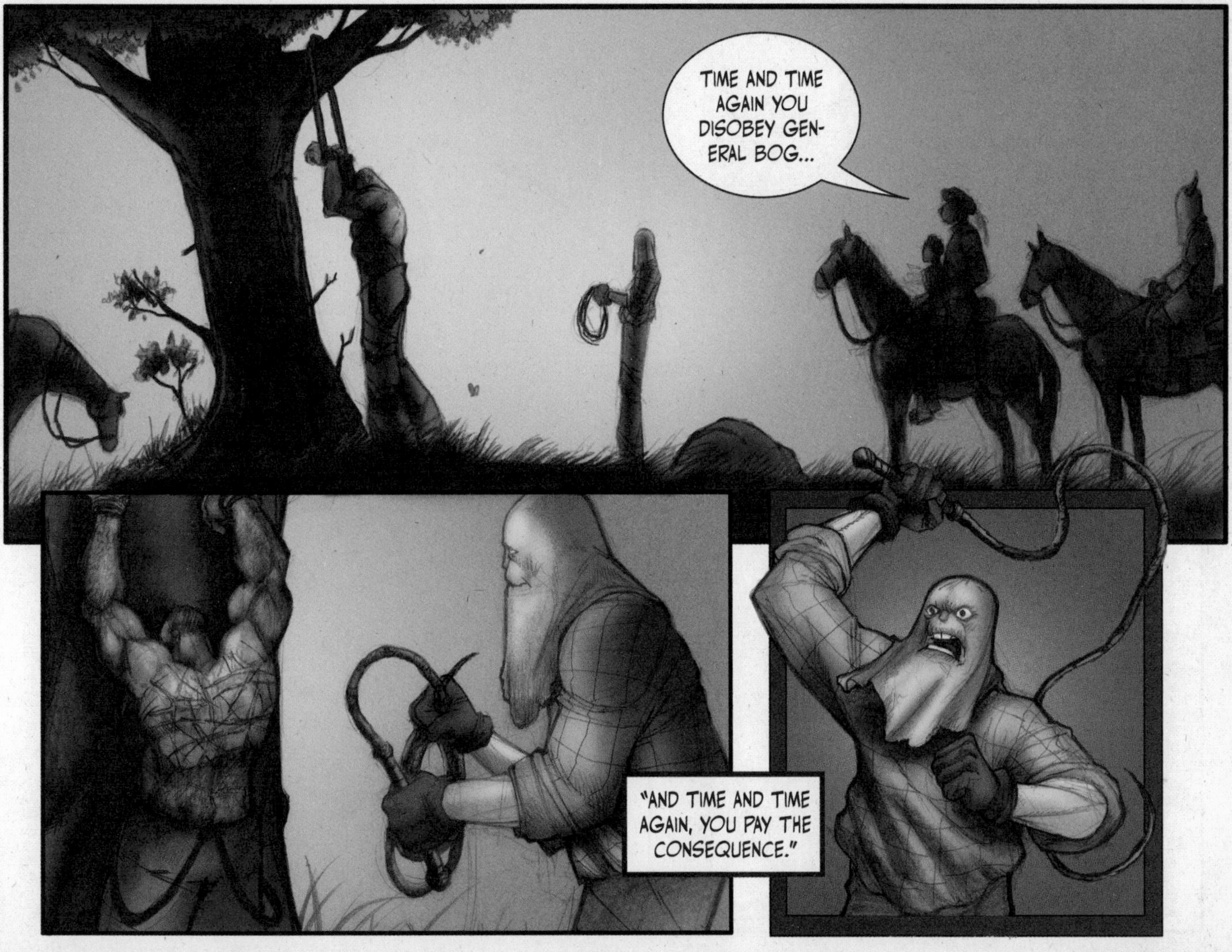
TIME AND TIME AGAIN YOU DISOBEY GEN- ERAL BOG...
"AND TIME AND TIME AGAIN, YOU PAY THE CONSEQUENCE."

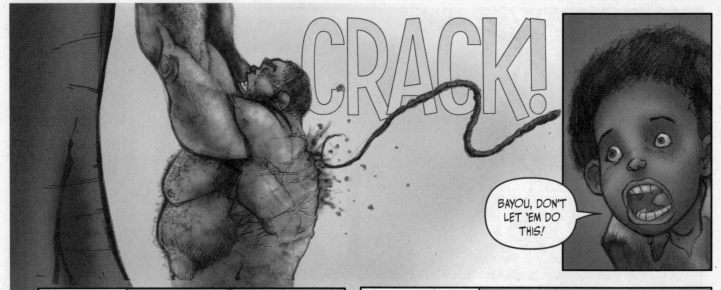

CRACK!

BAYOU, DON'T LET 'EM DO THIS!

WHAT CAN HE POSSIBLY DO? HE'S A SNIVELING COWARD,

AN OVERGROWN CHILD WHO MUST BE TREATED ACCORDINGLY.

YOU HAVE AN APPOINTMENT WITH THE GENERAL, LITTLE DARKIE.

NATHAN, MAKE HIM SUFFER!

CRACK!
BAYOU!! HELP ME!!
BAYOU!!!!
...

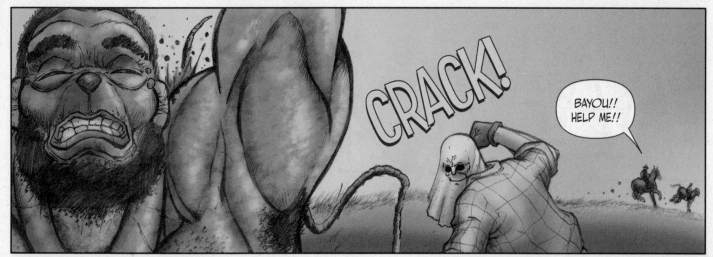

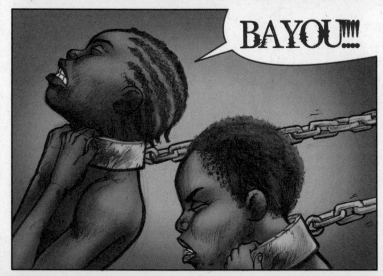

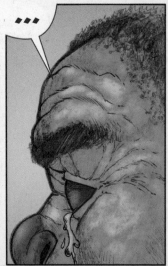

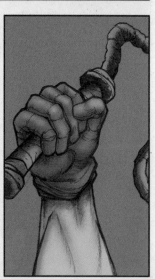

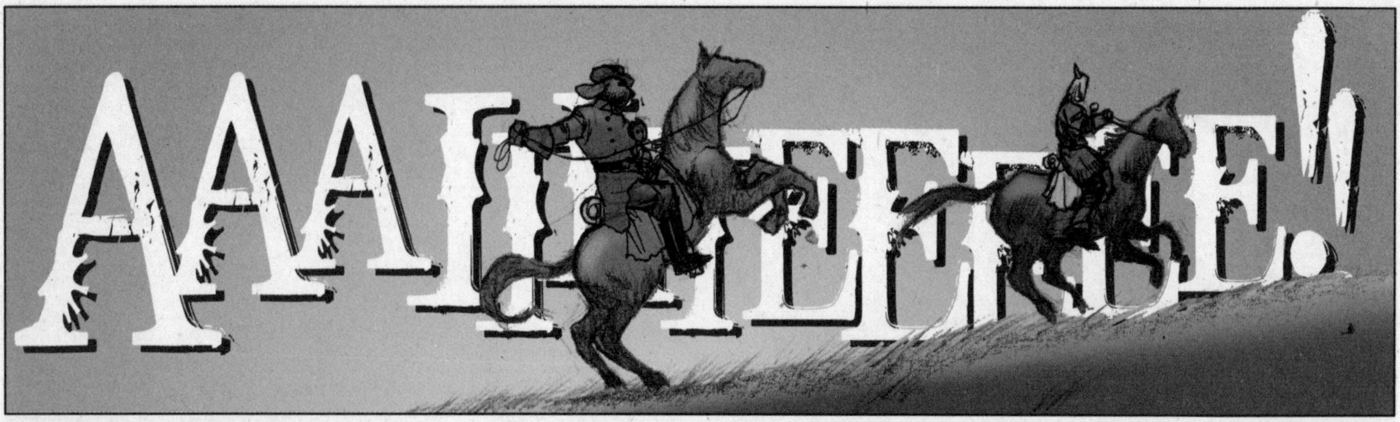

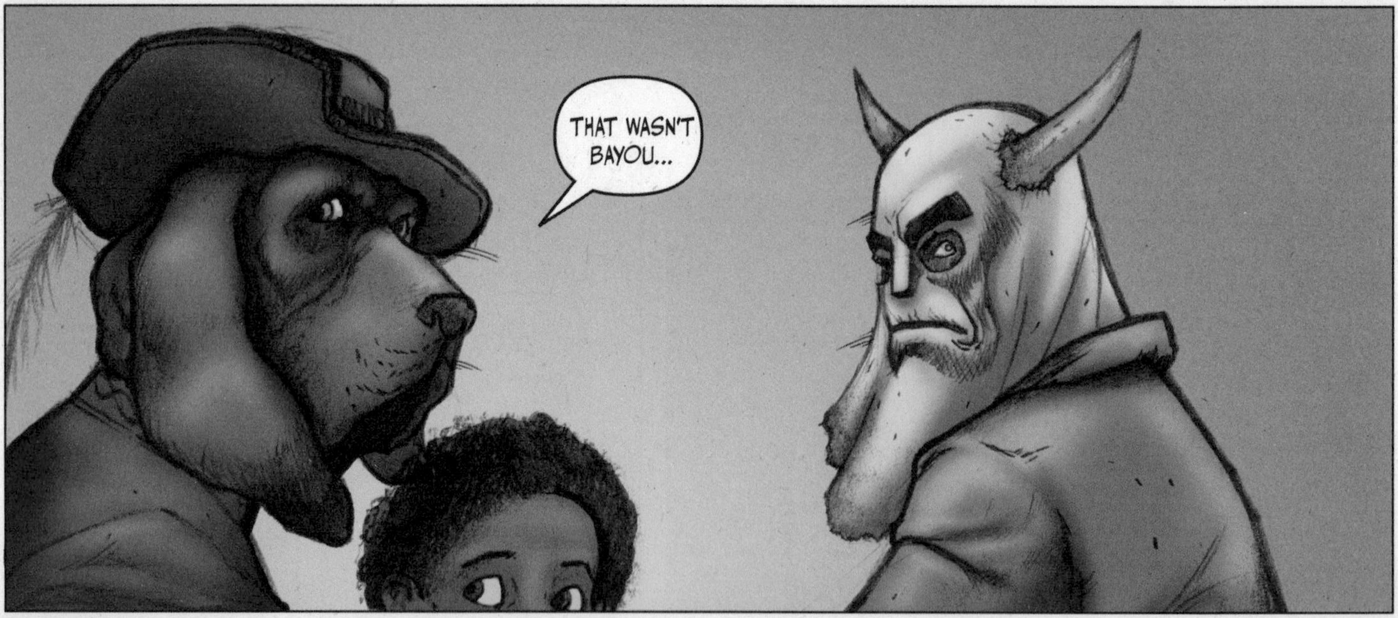
THAT WASN'T BAYOU...

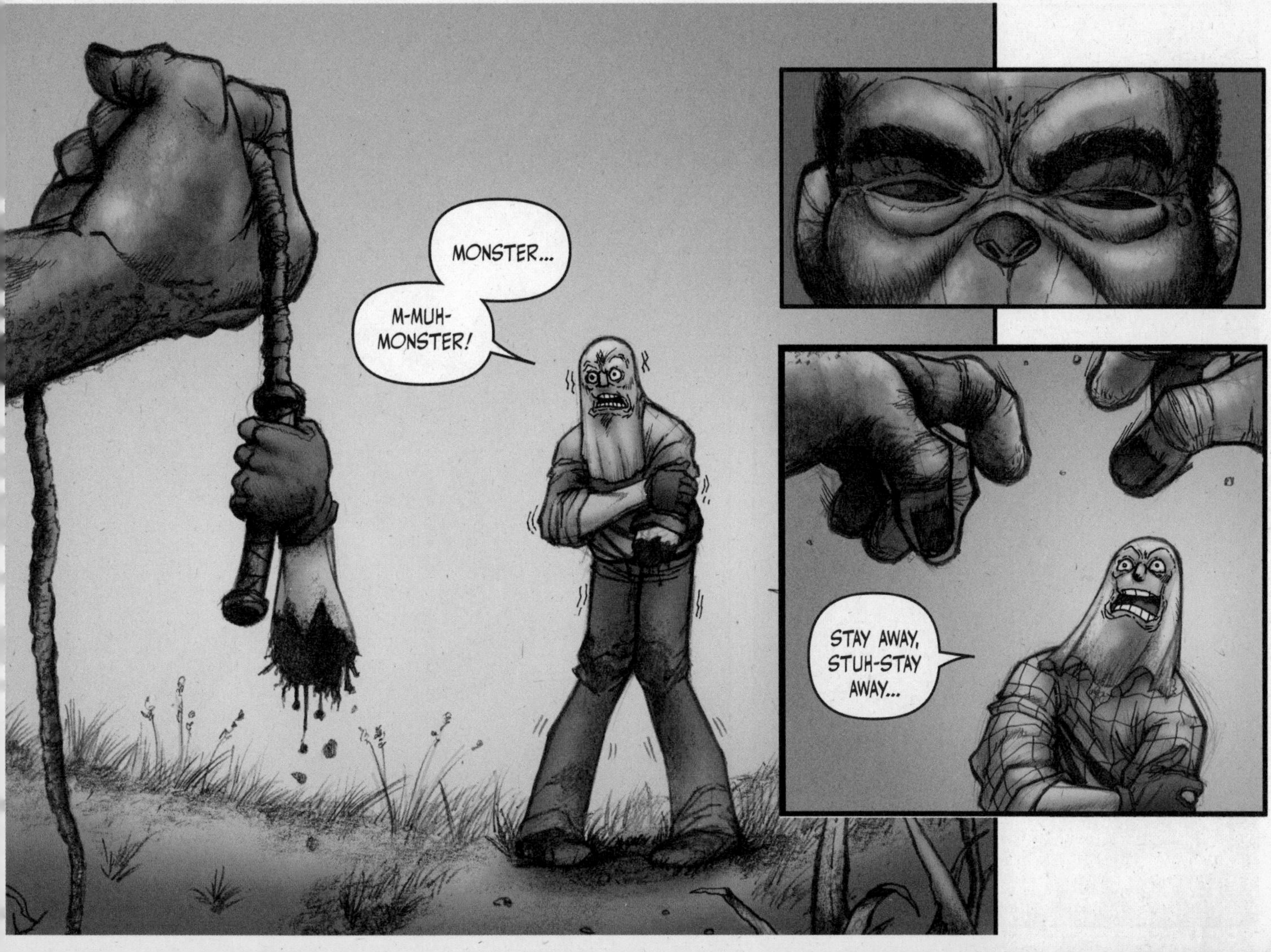
MONSTER...
M-MUH-MONSTER!
STAY AWAY, STUH-STAY AWAY...

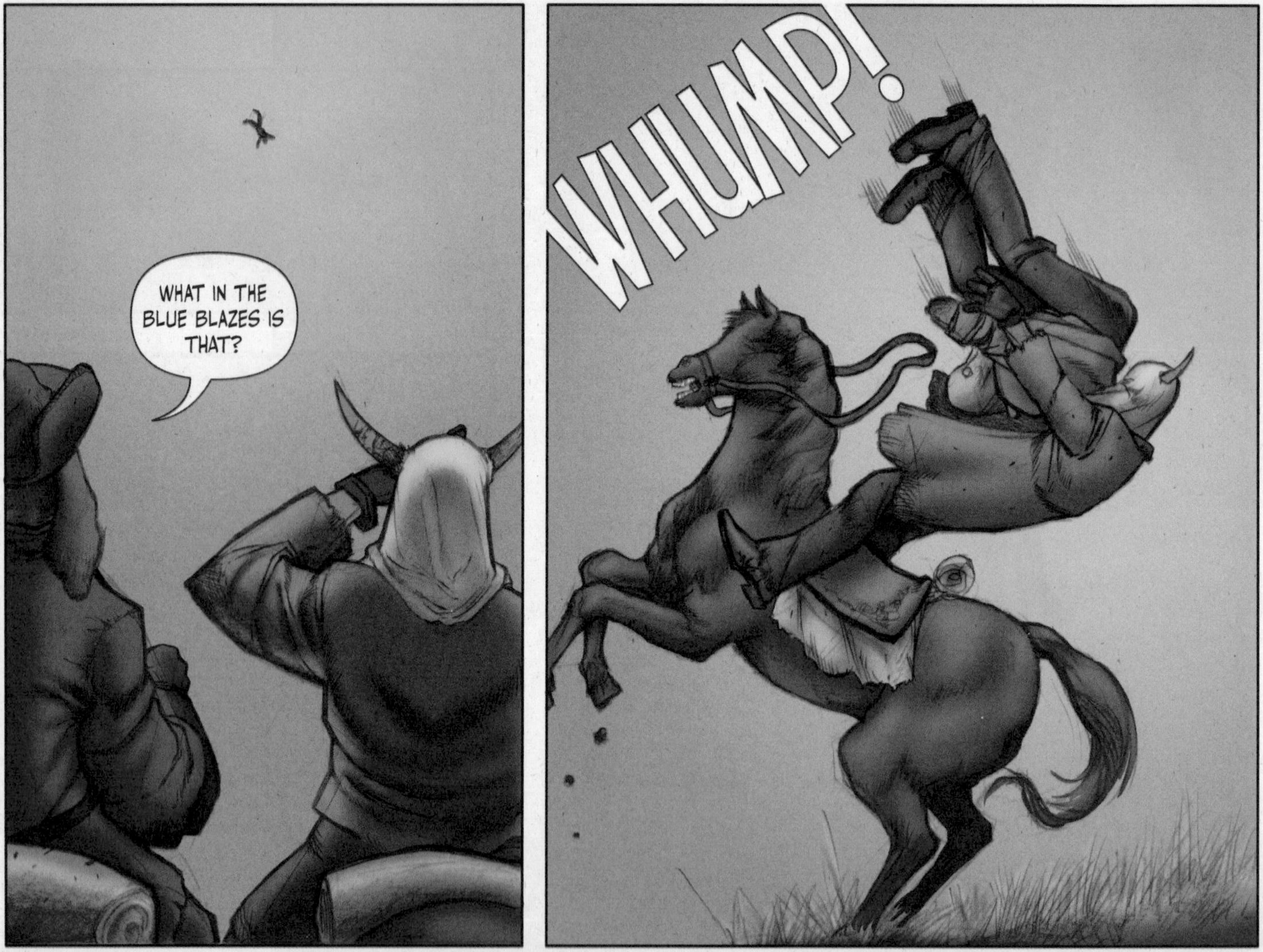
WHAT IN THE BLUE BLAZES IS THAT?
WHUMP!

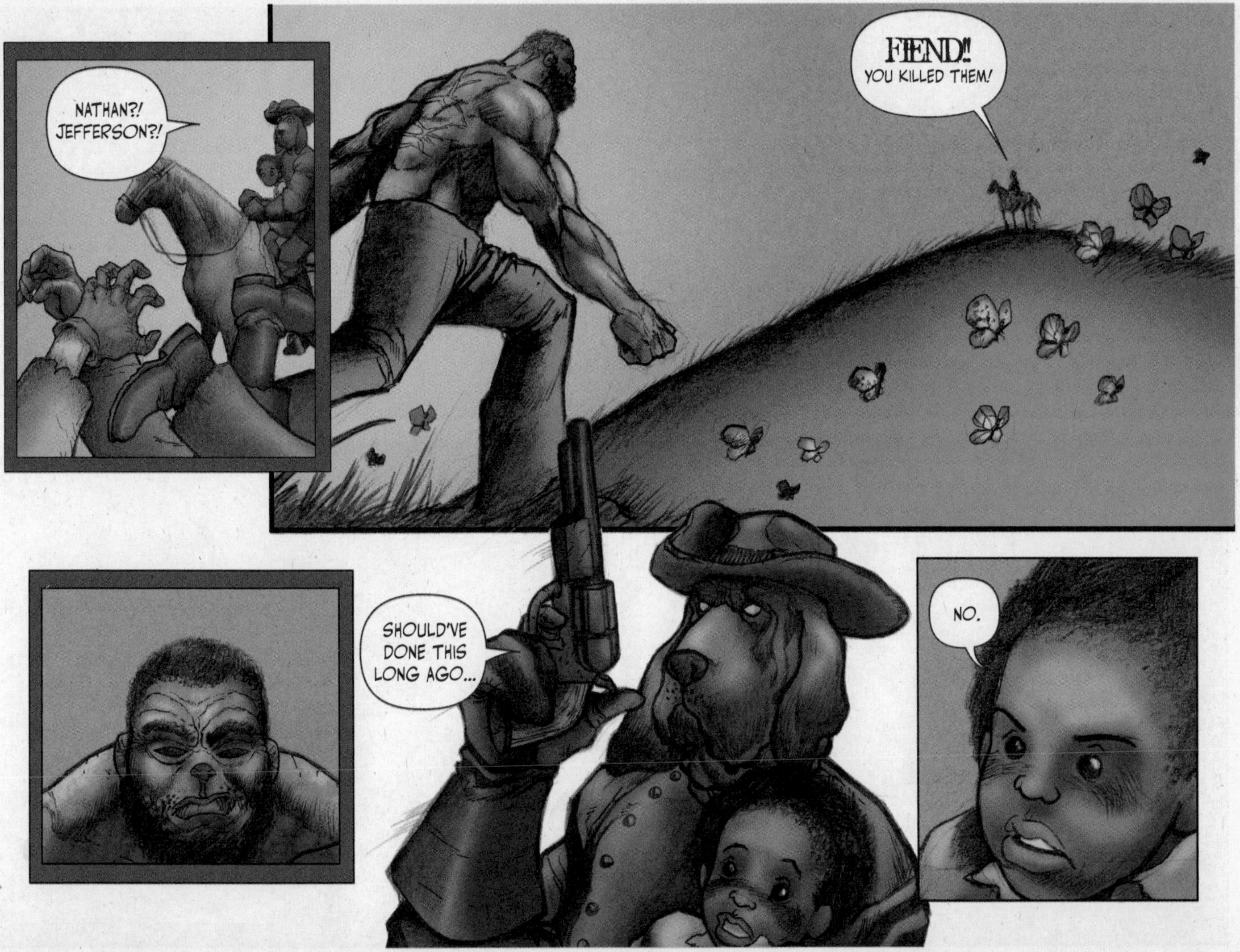

NATHAN?! JEFFERSON?!
FIEND!! YOU KILLED THEM!
SHOULD'VE DONE THIS LONG AGO...
NO.

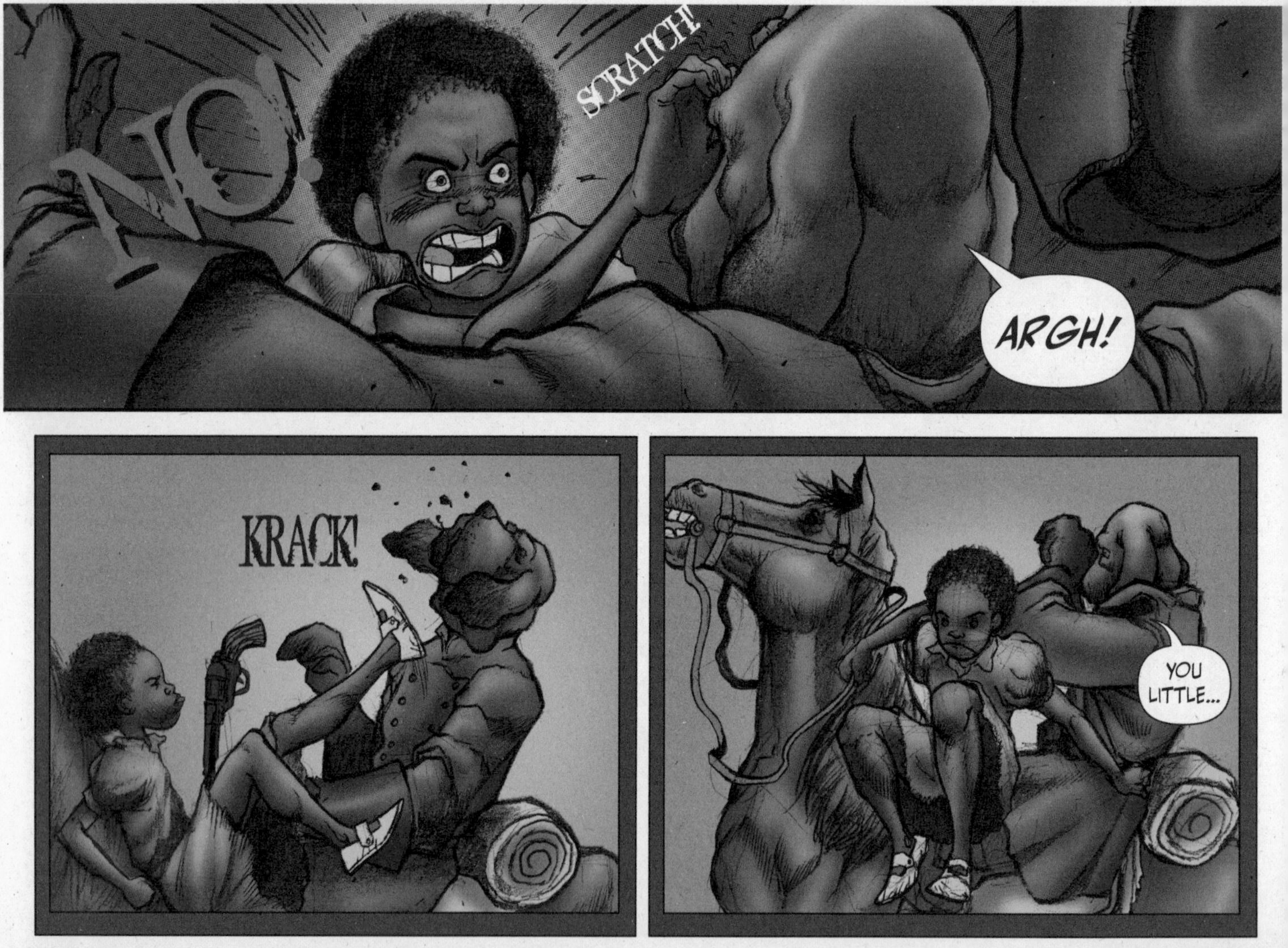
NO!
SCRATCH!
ARGH!
KRACK!
YOU LITTLE...

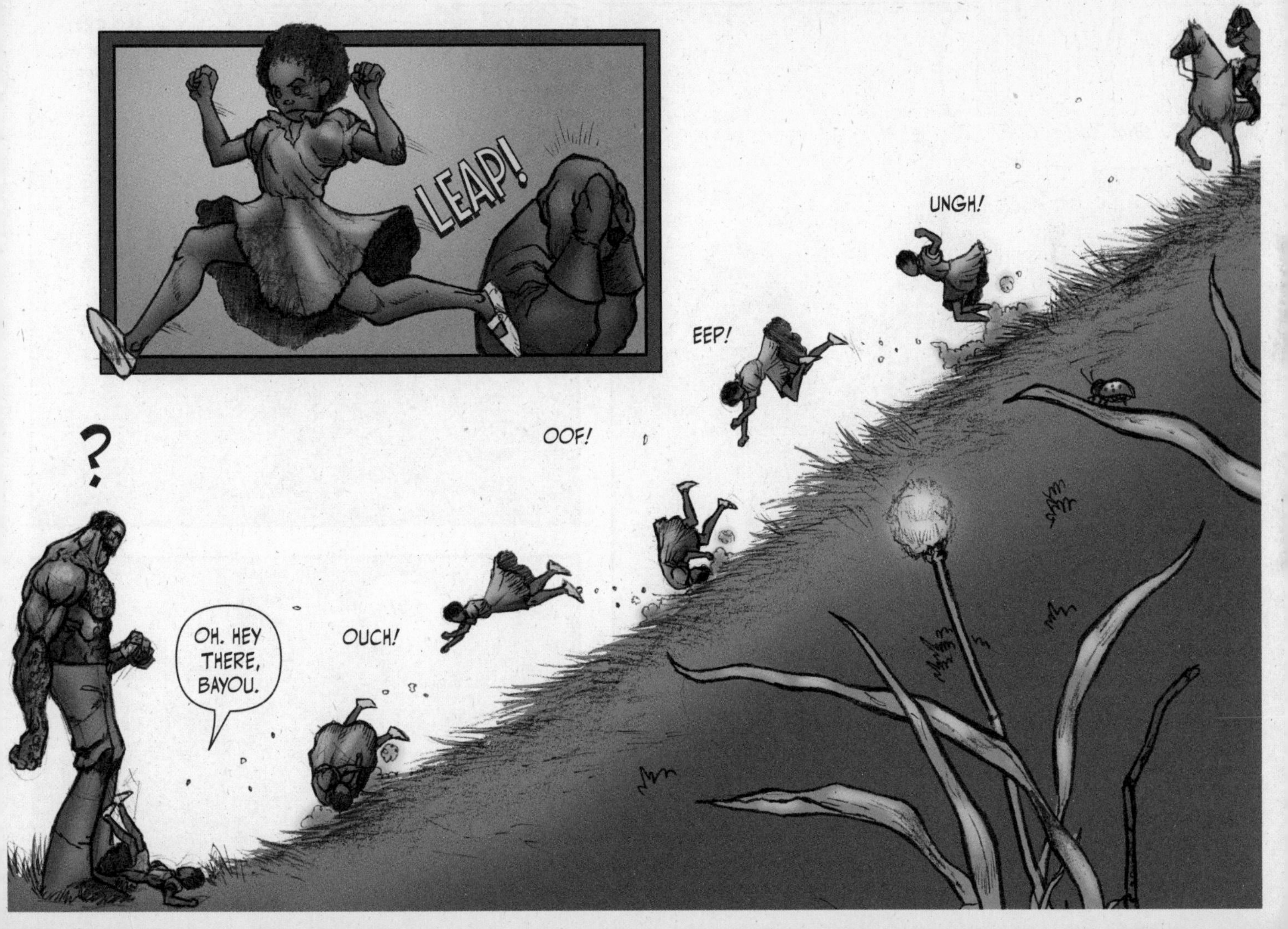
LEAP!
UNGH!
EEP!
OOF!
OUCH!
?
OH. HEY THERE, BAYOU.

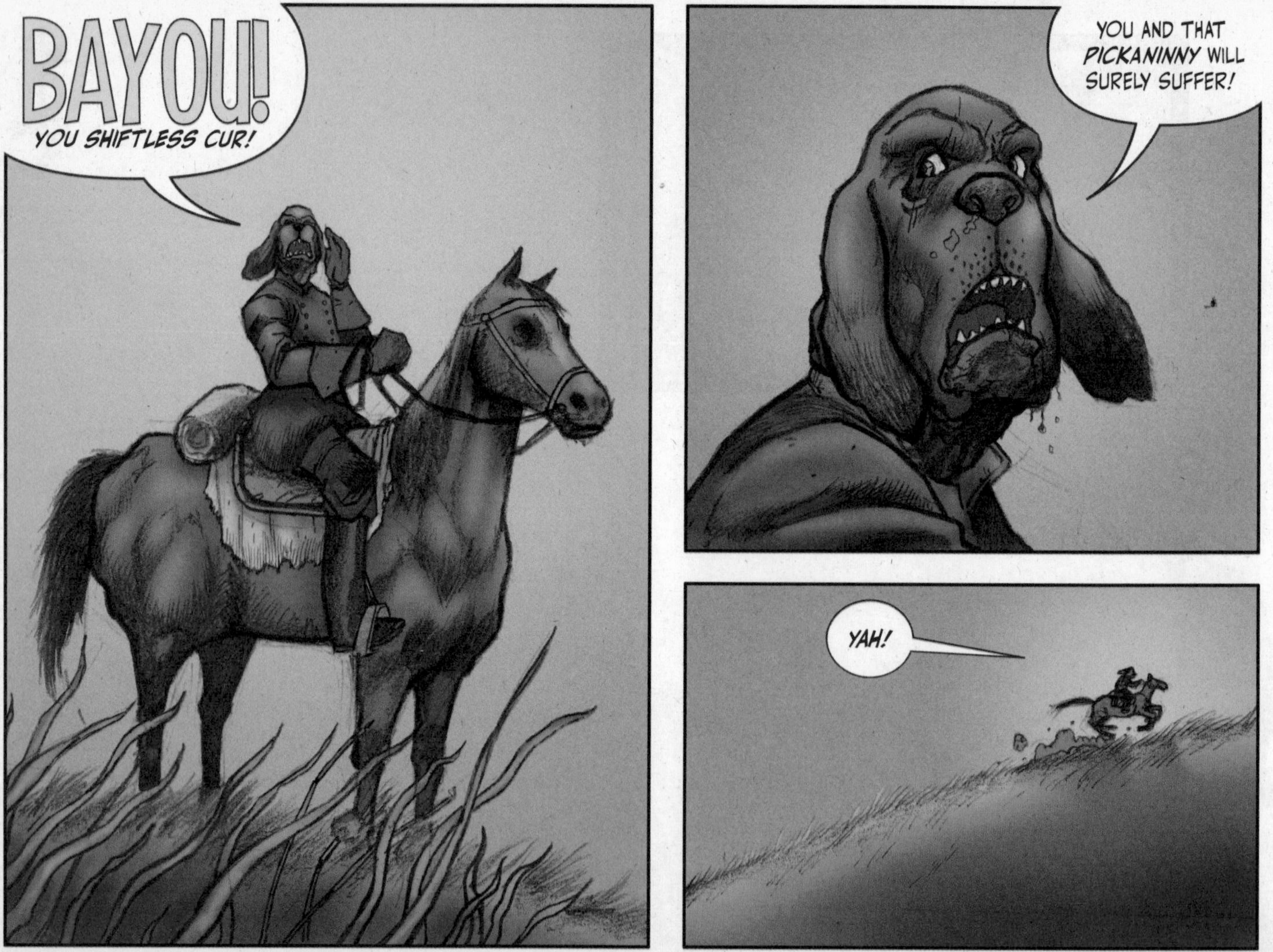
BAYOU!
YOU SHIFTLESS CUR!
YOU AND THAT PICKANINNY WILL SURELY SUFFER!
YAH!

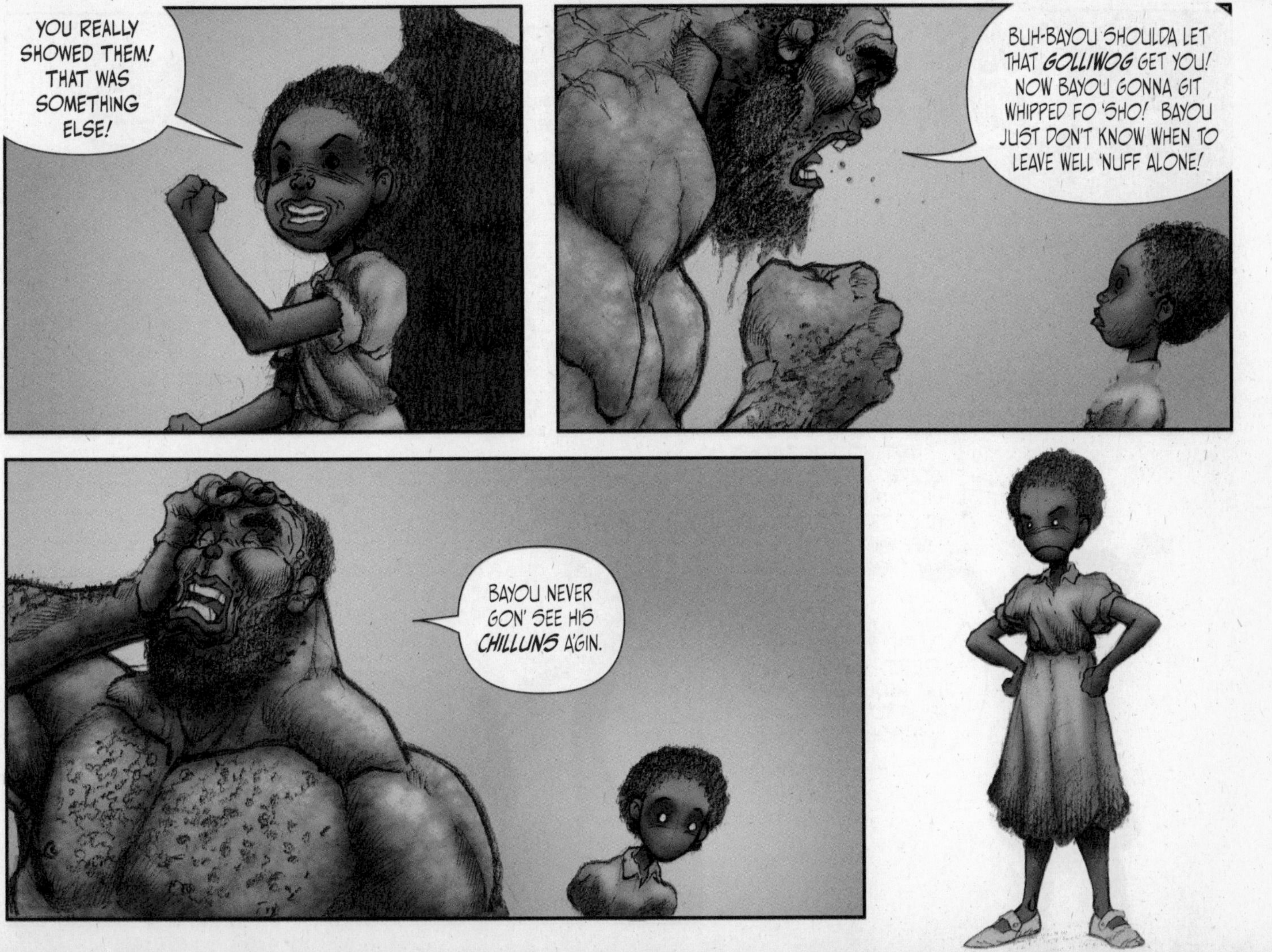
YOU REALLY SHOWED THEM! THAT WAS SOMETHING ELSE!
BUH-BAYOU SHOULDA LET THAT GOLLIWOG GET YOU! NOW BAYOU GONNA GIT WHIPPED FO 'SHO! BAYOU JUST DON'T KNOW WHEN TO LEAVE WELL 'NUFF ALONE!
BAYOU NEVER GON' SEE HIS CHILLUNS A'GIN.

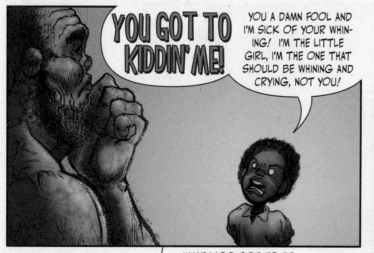

YOU GOT TO KIDDIN' ME!

YOU A DAMN FOOL AND I'M SICK OF YOUR WHINING! I'M THE LITTLE GIRL, I'M THE ONE THAT SHOULD BE WHINING AND CRYING, NOT YOU!

LOOK AT YOU! YOU A BIG OL' MONSTER WITH ARMS LIKE TREE TRUNKS! YOU CAN WHUP JUST ABOUT ANYTHING IN THE WHOLE WIDE WORLD!

WHATCHOO GOT TO BE SCARED OF SOME BOSSMAN FO'? IF I WAS BIG AS YOU, I'D BE THE BOSSMAN! YOU SEE WHAT YOU DID TO ALL THEM JOKERS BACK THERE?!

YOU SAID YOURSELF, THIS RABBIT FELLA KNOWS JUST ABOUT EVERYTHING THEY IS TO KNOW, RIGHT? WE SHOULD ASK HIM!

WE FIND YOUR BOSSMAN AND WE FIND LILY AND YOU CAN JUST MARCH RIGHT UP TO THAT OL' FOOL AND TELL HIM TO GIVE HIM YOUR CHILLUNS OR YOU GON' POUND HIM GOOD!

Miss Lee, what you talkin' sho' do make sense. Bayou reckons.

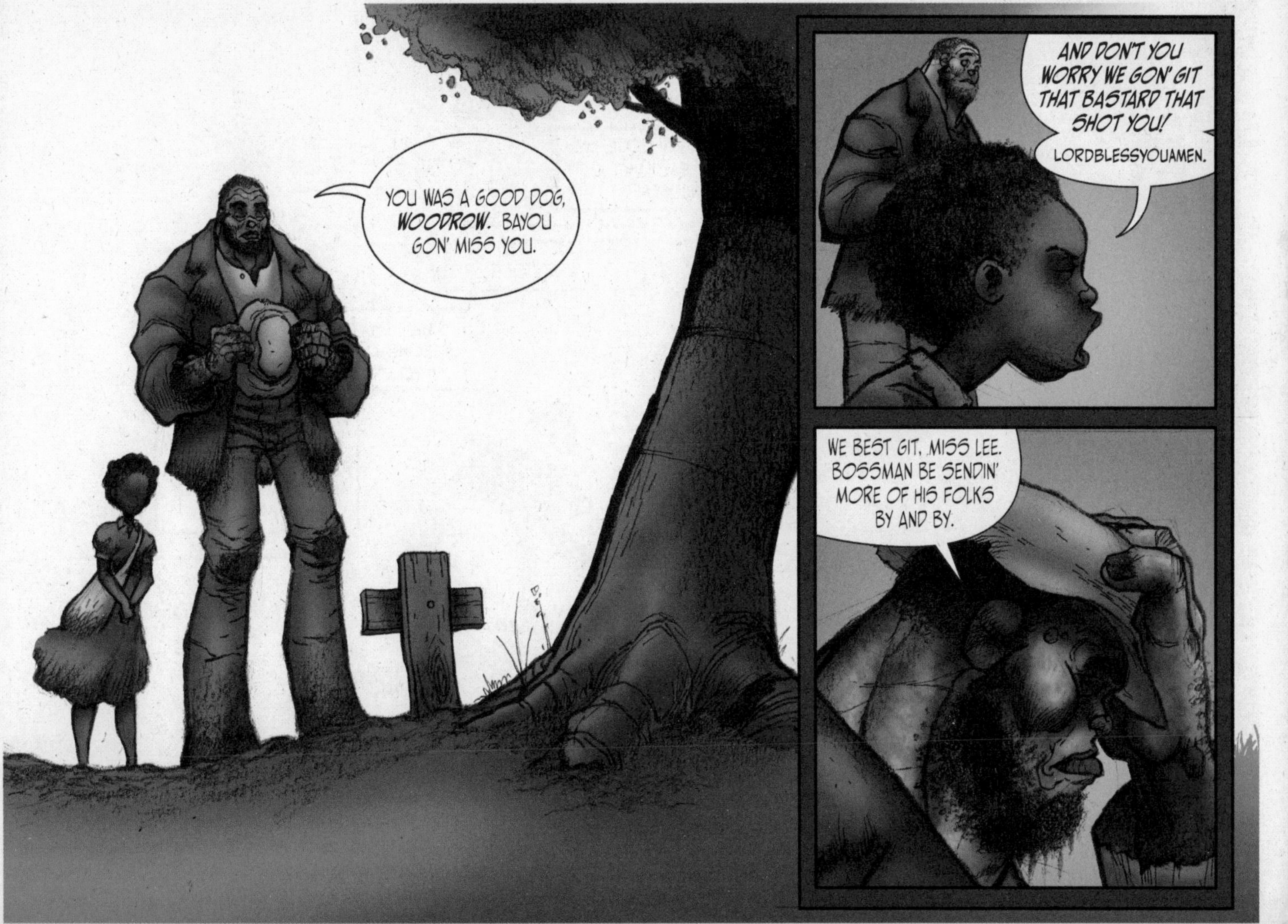
YOU WAS A GOOD DOG, **WOODROW.** BAYOU GON' MISS YOU.
AND DON'T YOU WORRY WE GON' GIT THAT BASTARD THAT SHOT YOU!
LORDBLESSYOUAMEN.
WE BEST GIT, MISS LEE. BOSSMAN BE SENDIN' MORE OF HIS FOLKS BY AND BY.

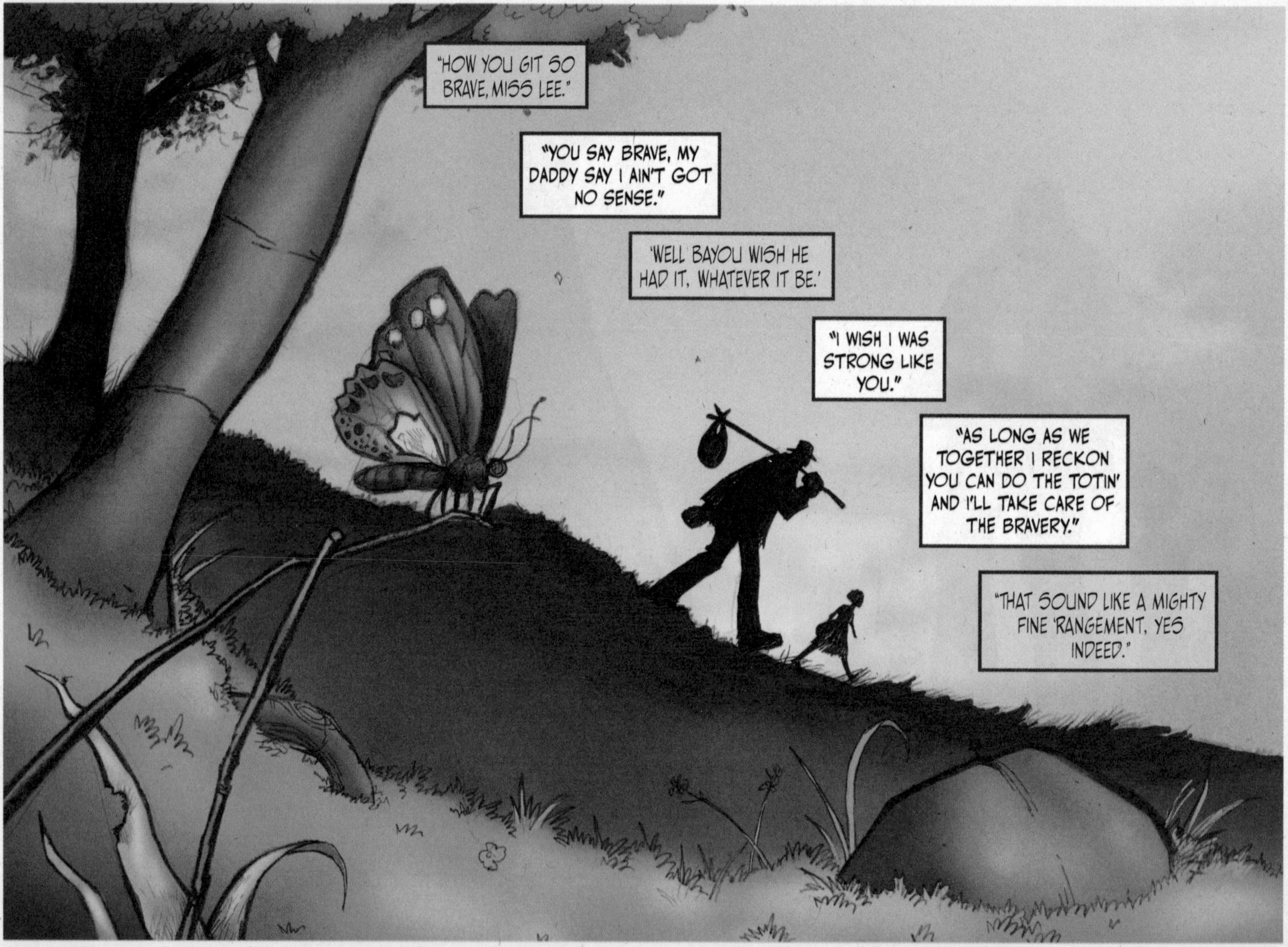
"HOW YOU GIT SO BRAVE, MISS LEE."
"YOU SAY BRAVE, MY DADDY SAY I AIN'T GOT NO SENSE."
'WELL BAYOU WISH HE HAD IT, WHATEVER IT BE.'
"I WISH I WAS STRONG LIKE YOU."
"AS LONG AS WE TOGETHER I RECKON YOU CAN DO THE TOTIN' AND I'LL TAKE CARE OF THE BRAVERY."
"THAT SOUND LIKE A MIGHTY FINE 'RANGEMENT, YES INDEED."

Bayou profile sketch from the original pitch.

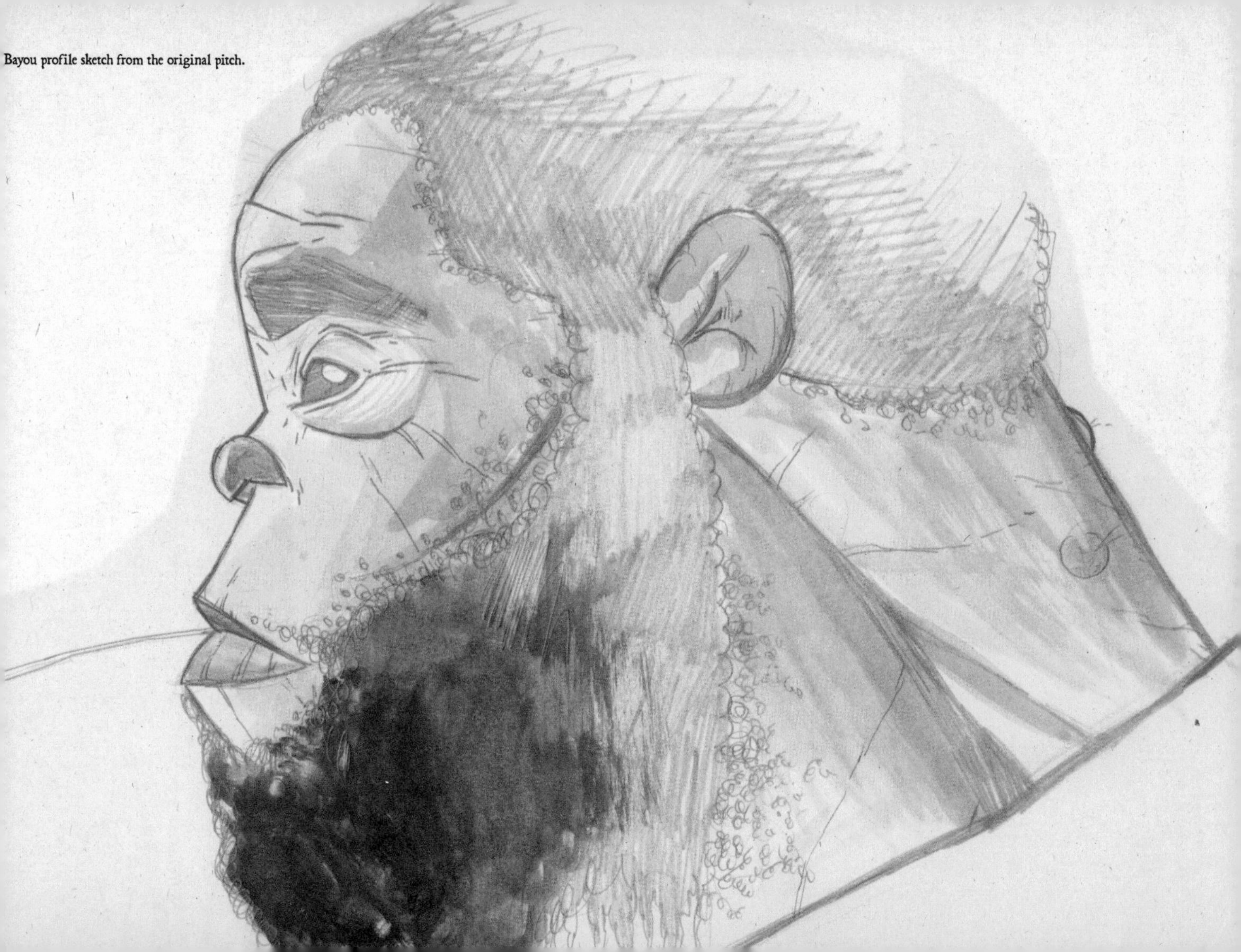

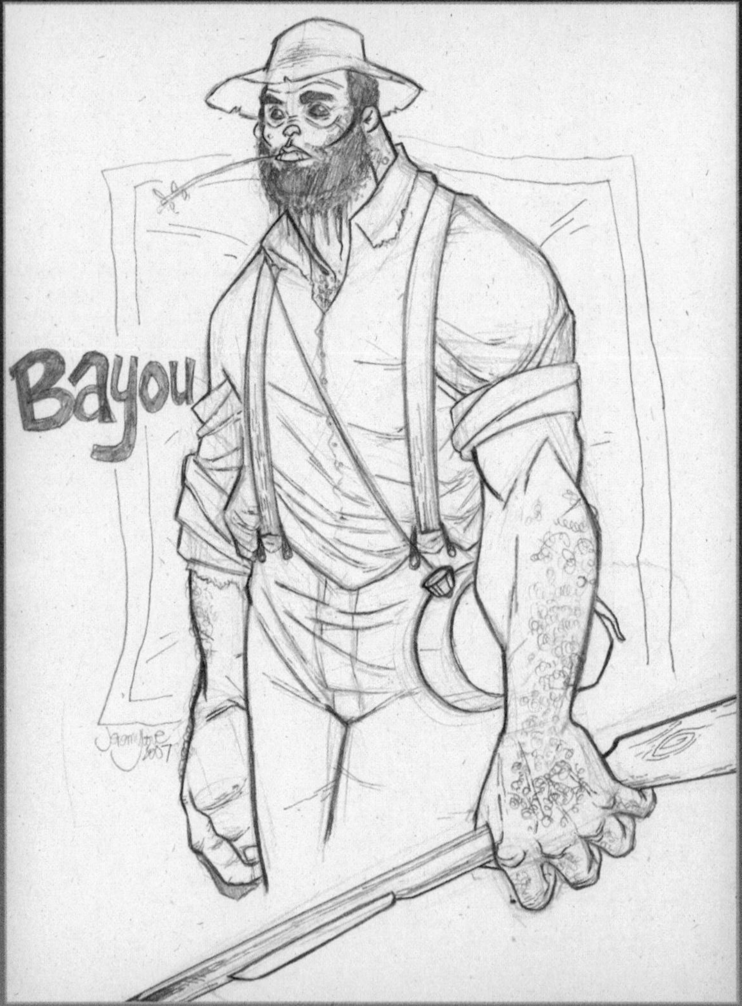
Bayou

Original Bayou concept sketch. He looks pretty much exactly as he appears now.

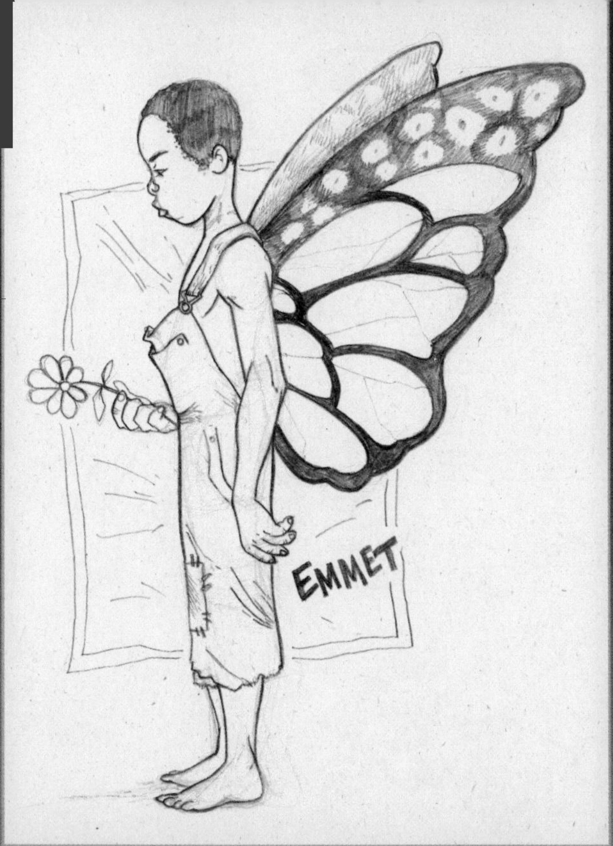
EMMET

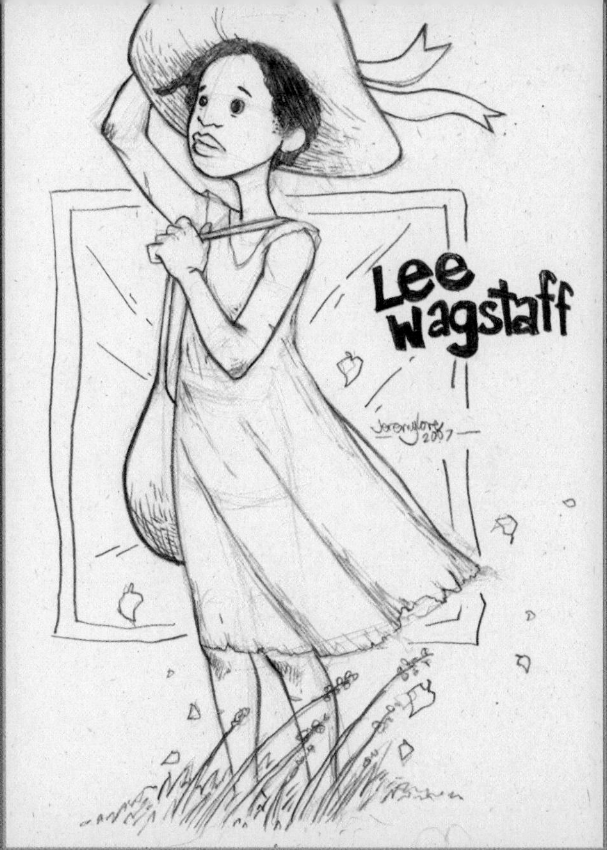
Lee
Wagstaff

Designs for Billy Glass and Lee Wagstaff. Notice Billy's original name was not "Billy."

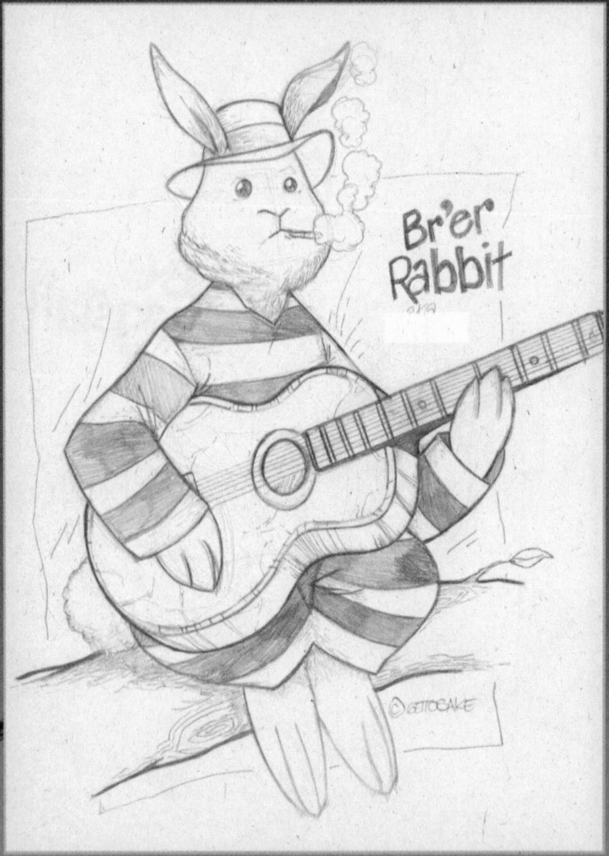
Br'er Rabbit

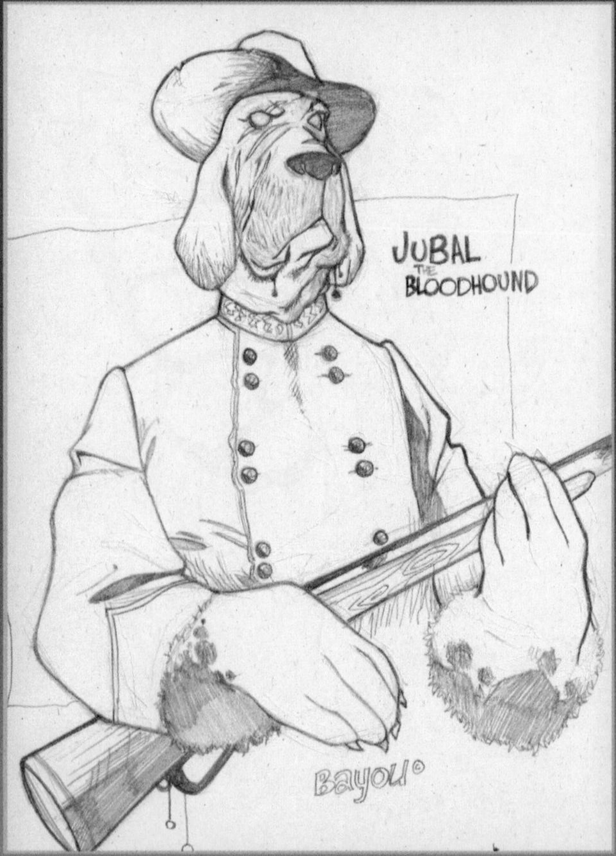
JUBAL THE BLOODHOUND
Bayou©

Initial designs for the cantankerous Rabbit and Jubal.

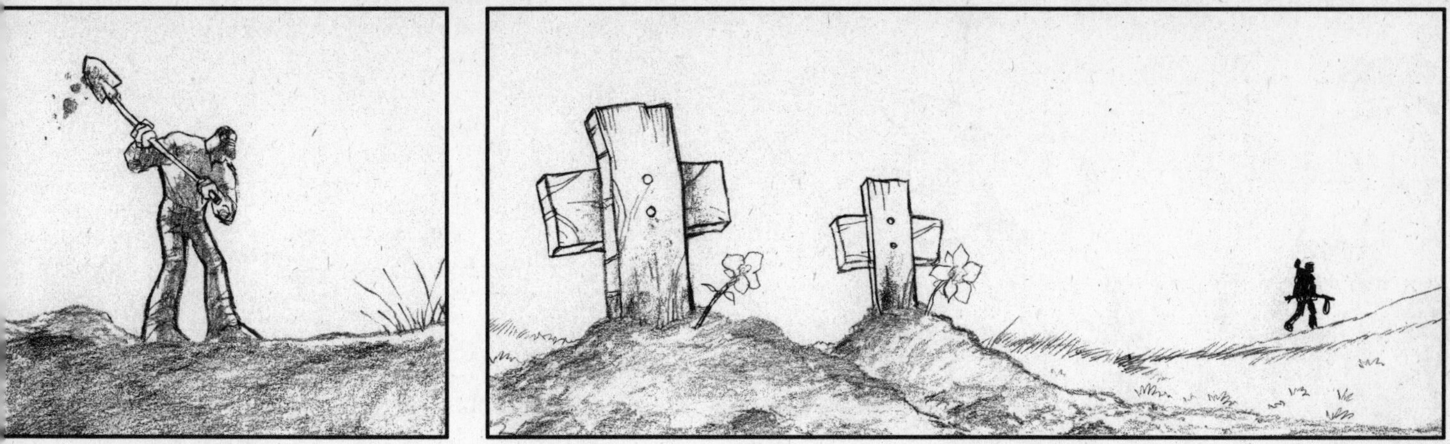

One of many somber moments in Bayou.

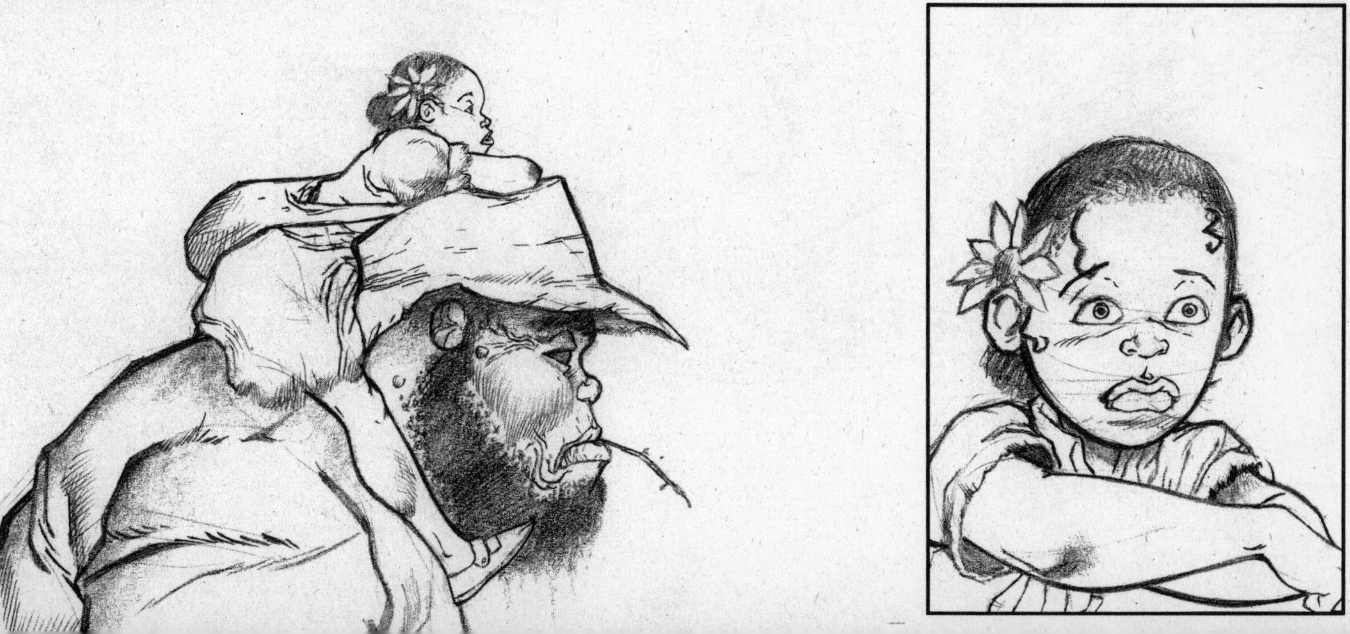

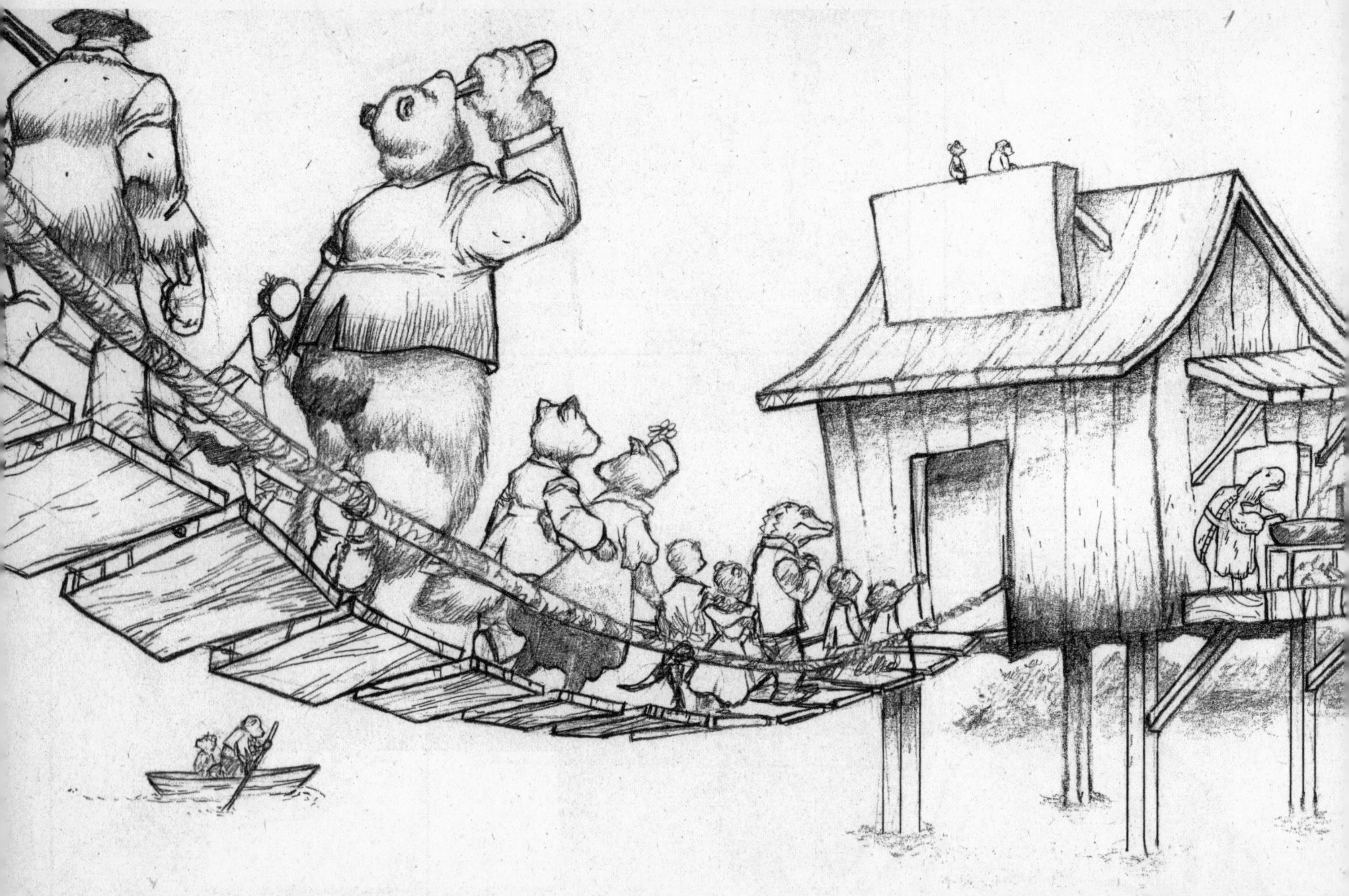

The juke joint where Bayou and Lee search for Rabbit.